D1257647

*Air War Over Korea*

# *Air War Over Korea*

*Robert Jackson*

Charles Scribner's Sons
New York

Printed in Great Britain
Library of Congress Catalog Card Number 74–19687
ISBN 0–684–14193–0

# Contents


Introduction page 6

1 The North Koreans Attack 9
2 The Battleground 21
3 The Battle for Pusan 32
4 On the Offensive 44
5 Strategic Bombing of North Korea, July–September 1950 56
6 The Battle over the Yalu 60
7 The Winter of Defeat 72
8 The Red Air Offensive, January–July 1951 84
9 The Battle of the Lifelines 99
10 Battlefield Support, 1951 106
11 The New Communist Bid for Air Superiority 117
12 The Railway Battle, September 1951–July 1952 134
13 The Mounting Offensive 141
14 North Korea's Dams: The UN's Last Target System 156
15 The Reckoning 161

Appendices
1 The Korean Aces 165
2 FEAF Order of Battle, July 1st, 1950 168
3 Fifth Air Force Order of Battle, December, 31st 1950 169
4 UN Air Forces' Order of Battle, July 31st, 1953 170
5 Statistics 171
6 British Commonwealth Air Units Supporting Korean Operations 173

Abbreviations 174
Bibliography 175

# Introduction

In November 1943, Prime Minister Winston Churchill, President Theodore Roosevelt and Generalissimo Chiang Kai-shek met in Cairo to thrash out plans for the re-shaping of the Far East after Japan's defeat. The Soviet Union, which at that time was not committed to the Pacific War, was not represented.

Among the pledges made at the Cairo Conference was that Korea, annexed by Japan in 1910, should once again become a free and independent state. So was laid the foundation of the issues that were to dominate international relations throughout the early 1950s, and which would bring the hitherto obscure name of this Asian peninsula to the front pages of the world's newspapers for three long and bloody years.

After the collapse of Japan in September 1945, the Soviet Union—exploiting the advantages of her belated entry into the war in the Far East—occupied the northern half of Korea. United States forces occupied the southern half, and in order to facilitate the surrender of Japanese troops in Korea the United States and Russia agreed—purely for military purposes—that their respective zones of occupation would be separated by the 38th Parallel of latitude.

This demarcation was to have been a temporary measure until the promise of a unified, independent Korea—a promise later underwritten by Russia on her entry into the Pacific War—became reality. But two years of haggling and bargaining achieved nothing; all attempts by the United States and Soviet Union to reach agreement on the Korean independence proposals and the withdrawal of their respective forces of occupation ended in failure. In 1947 the talks broke down completely, and in September of that year the US Government laid the whole question of Korea's future before the General Assembly of the United Nations. By this time Korea had become yet another pawn in the growing and world-wide power struggle between Russia and America, and the rift between the two halves of the country was growing rapidly wider; the 38th Parallel, now far removed from a simple demarcation line running east–west across the waist of Korea, had been turned into a strongly-fortified defensive wall.

A majority at the United Nations favoured all-Korean elections to unite the country, but the Russians rejected this outright and claimed that the future of Korea was a matter to be decided by the four signatories to the Cairo agreement. The United Nations nevertheless went ahead and formed a Commission to supervise the elections for a Korean National Assembly—but the Russians refused to allow the Commission into the Soviet-occupied zone. The result was that UN-supervised voting was held only in the south, and in August 1948 it led to the establishment of the Republic of Korea under the presidency of Dr Syngman Rhee. A month later, in the north, the Communist Democratic People's Republic of Korea came into being at Pyongyang. Its premier was Kim Il Sung, a former guerrilla leader.

The majority of the western nations recognised the Republic of Korea, while the Democratic People's Republic had the recognition and overwhelming support of the Soviet Union and her satellites. The two republics faced each other across the Parallel, each antagonistic towards the other, each claiming jurisdiction over the entire country, and each backed by the political, economic and military power of a giant nation.

North Korea was now almost completely sealed off. The American intelligence network there was virtually non-existent, and consequently neither the ROK nor US governments were aware of the extent of the military build-up that was taking place north of the Parallel. Although there was no denying that a very real threat to the security of South Korea existed—sporadic fighting along the 38th Parallel had become an almost daily occurrence by the winter of 1949–50—the Americans believed that it would take the form of terrorism, psychological warfare and guerrilla attacks.

The Americans, in fact, were so confident that there would be no conventional Communist invasion of the South—at least for the forseeable future—that they withdrew their troops in the summer of 1949. In any case, American strategic planning was dictated by the belief that any future conflict would be global, and the US Joint Chiefs of Staff considered Korea to be outside the US defensive perimeter in the Pacific.

They apparently failed to appreciate the fact that Russian military planners were thinking along somewhat different lines. The Russians were well aware that Communist domination of South Korea would greatly strengthen their own Pacific defences; moreover, a communist takeover would in all probability lend weight to anti-American factions in Japan at a time when the United States was negotiating a peace treaty with her old enemy.

Such, in brief, was the course of events that was to precipitate the Korean War. But if the Americans had made their mistakes, so had the Russians. In the early hours of June 25th, 1950, when eight North

Korean divisions stood poised for an invasion of the South, the architects of the offensive, in Pyongyang and Moscow, did not consider it likely that the armed Communist aggression in South Korea would be resisted by force from outside.

They were wrong.

CHAPTER ONE

# The North Koreans Attack

Sunday, June 25th, 1950, 04.00hrs.

The assault came without warning. The North Korean infantry divisions attacked out of the dawn, spearheaded by squadrons of Russian-built T-34 tanks. The Communist troops stormed across the 38th Parallel through the gaps torn by their armour and artillery, sweeping resistance aside and flooding into the Republic of South Korea. Taken completely by surprise the lightly-armed ROK forces wavered and broke. While the T-34s rumbled on towards their first objectives, Kaesong and Chunchon, more North Korean infantry and marines poured ashore on Korea's east coast near Kangnung from an armada of small craft. Kaesong fell at 09.00hrs and the seaborne columns pushed their way steadily inland. It was now evident that this was something far bigger than one of the numerous skirmishes which had taken place along the 38th Parallel during the previous year. The full-scale Communist invasion of South Korea had begun.

Five hundred miles east of the Korean battlegrounds, over Japan, June 25th dawned with the promise of rain. Although the skies were still clear for most of the time, oppressive heat and occasional showers heralded the start of the monsoon season. Ever since the collapse of Japan five years earlier, these Japanese Home Islands had been the home base of the United States Fifth Air Force; spread out in a defensive arc from Kyushu in the south to northern Honshu, the Fifth Air Force's combat squadrons formed the front line of America's air defences in the Far East against the potential air threat from the Soviet Union. The mainstay of the Fifth's defensive capability was the Lockheed F-80C Shooting Star jet interceptor; the type equipped the 35th Fighter-Interceptor Wing at Yokota, near Tokyo, the 68th Fighter Bomber Wing at Itazuke Air Base on Kyushu, and the 49th Fighter Bomber Wing at Misawa on northern Honshu. The jet squadrons were backed up by two all-weather fighter units operating North American F-82 Twin Mustangs; these were the 68th Fighter All-Weather Squadron at Itazuke, and the 339th Fighter All-Weather Squadron at Yokota. Also at Yokota were the RF-80A photo-reconnaissance aircraft of the 8th Tactical Reconnaissance Squadron. Two tactical light bomber squadrons of the 3rd Bombardment Wing, equipped with Douglas B-26s, were based at Johnson Air Base, north of Tokyo. The Fifth Air Force's line-up of units was completed by the 374th Troop Carrier Wing, which operated out of Tachikawa Air Base with two squadrons of C-54 transport aircraft.

The Fifth Air Force, commanded by Major General Earle E. Partridge—known universally as Pat—had been formed in September 1942 in Australia, and during the years that followed it had been honed to a razor's edge of combat efficiency as Allied forces leap-frogged across the chain of Pacific Islands in the relentless drive towards Japan. Since 1944 it had formed part of the United States Far East Air Forces, an organisation which in 1950—although far removed from the mighty war machine that had pounded Japan to destruction during World War II—nevertheless possessed a high degree of combat efficiency and was well equipped to carry out its task as part of America's bastion in the Pacific. The Fifth Air Force, holding as it did a position of vital importance at the very edge of the defensive shield, was the largest of the Far East Air Forces' subordinate commands. The other units of the Far East Air Forces were the Twentieth Air Force, based in Okinawa and the Marianas, and the Thirteenth Air Force in the Philippines. In addition to the fighter interceptor and fighter all-weather units equipped with F-80 and F-82 aircraft, the Twentieth Air Force also possessed two squadrons of Boeing B-29 Superfortress long-range medium bombers. These belonged to the 19th Bombardment Wing and were based at Anderson Air Base on Guam in the Marianas. Also attached to the Twentieth Air Force was a United States Strategic Air Command unit, the 31st Photo-Reconnaissance Squadron, equipped with long-range RB-29s and based at Kadena on Okinawa. Also at Okinawa were the 51st Fighter-Interceptor Wing and the 4th Fighter All-Weather Squadron, the first equipped with F-80 Shooting Stars and the second with F-82s. Southward in the Philippines, the Thirteenth Air Force consisted primarily of the 18th Fighter-Bomber Wing equipped with F-80s and based at Clark Air Base, although the Douglas C-54s of the 21st Troop Carrier Squadron gave it a small transport capability.

The Commander-in-Chief of FEAF, General George E. Stratemeyer, and his subordinate commanders were well aware of their fearful responsibilities. The United States no longer had the monopoly of nuclear weapons; the Soviet Union had detonated its first atomic bomb less than a year earlier, in the autumn of 1949, and the early months of 1950 had been accompanied by a dramatic rise in international tension. It needed only a slight push to topple the great nations of East and West over the brink into the abyss of total war, and if that happened the FEAF would find themselves in the forefront of the battle. A high degree of combat readiness along the units of FEAF was therefore

UN air bases in Japan.

imperative; this was particularly true in the case of the Fifth Air Force, whose Japanese bases would be the first to be hit by a Communist air attack from the mainland of Asia. The silent radar scanners carried out their never-ending search of the threatening sky to the north; on the Fifth Air Force's fighter bases alert crews stood by twenty-four hours a day seven days a week, ready to scramble instantly by day or night to intercept any unidentified aircraft approaching from the hostile sector of the sky.

On the morning of June 25th, 1950, however, there was no escaping the fact that the Fifth Air Force's state of readiness was not as high as it might have been. Many personnel—including General Partridge himself, who was in Nagoya with his family—were on weekend leave, and there was a prospect of a dull and boring week ahead; a front, coming in over the sea of Japan with low clouds and heavy rain, would severely curtail operational flying. One way and another, there were a lot of gaps in the Fifth Air Force's state of alert; in many ways, it was rather grimly reminiscent of another Sunday morning, twenty years earlier, when Japanese carrier aircraft had swept across the Hawaiian Islands to attack Pearl Harbour.

The first report of the North Korean attack, telegraphed by the duty officer at the Office of Special Investigations in Seoul, did not reach the headquarters of the FEAF until 09.45hrs. The initial American reaction was one of confusion; other than flashing the news immediately to the headquarters of the Fifth, Thirteenth and Twentieth Air Forces, there was not a great deal that could be done in the way of immediate decisions on how to meet the situation. General Stratemeyer, the C-in-C, had been attending a conference in Washington, and at this moment was somewhere over the Pacific en route from San Francisco to Hawaii. His second-in-command, General Partridge, did not receive the news until 11.30hrs. Even then—although by this time reports were indicating that the situation in Korea was precarious and that the North Koreans had launched a full-scale war—General Partridge was powerless to order his substantial air power to intervene on behalf of the hard-pressed ROK ground forces. The Fifth Air Force's firmly-dictated task, in the event of an outbreak of hostilities in Korea, was to assure the evacuation of the American nationals, and even that could only be carried out at the direct request of the United States Ambassador. Only if the North Koreans attempted to interfere with the evacuation would the Fifth Air Force be permitted to release its aircraft for attacks on enemy ground targets, and this could only be done on the direct orders of General Douglas MacArthur.

Detailed plans for the airlift of United States personnel from Korea in the event of an emergency had already been in force for several months, and General Partridge lost no time in deploying his units in readiness to carry them out. Colonel John M. Price, Commander of the 8th Fighter-Bomber Wing, was to be in command of the operation. F-80 and F-82 fighters were to provide air cover over the South Korean airfields and ports from which the evacuation was to take place, while a flight of B-26s of the 3rd Bombardment Wing, operating out of Ashiya Air Base, was to maintain standing patrols over the sea areas off the Korean coast. By the end of the afternoon, in addition to the 8th Wing's F-80s and F-82s, Colonel Price had assembled a force of ten B-26s, twelve C-54s and three C-47s. He then informed the Fifth Air Force operations centre that his units would be ready to begin the evacuation at 03.30hrs the following morning, which would allow the first of his transports to reach Kimpo airfield, near Seoul, before dawn. There was nothing to do now but wait for MacArthur's order for the operation to go ahead.

Meanwhile the disjointed reports that were coming in from Korea were taking a more optimistic turn. The initial impetus of the North Korean drive appeared to have exhausted itself, and American observers with the ROK forces reported that the latter were holding in several places and that there was a chance that the front line might shortly stabilize. In the early afternoon, however, one critical deficiency in the South Korean defences became apparent when two North Korean Yak-9 fighters appeared over Kimpo and Seoul Airfields and circled leisurely for several minutes at low altitude before flying away northwards. The South Koreans had nothing capable of intercepting the enemy aircraft; in June 1950, the Republic of Korea Air Force consisted of only 60 aircraft, all trainers; 8 L-4s, 5 L-5s and 3 T-6 Texans. These were based on Kimpo and Seoul Airfields.

The pitifully inadequate state of the ROK Air Force was a direct result of United States policy; following repeated pleas by President Syngman Rhee, Major-General Claire L. Chennault had drawn up a plan for a South Korean Air Arm consisting of 99 aircraft, including 25 F-51 Mustang fighter-bombers, but this had been rejected by General MacArthur, who believed that the build-up of such a force would serve to increase the tension that already existed between North and South Korea and would lend weight to the Communists' claim that the United States was deliberately seeking to promote an arms race in the area. The result of this policy was that when the Communists finally did attack, they enjoyed complete and overwhelming air superiority.

On June 25th, 1950, the North Korean Air Force possessed a total of 132 combat aircraft, comprising 62 Ilyushin Il-10 ground attack machines, and 70 Yak-3, Yak-7B, Yak-9 and La-7 fighters. There were also 22 Yak-18 twin-engined light transports, and 8 Polikarpov Po-2 trainer aircraft. The majority of the combat types were concentrated on two principal airfields at Pyongyang and Yonpo, but by the time the war broke out several flights had been moved forward to hurriedly prepared advance bases near the 38th Parallel. Unlike the North Korean Army, which consisted largely of conscripts, the pilots of the infant NKAF were all volunteers and although they lacked operational experience their eagerness and willingness to fight was not in doubt. The NKAF's Russian instructors were all carefully selected veterans of World War II and the North Korean students were given a thorough grounding in the tactical lessons learned by the Soviet Air Forces on the eastern front between 1941 and 1945.

It was not long before the North Korean pilots demonstrated their aggressive ability. At 15.00hrs on June 25th two Yak-9s raced low over Kimpo, spraying the field with cannon and machine-gun fire. Cannon shells shattered the control tower and found their mark in a fuel dump, which exploded in a tremendous mushroom of smoke and flame. An American Military Air Transport Service C-54 was also hit and damaged. While this attack was in progress four more Yaks strafed Seoul, damaging seven trainer aircraft, and at 19.00hrs a second attack was made on Kimpo. This time the North Korean pilots concentrated on the C-54 transport damaged in the earlier raid, and this was sent up in flames. These attacks underlined an urgent plea made earlier in the day to the United States Ambassador by President Rhee, who requested the immediate delivery of ten F-51 Mustangs, complete with bombs and rockets, for use by South Korean pilots.

Shortly before midnight, with North Korean tanks only seventeen miles north of Seoul, the United States Ambassador—John J. Muccio—ordered the evacuation of all American women and children from the South Korean capital and from Inchon. On his orders several freighters were already standing by in Inchon harbour, ready to embark the refugees and take them to Japan. In the early hours of June 26th General MacArthur ordered General Partridge to provide fighter cover over Inchon during the embarkation and subsequent withdrawal. The fighters were not to venture over the Korean mainland, and were to engage in combat only if the freighters were directly threatened.

The only aircraft really suitable for carrying out this patrol task, because of the distances involved, was the F-82 Twin Mustang. Colonel Jack Price had at his disposal twelve serviceable F-82s of the 68th Fighter All-Weather Squadron, but these were too few to carry out effective standing patrols. The only other unit based on Honshu that might have been able to help was No 77 Squadron, Royal Australian Air Force, which operated F-51 Mustangs out at Iwakuni Air Base. However, the reaction of the British Commonwealth to the recent events in Korea was not yet known, and although No 77 Squadron was technically at the disposal of the Supreme Commander Allied Powers, General MacArthur, the idea of asking for Australian assistance at this stage was rejected. In an effort to solve the problem, General Partridge ordered the 339th All-Weather Squadron to transfer its F-82s from Yokota to Itazuke, and also requested the Twentieth Air Force to dispatch eight F-82s of the 4th Squadron to Itazuke from their base on Okinawa.

The evacuation began in earnest at first light on June 26th, the majority of the refugees embarking on a Norwegian merchantman. Overhead, the F-82s circled watchfully in flights of four, a few hundred feet below the cloud base. The evacuation went ahead without incident during the morning, but at 13.30hrs there was a sudden alarm as a North Korean La-7 fighter suddenly dropped down out of the clouds and dived straight through the middle of an F-82 flight, its cannon blazing. The American pilots took violent evasive action and after this one firing pass the enemy fighter climbed steeply back into the clouds and disappeared. The F-82s continued to provide air cover throughout the remainder of the day, sometimes—in accordance with the new orders—venturing inland to cover refugee convoys on their way from Seoul to Inchon. After dark the fighters continued to accompany the merchant vessel as it headed out into the Yellow Sea, only breaking off their patrols when the ship was met by an escort of American destroyers.

The airlift of refugees from Seoul and Kimpo finally got under way on the morning of June 27th. Finding transport aircraft had presented something of a problem; the C-54s of the 374th Wing were widely dispersed on routine duties, and only two were immediately available to Colonel Price. The situation was saved by the arrival of eleven C-47s, hastily scraped together from various FEAF transport units. The first transports took off from Itazuke before dawn, escorted by a formation of F-82 Twin Mustangs. At daybreak, while the transports touched down at Kimpo and Suwon airfields and the F-82s orbited overhead at low altitude, two flights of F-80 Shooting Stars of the 8th Fighter-Bomber Wing arrived over the Han River and began a high-level patrol, covering the approaches to the South Korean capital.

The patrolling fighters encountered no enemy opposition until mid-day, when five Yak-7s appeared over Seoul and began a long, slanting dive towards Kimpo airfield. They were immediately pounced on by five F-82s of the 68th and 339th Squadrons, and in a brief one-sided dogfight lasting less than five minutes three of the enemy aircraft were shot down in flames. In the first few seconds of the battle a well-aimed burst of fire brought Lieutenant William G. Hudson of the 68th Squadron the distinction of destroying the first Communist aircraft over Korea. The other American pilots who scored were Major James W. Little and Lieutenant Charles B. Moran. An hour later the North Koreans tried again, this time with eight Il-10 fighter-bombers. The intruders were spotted over Seoul by the pilots of four F-80s of the 35th Fighter Bomber Squadron, who dived down to intercept. It was a massacre. Two of the Il-10s were destroyed by Lieutenant Robert E. Wayne, while Captain Raymond E. Schillereff and Lieutenant Robert H. Dewald shot down one each. Unnerved, the other four Communist pilots turned tail and ran. The Americans, with no orders to pursue, climbed away and resumed their patrol. There were no further attempts to interfere with the air evacuation during the remainder of that day.

On the evening of June 27th, the United Nations Security Council adopted a resolution in favour of supplying such aid as might be necessary to enable South Korea to repel the Communist attack. The United States Government immediately authorised General MacArthur to employ, at his discretion, United States Naval and Air Forces in support of the South Koreans. Only by launching an immediate series of large-scale air strikes against the enemy ground forces could he hope to buy time for the crumbling South Korean army, restoring at least some of its shattered morale and giving it time to regroup. He accordingly directed General Partridge to employ the Fifth Air Force's B-26s, F-80s and F-82s against enemy armour, artillery, military convoys, supply dumps, bridges and troop concentrations; in short, the American pilots were to be given licence to range over the ground between the front line and the 38th Parallel and to shoot up everything that carried a red star. The 374th Troop Carrier Wing, now that its primary task of evacuating American non-combatants was completed, was to begin an immediate airlift of ammunition and war material to South Korea.

Putting this sweeping directive into effect was not easy. For a start, the 3rd Bombardment Wing's 8th Squadron—which had been earmarked to carry out the first ground attack mission under cover of darkness—had only four available B-26s; the other six were engaged in patrol duties over the Yellow Sea. The four that did take off to attack enemy armour north of Seoul returned to base with their bombs still on board, unable to find their target in darkness and badly deteriorating weather. A second B-26 mission also had to be abandoned for the same reasons. However, the Met report for the following morning lent some encouragement; though there would be low clouds and heavy rain over the Fifth Air Force's Japanese bases, a weather reconnaissance report brought back by a RF-80A jet at dawn indicated that the weather over Korea was clearing slightly, and that if the strike aircraft could get airborne there was a good chance that they might be able to find and hit their targets.

The first strike on June 28th was launched at 07.30hrs, when twelve B-26s took off from Ashiya to attack the rail complex at Munsan near the 38th Parallel. This target was successfully bombed, the B-26s afterwards attacking enemy troop concentrations and motor transport in the area with rockets and machine gun fire. The enemy suffered heavily, but almost all the B-26s were damaged to some extent by intense ground fire. One had to make an emergency landing at Suwon; a second got back to Japan all right but was found to be so badly damaged it had to be scrapped, and the third crashed on landing at Ashiya, killing its crew. Nine more B-26s, which attacked targets north of Seoul later that day, all returned safely to base. During the afternoon the programme of strikes was continued by the Fifth Air Force's F-82s and F-80s, the latter doing particularly good work despite the fact that their time in the target area was restricted to only a few minutes. Shortly before dusk four B-29s of the 19th Bombardment Group arrived over Korea from Guam and bombed road and rail communications north of Seoul.

In the afternoon of June 28th the North Korean Air Force again put in an appearance. While the Fifth Air Force's fighter bombers were fully committed to attacks on enemy ground targets, four Yak-9s slipped through and attacked Suwon airfield at 13.30hrs, destroying the 8th Squadron B-26 and also an F-82 of the 68th Squadron, which had been compelled to land there earlier in the day. At 18.30hrs, three pairs of Yaks arrived over the same airfield and attacked a C-54 of the 22nd Troop Carrier Squadron that was coming into land; the transport was badly damaged but the pilot managed to get away and returned to Ashiya, where he made a successful emergency landing. The same Yaks then made a strafing pass over the airfield, setting another C-54 of the same squadron on fire.

To co-ordinate and control all American military activities in Korea, an Advance Command and Liaison Group (ADCOM) under the command of Brigadier General John H. Church arrived at Suwon in the evening of June 27th and set up a command post alongside the headquarters of the Republic of Korea Army. The task facing ADCOM was heartbreakingly difficult. For a start, General Church had only scant information on the course of events at the battlefront; even the South Korean C-in-C had no real idea where most of his units were located. What he did know was that his forces had suffered forty per cent casualties in forty-eight hours, and that up to seventy per cent of the ROK's automatic weapons and field guns had already fallen into North Korean hands. It was a gloomy picture, but General Church refused to give way to undue pessimism. He believed that once the shock of the initial enemy attack had worn off the South Koreans would be capable of holding, and he advised the ROK Commander to establish a defensive zone along the line of the Han River, north of Suwon.

Throughout that night and the following day, Church and his staff worked like slaves to pave the way for the arrival of further American aid. Under the direction of a young USAF Lieutenant-Colonel named

John McGinn, facilities were rapidly set up on Suwon airfield to receive the first transport aricraft from Itazuke. These arrived the following morning, laden with arms and ammunition. McGinn also drew up lists of priority front-line targets, which he sent back to Itazuke with the transport crews for evaluation. During this time, Suwon was virtually cut off from the outside world; it was not until June 29th that a high-frequency radio set, with sufficient range to reach Tokyo, was flown in. Meanwhile, Lieutenant-Colonel McGinn used the only two radios at his disposal—a pair of short-range VHF sets—to establish an efficient ground–air link with American fighters and fighter-bombers operating in the area.

Under the direction of ADCOM, American air operations in support of the South Korean ground forces began in earnest on June 29th. The first mission of the day, however, was carried out independently of ADCOM. At 08.00hrs, on the orders of General MacArthur, nine B-29s of the 19th Group at Kadena droned over Kimpo airfield—now in North Korean hands—at three thousand feet and released their loads of 500lb bombs on the runways and installations. The formation was attacked by three enemy fighters, one of which, a Yak-9, was shot down and a second damaged.

In the early afternoon the Fifth Air Force's B-26 light bombers entered the fray, attacking bridge targets along the Han River at the request of General Church. At the same time, F-82 fighter bombers bombed and strafed concentrations of enemy troops along the banks of the river, the 68th Squadron attacking with napalm for the first time in Korea. A few ground attack missions against enemy transport were also flown by F-80 Shooting Stars in the course of the afternoon, but the primary task of the jet fighters was to maintain standing patrols at ten thousand feet over the Han. The fighters successfully broke up five separate attempts by the North Korean Air Force to attack Suwon airfield, shooting down an La-7 and an Il-10, but at the sixth attempt a flight of three Il-10s managed to slip through and destroy a C-54 on the ground.

The biggest American fighter effort of the day was laid on in mid-afternoon, when F-80s of the 8th Fighter Bomber Wing, together with a flight of Mustangs, which were about to be turned over to the South Korean Air Force, orbited in relays over Suwon to cover the arrival of a C-54 carrying General MacArthur, who had decided to fly to Korea to make an on the spot survey of the situation. An hour after his arrival, MacArthur was treated to a grandstand view of an air battle as four Yak-9s attempted to attack Suwon airfield. The enemy fighters were intercepted by the Mustang Flight and not one of them escaped; two were shot down very quickly by Lieutenant Orrin R. Fox of the 8th Squadron, a third by Lieutenant Harry T. Sandlin of the same unit, and the fourth by Lieutenant Richard J. Burns of the 35th Squadron.

This incident convinced MacArthur of the imperative need to destroy the North Korean Air Force before it could inflict serious damage. While still at Suwon, he got in touch with General Stratemeyer and gave him verbal orders to authorise the Far East Air Forces to begin immediate air attacks on NKAF airfields north of the 38th Parallel. The first of these was carried out at dusk by eighteen B-26s of the 3rd Bombardment Group, which hit the North Korean airfield at Pyongyang with fragmentation bombs and destroyed about 25 enemy aircraft on the ground. The eight bombers were attacked by a solitary Yak-3, which was shot down. The majority of the North Korean military airfields north of the Parallel were photographed by RF-80As of the 8th Tactical Reconnaissance Squadron soon after first light on June 30th, but there was no immediate large-scale offensive against them; instead most of the American air effort throughout the day was devoted to concentrated attacks on massive North Korean troop concentrations along the North bank of the Han River.

In the course of the morning, fifteen B-29s of the 19th Bombardment Group, originally scheduled for a strike on Wonsan Airfield, were diverted to carry out attacks on enemy forces north of the river with 260lb fragmentation bombs. Meanwhile, eighteen B-26s of the 3rd Bombardment Group carried out intensive attacks on enemy convoys in the Seoul area; during one of these, the American pilots located a long convoy of armoured and soft-skinned vehicles piled nose to tail along a stretch of roadway leading to a bridge that was under repair, and wiped it out in a five minute attack using rockets and machine guns. The F-80s, meanwhile, continued to fly combat patrols over the battle area. The American pilots saw little in the way of enemy aircraft, although in the afternoon of June 30th two Yak-9s were shot down by Lieutenants Charles A. Wurster and John B. Thomas of the 36th Squadron. That same afternoon, the 36th Squadron suffered the first American jet casualty of the Korean War when one of its pilots, diving down to attack an enemy ground target towards the end of his patrol, flew through high tension cables and lost part of his wing. He was left with just enough control to allow him to limp back over friendly territory before bailing out.

Generally speaking, the relatively small number of ground attack missions flown in support of the ROK forces on June 30th produced no effective result, and it was clear that they would continue to be ineffective as long as the American fighter-bombers operated from Japanese bases. Accordingly, on the evening of the 30th, General Stratemeyer directed the Fifth Air Force to establish combat units on Korean airfields, principally at Suwon. By the time this order was received, however, it was already clear that the American position on Suwon was quickly becoming untenable. The ROK defensive line along the Han River was rapidly crumbling, and the North Koreans had already succeeded in establishing bridgeheads on the south bank of the river. At 18.00hrs, General Church told the assembled members of ADCOM that he had no alternative but to order the evacuation of Suwon, and at 21.30hrs the American personnel set off for Taejon in convoy. A matter of hours later, in darkness and pouring rain, the first units of North Korean infantry infiltrated on to Suwon airfield.

Meanwhile, following high level discussions between US Headquarters in Tokyo and the Pentagon, the decision had been taken to establish a new defensive line in Korea in the event of a massive North Korean breakthrough across the Han River. New defences were to be established along the line of the 36th Parallel, running east–west across Korea, north of Taegu. Priority was to be given to the defence of the vital port of Pusan, and to the airfields at Pusan and Taegu. To assure the defence of these positions, President Truman authorised American combat troops to be sent to South Korea from Japan, although he emphasised that such troops were not to be used directly in combat against North Korean forces. The latter decision ran contrary to the wishes of General MacArthur, who, following his tour of the South Korean defences along the Han River, was more than ever convinced that only the injection of large numbers of American combat troops into the battle area would enable the South Koreans to hold. In his report to the Pentagon, MacArthur advocated that once the North Korean advance had been checked in the Suwon area with American help, plans should be laid for a rapid counter-offensive with the help of two divisions of American infantry from Japan. There was no mistaking the urgency that lay behind MacArthur's recommendations, underlined as they were by continual reports of the deteriorating situation in Korea. On the morning of June 30th, President Truman relented and authorised MacArthur to transfer a regimental combat team to the Suwon combat area, and also promised to make an early decision on whether to commit larger numbers of American forces to the conflict.

The Presidential decision to allow General MacArthur to commit his available land forces to the battle in Korea came at 10.00hrs on June 30th. By that time, units of the 24th United States Infantry Division were already standing by on Kyushu for immediate transfer to Pusan. At the same time units of the United States Navy headed out into the Yellow Sea and the Sea of Japan, with orders to establish a blockade of the North Korean coast. Less than five years after the guns fell silent in the Pacific, America was once again going to war.

CHAPTER TWO

# The Battleground

Although the 374th Transport Wing's fleet of C-46s, C-47s and C-54s was standing by at Itazuke from dawn on July 1st, plans for the rapid airlift of the 24th Division to Korea were initially hampered by bad weather. Six C-54s managed to get through to Pusan with their loads of troops during the afternoon, but then the weather deteriorated to such an extent that the major part of the operation had to be postponed until the following morning.

Then another problem arose; Pusan's primitive runway took such a pounding from the heavily-laden C-54s during the morning of July 2nd that by now it was virtually unusable. Major-General Edward J. Timberlake, Acting Commander of the Fifth Air Force in the temporary absence of General Partridge, accordingly ordered the 374th Wing to continue the operation with lighter, twin-engined C-46s and C-47s. The runway held, and by nightfall on July 4th the Wing had flown in the two battalions of the 24th Division, as well as the Divisional Headquarters and a Regimental Combat Team of the 21st Infantry Division.

All told, the airlift had proceeded with remarkably few hitches. In fact, it was one of the very few operations that did unfold with any reasonable degree of efficiency during this initial phase of the American commitment; activities during the first week of July revealed a regrettable lack of co-ordination at most levels, and it was to be some days—in some cases, weeks—before the machine began to function more or less smoothly.

Nowhere was this deficiency more apparent than in relations between the Army and Air Force. The vital importance of full ground–air co-operation, a lesson learned the hard way during the grim days of World War II, appeared to have been forgotten in the space of five short years. Military and air commanders quickly realised to their dismay that no firm plans existed either for the deployment of troops to Korea by air, or for the support of those troops by tactical aircraft once they entered combat; a formula for effective air–ground co-operation had to be thrashed out from scratch and in the meantime the American effort was sustained largely as the result of personal initiative on the part of certain commanders. A good example of this was the decision taken by General Hoyt S. Vandenberg, the USAF's Chief of Staff, to authorise the immediate move of two medium bombardment groups—the 22nd and 92nd—to the Far East from their bases in the United States. Both these B-29 Groups belonged to the Strategic Air Command's Fifteenth Air Force, and although their transfer meant that SAC's striking capability would be temporarily depleted, General Vandenberg believed that he was justified in taking the risk. On July 8th the two groups—together with the 19th Bombardment Group and the 31st Strategic Reconnaissance Squadron—were formed into a Far East Air Forces Bomber Command at Yokota under the command of Major-General Emmett O'Donnell, Jr.

The lack of co-ordination was particularly apparent in the time it took to get messages from the ADCOM in Korea to the Advance Headquarters of the Fifth Air Force at Itazuke. Requests for air support of any kind had to follow a tortuous route through GHQ in Tokyo and FEAF before they finally reached Itazuke; and delays of up to four hours, even involving urgent messages, were normal.

On July 4th, in a determined effort to overcome this ridiculous situation, General MacArthur ordered the establishment of a new ground command; United States Army Forces in Korea (USAFIK), under the command of Major-General William F. Dean. The latter was ordered to by-pass the usual circuitous channels and communicate directly with the Commanders of FEAF and Naval Forces Far East whenever he needed air and naval support. The next essential step was the creation of a joint operations centre; this opened on July 5th in Taejon, and consisted of two operations sections, one run by the Air Force and the other by the Army. Their function was to collate and co-ordinate all available intelligence; actual control of tactical air power was to be exercised by a tactical air control centre, operating in close conjunction with the Joint Operations Centre. In these early stages, however, the JOC was run almost entirely by Air Force personnel—some 45 in all, under the command of Lieutenant-Colonel John R. Murphy—and there was little in the nature of a joint enterprise about it. The situation at the battlefront was so confused that is was almost impossible to draw an accurate intelligence picture, and, because the communications problem was still far from solved, such information as was available was more often than not out of date by the time it filtered through to Fifth Air Force Advance Headquarters at Itazuke.

The dangers attending this general lack of communication were tragically highlighted on July 3rd, when a report that a strong North Korean convoy was pushing southwards between Osan and Suwon was received at Fifth Air Force Advance Headquarters. Five Mustangs of No 77 Squadron, RAAF, now released for duty by the Australian government, were immediately detailed to take off and attack the convoy. What the Australian pilots did not know was that it was at least five hours since the original report had been sent out, and that the location they had been given was an estimated one. Arriving over the sector indicated to them by Fifth Air Force Operations, the Australians spotted a long line of soft-skinned vehicles moving slowly southwards along a road near Suwon, and attacked it. Later, they learned that their target had been an ROK convoy filled with retreating troops, who had suffered severe casualties as a result of their attack. It was only No 77's second mission over Korea, and the incident spread an air of gloom over the Squadron's activities for days. One immediate result was that General MacArthur ordered the ROK forces to paint large and distinctive white stars on the bonnets of their vehicles so that the latter could be easily identified from the air.

By the end of the first week of July, it was apparent that the plan to stiffen the resistance of the ROK forces with the aid of the 24th Infantry Division had failed. Lightly armed American infantry, outnumbered by ten to one, lacking supporting artillery and armour, were no match for the North Koreans' T-34 tanks. On July 6th the American forces, dazed and bewildered by the battering they had received, were in full retreat towards Chonan. This position also had to be evacuated less than twenty-four hours later; the situation was now extremely critical, and General MacArthur expressed his fear to the joint Chiefs of Staff that unless more American combat units could be rushed to Korea with the least possible delay the Allies might not be capable of holding the Pusan perimeter. Tactical air power was now the only trump card the Americans had left, and they were prevented from using even this to the fullest advantage by the ever present problem of range.

It was an unfortunate handicap, for the North Korean People's Army—strung out as it was in long convoys along the country's roads in its headlong drive southwards—was extremely vulnerable to hostile air attack. The North Koreans appeared to be completely unaware of the havoc that could be wrought by ground attack aircraft or else they chose to ignore it; more often than not, when American fighter-bombers appeared, the enemy infantry—instead of diving for cover—stood up in their trucks and fired back with every available weapon. American pilots seldom returned from a mission without reporting some success against enemy ground forces. Among the most successful of all were the crews of the 3rd Bombardment Wing, whose B-26s carried sufficient fuel to permit a leisurely reconnaissance of enemy territory and selection of the most likely-looking targets. Most of the Group's aircraft were hard-nosed B-26Bs, and in addition to the usual load of bombs and rockets these carried a powerful punch in the shape of up to fourteen fixed forward-firing machine guns. These aircraft accounted for a high proportion of the 197 trucks and 44 tanks knocked out in the area between Pyongtaek and Seoul during the three days between July 7th and 9th.

A good seventy per cent of all combat missions over Korea during the first two weeks of July, however, were flown by the Fifth Air Force's F-80 Shooting Stars. Although they had next to no experience in ground attack techniques the F-80 pilots quickly built up a high degree of proficiency in their unaccustomed fighter-bomber role, particularly in the use of the 5in high velocity aircraft rocket (HVAR) against the enemy armour. Each Shooting Star could carry up to sixteen of these projectiles in addition to its primary armament of eight 0·5 machine guns. The Fifth Air Force pilots were unanimous in their praise of the F-80 as a ground attack aircraft; the high speed gave it the all-important element of surprise, and because there was no propeller torque to cope with it was a far better gun platform than any conventional propeller driven machine.

The F-80C could also carry a pair of 1,000lb bombs in place of its 165 gallon tip tanks, but this reduced its radius of action to approximately 100 miles. Normally, with a full fuel load and sixteen rockets the radius of action was 225 miles; in this configuration the aircraft had a loiter time over the target of something like fifteen minutes. It was not enough, and General Partridge—conscious of the fact that a few more minutes in the target area would double the F-80s success rate—gave the 49th Fighter-Bomber Wing the task of working out some kind of solution.

It was not long before the 49th's engineer officers came up with an answer. They found that the two centre sections of a Fletcher fuel tank could be fitted into the middle of the standard Lockheed tank carried by the Shooting Stars, creating a longer tank capable of holding 265 gallons of fuel. Tests showed that the F-80 was quite capable of carrying the modified tanks, and although there were fears that the heavier load would overstress the aircraft's wing tips, Far East Air Force ordered manufacture of one pair of tanks for every Shooting Star in the Far East Command to go ahead. About twenty-five per cent of the Japan-based F-80 units had received the modified tanks by the end of July, and pilots now found that they were able to spend up to forty-five minutes in the combat area.

The problem of range and endurance would have been overcome far more satisfactorily had the Fifth Air Force's F-80 groups been able to re-equip with the more modern Republic F-84E Thunderjet, a type which—in 1950—equipped a large proportion of the USAF's fighter-bomber units. With its ability to carry up to 32 HVAR rockets, coupled with a combat radius of 850 miles, the F-84E would have more than adequately fulfilled the Fifth Air Force's ground attack requirements in Korea; the only thing that prevented its operational deployment in

Japan was the inadequacy of the Japanese airfields themselves, only four of which had the 7,000-foot runways necessary for the safe operation of aircraft of this type. For the time being, the Shooting Star—with all its inadequacies—was the most advanced combat aircraft the Fifth Air Force was capable of handling.

A request for an additional 164 F-80Cs, in fact, headed the list of urgent aircraft requirements sent to Washington by General Stratemeyer on June 30th. The list also included an additional 64 F-51 Mustangs and 21 F-82s, both of which types were eminently suitable for long range ground attack work. The Mustangs were to be used to build up a new fighter-bomber group, which was to be based at Iwakuni; meanwhile General Stratemeyer ordered the Thirteenth Air Force to form an F-51 Squadron at Johnson Air Base with the aid of thirty Mustangs pulled out of storage. All the other aircraft on Stratemeyer's list were needed for existing FEAF units, some of which were seriously under strength; a second requirements message, dated July 1st, requested the immediate despatch to Korea of one Medium Bombardment Wing, two Mustang Wings, two F-82 all-weather Squadrons, a B-26 Wing and finally two B-26 Squadrons to reinforce the 3rd Bombardment Wing. A few days later the requirement was extended to include an RF-51 Reconnaissance Squadron, an RB-26 Night Photographic Reconnaissance Squadron and a Tactical Air Control Squadron.

Meeting these requirements, however, presented a major problem. For a start, F-80C Shooting Stars were in short supply, and although there were more than 300 F-80As and F-80Bs that could be brought up to C standard by Lockheeds, this could only be done at a rate of 27 a month. Also the USAF was totally unable to meet the requirements for additional F-82 Twin Mustangs; there were only 168 of these aircraft in USAF service, and this fact—together with a critical shortage of spares—prevented any hope of making good combat attrition suffered by the Fifth Air Force's F-82s in combat over Korea. As far as the F-51 Mustangs were concerned, the position was a little rosier; 764 of these aircraft were in service with Air National Guard units, and a further 794 were in storage. Upon receipt of Stratemeyer's requirements list 145 F-51s were recalled from the Air National Guard, and made ready for shipment to Korea aboard the aircraft-carrier USS *Boxer*, together with their pilots and ground crews. The plan was to deploy a proportion of these aircraft on the South Korean airfields as soon as possible after their arrival in the Far East.

Before this deployment could take place, however, steps would have to be taken to remedy the deplorable condition of the South Korean airfields still held by the Allies. In July 1950 the only South Korean airfield suitable for operations even by piston-engined combat aircraft was Taegu, and even that had little to offer; the runway was a bumpy pilot's nightmare of packed earth and gravel, and amenities consisted of a few ramshackle buildings. Since June 30th Taegu—known also under the military designation of K-2—had been the home of the ten worn-out Mustangs supplied to the Republic of Korea on the request of President Rhee. This unit, manned by a mixed bunch of South Korean and American pilots under the command of Major Dean Hess, was in action almost continually during the early days of July, although its effectiveness was hampered by the fact that many of the South Korean pilots lacked sufficient experience to handle the F-51 and also by the lack of a suitable tactical air control system. Nevertheless, because of its location the Mustang squadron was the only Allied unit capable of ranging along the whole length of the front and of patrolling the battle area for between two and three hours at a stretch. It was comforting for the commanders of the hard-pressed 24th Division and the ROK forces to know that a flight of Mustangs could be overhead within minutes of a request for help being sent out.

Meanwhile, there were indications that the Communists were at last beginning to feel the effect of the growing weight of air power that was being directed against them. This was apparent in the fact that they were forced to rest and regroup after the capture of Chonan on July 8th; had they been able to push on immediately, they might well have succeeded in rolling up the remnants of the 24th Division and annihilating them. Since July 2nd, the Fifth Air Force's fighter-bombers had been joined by naval aircraft from the carriers USS *Valley Forge* and HMS *Triumph*, on station in the Yellow Sea. The *Valley Forge* and her escorts formed a fast carrier striking force, known as Task Force 77, the offensive power of which had virtually been doubled with the arrival of HMS *Triumph* from Hong Kong on June 30th, together with two cruisers, two destroyers and three frigates.

The carrier aircraft—Corsairs and Skyraiders from the *Valley Forge*, together with Fireflies and Seafires from *Triumph*—launched their first strikes of the war on July 3rd. For two days they pounded the Communist airfields at Pyongyang and Onjong-ni, and in addition to the damage inflicted on ground installations, naval pilots—Lieutenant J. H. Plog and Ensign E. W. Brown, flying F9F Panthers of VF-51—shot down two Yak-9s and damaged ten other Communist aircraft on the ground.

The appearance of the British aircraft, with their unfamiliar outlines, posed an immediate problem of identification; this was particularly true of the Seafire, which, when viewed from certain angles, bore more than a passing resemblance to the Communist Yak-9. The Fleet Air Arm aircraft were frequently fired on by friendly ground forces, and on one occasion—on July 28th—a Seafire of HMS *Triumph*'s No 800

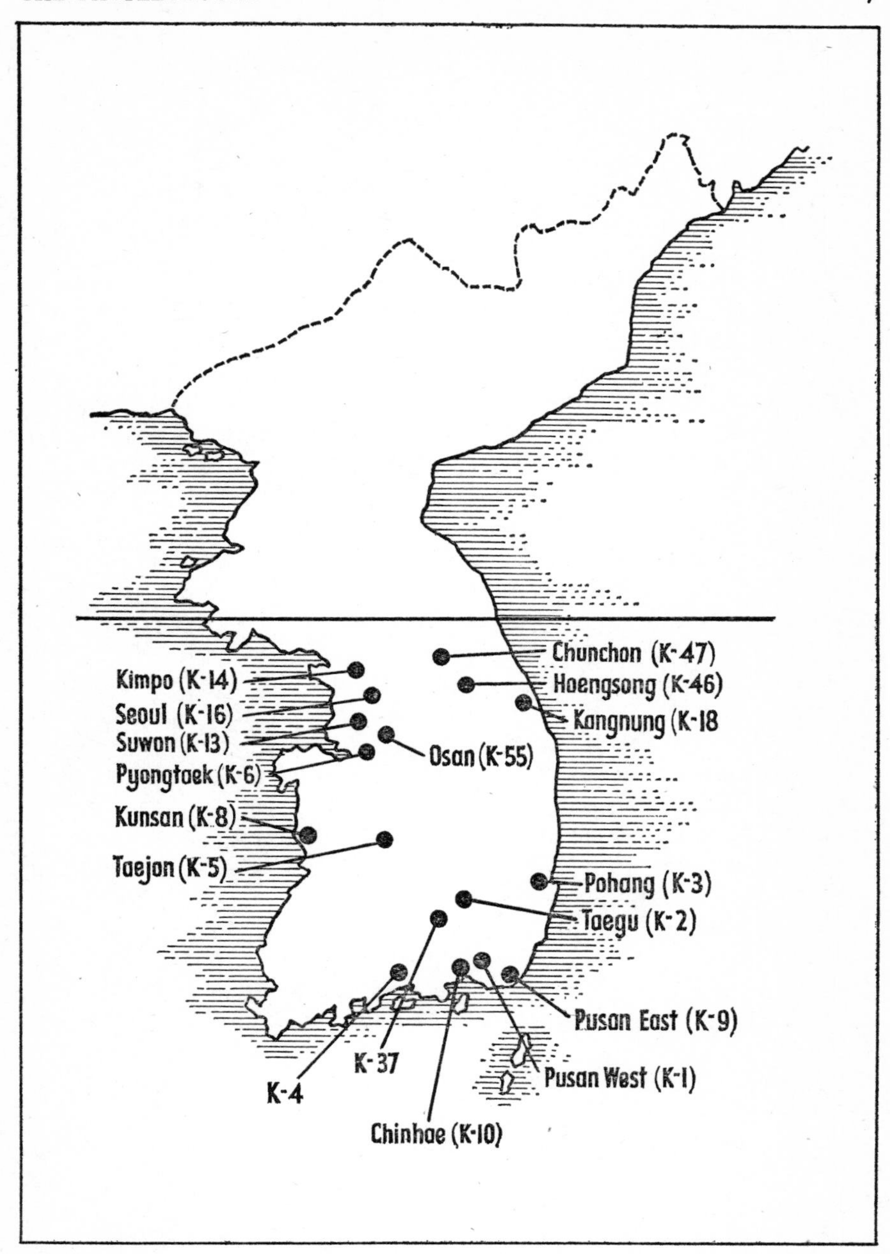


Location of main UN airfields in South Korea, 1950–53.

Squadron was shot down in error by the gunners of a B-29 formation of the 22nd Bombardment Group. Fortunately, the British pilot bailed out and was picked up safely.

The naval air strikes against the Communist airfields early in July heralded the start of a determined effort by the United Nations to eliminate North Korea's small air force once and for all. The importance of such a step was underlined on July 10th when four Yak-9s attacked elements of the United States 19th Regiment near Chongju and inflicted some casualties. The following day, more Yaks attacked a flight of F-80 Shooting Stars engaged in strafing ground targets in the same area, and the American pilots—short of fuel—barely managed to escape unharmed. This incident was repeated the following day, near Chochiwan; once again the American pilots were able to get away, but a B-29 of the 19th Group, engaged in bombing railway targets near Seoul, was not so lucky. It was trapped by three Yaks, and after a brief one-sided encounter was shot down in flames. A small L-4 liaison aircraft was also destroyed by a pair of Yaks towards the end of the day. On July 15th two more Yaks came up to intercept a flight of four B-26s over Seoul; they harried the bombers for ten minutes with a series of determined attacks, severely damaging one of them.

American Intelligence indicated that seven or eight Yaks were operating out of Kimpo, and in the afternoon of the 15th, on the orders of General Partridge, this was attacked by a flight of F-80s. Later in the day Kimpo was also bombed by three B-29s. The majority of the Communist aircraft, however, were reported to be concentrated on the airfields of Pyongyang and Yonpo, and on July 18th and 19th these were the targets of the carrier aircraft of Task Force 77. In two days of operations, the naval pilots claimed a destruction of 32 enemy aircraft on the ground, together with thirteen damaged. Also on the 19th, seven F-80s of the 8th Fighter-Bomber Group launched a concentrated strike on the satellite airfield near Pyongyang, destroying fifteen aircraft in one whirlwind firing pass. The next day, fourteen B-29s followed up these strikes by bombing the runways of the Communist airfields clustered around Pyongyang. During this same period—between July 17th and 20th—F-80 pilots of the 8th Group also destroyed six enemy fighters in the air to air combats over the front line.

By July 21st, although the NKAF had still not been totally destroyed, it had become almost completely ineffective as a fighting force. Wherever reconnaissance located enemy aircraft, they were immediately neutralised by air strikes. By August 10th allied pilots had claimed the destruction of 110 Communist aircraft in the air and on the ground. There was some doubt as to the validity of this figure, for it was known that some of the enemy aircraft claimed as destroyed had in fact been dummies deployed by the Communists on their airfields;

nevertheless the absence of the North Korean Air Force in combat during the first week of August indicated that the enemy had, to all intents and purposes, been knocked out of the fight. Communist aircraft did in fact continue to put in an occasional appearance—on August 15th, for example, a solitary La-7 attacked a B-29 of the 307th Bombardment Group without inflicting any damage—but such incidents were few and far between.

The elimination of the NKAF meant that the FEAF's medium bomber groups could now range freely over the whole of North Korea without fear of interference from hostile aircraft. The first strategic mission of the newly constituted Far East Air Forces Bomber Command had been flown on July 13th, when B-29s of the 22nd and 92nd Bombardment Groups bombed the marshalling yards and oil refinery at Wonsan, through cloud with the aid of radar. The number of strategic missions of this kind was stepped up during the remainder of July, as the increasing successes of the Fifth Air Force's fighter-bombers against the advancing Communists enabled more medium bombers to be diverted from the tactical support role, a task for which they were totally unsuited.

Although the Japan-based fighter-bombers of the Fifth Air Force were already inflicting great devastation on the North Korean columns by the end of the second week in July—on July 10th, for example, a convoy of 150 enemy vehicles was wiped out near Pyongtaek in a massive air strike by B-26s, F-82s and F-80s—the real turning point in the air-ground offensive came in mid-July, with the establishment of the Mustang-equipped 51st Fighter Squadron at Taegu. This squadron, which also absorbed the battle-weary surviving aircraft of Major Dean Hess's composite South Korean/American Unit, flew its first ground attack mission on July 15th.

Meanwhile Air Force engineers had been working flat out to extend the runway facilities of an old wartime Japanese airfield near the town of Pohang, on the east coast of Korea. Their work was completed by July 14th, and two days later the Mustangs of the 40th Fighter Squadron flew in from Ashiya. This squadron was the first Fifth Air Force Unit to exchange its F-80 jets for piston-engined F-51s, and the pilots had completed their conversion to the older type in record time.

It was not long before the two squadrons, with their ability to be over the front line within minutes of a call for assistance being received, had begun to take a heavy toll of enemy troops and transport. Beginning on July 17th, the 40th Fighter Squadron—bereft of almost all communications with the outside world—began what virtually amounted to a private war against a strong force of North Korean regular troops advancing down the east coast towards Pohang. Within three days the enemy force had lost all its transport, and the troops, threatened by continual air attack, were forced to restrict their movements to night time. The North Korean armour suffered particularly heavy losses. The Russian-built T-34 tanks were found to be extremely vulnerable to napalm attacks, and both the 51st and 40th Squadrons made extensive use of this weapon.

Although the continual air onslaught slowed down the Communist advance, it could not stop it. The North Korean forces continued to advance along the entire front, with a main drive directed towards Taejon. On the morning of July 19th the Communists opened a large-scale assault against the city, which was defended by the battered United States 24th Infantry Division. The task of the 24th Division was to fight a delaying action, buying time for two more divisions—the 25th Infantry Division and the 21st Cavalry Division, which had landed in Korea on July 15th and 18th respectively—to deploy their forces to the south and east. It was hopeless. In the early hours of the 20th the first Communist T-34s rumbled into the city, and although fifteen of them were knocked out in the course of the day with the aid of new 3·5in bazookas which had been flown into Korea from the United States, and were now being used in action for the first time, the odds proved too great for Major-General Dean to hold the city with the force of four thousand men at his disposal. Before the end of the day the remnants of the 24th Division were withdrawn from the shattered town, leaving behind a small force to fight a gallant rearguard action. The rearguard was commanded by Dean himself, standing amid the smoke and flames and coolly directing bazooka fire on to enemy tanks only a few yards away. When the city fell Dean, along with the other survivors, managed to break out of the trap and spent more than a month wandering in the neighbouring hills. He was finally captured by the enemy and spent the rest of the war in North Korean prisoner of war camps, stubbornly resisting every attempt by the Communists to brainwash him.

With the United States and ROK forces being driven back relentlessly towards the Pusan perimeter, the need for close support aircraft to operate from Korean airfields was now imperative. On July 23rd, two days after the fall of Taejon, the aircraft-carrier USS *Boxer* arrived at Tokyo and unloaded 145 F-51 Mustangs, pulled in from Air National Guard units all over the United States in accordance with General Stratemeyer's request. These aircraft were assembled by the Far East Air Material Command in record time and flown to Tachikawa to await collection by fighter-bomber pilots, who were going through a rapid conversion course at Johnson Air Base. The first batch of combat-ready Mustangs was delivered to the 40th and 51st Squadrons in Korea on July 30th, bringing the strength of each unit up to twenty-five aircraft, and preparations were made to move another Mustang unit—the 67th Squadron of the 18th Fighter-Bomber Group—to Taegu from Ashiya. This move was in fact delayed for a while because the Air Force engineers were still hard at work extending Taegu and the airfield was not yet ready to receive a second Mustang Squadron. In the event, the third Mustang Squadron to arrive in Korea was the 39th, which exchanged its F-80 jets for Mustangs during the first week of August and moved to Pohang on the 7th of the month. Four days later the 8th Group's 35th and 36th Squadrons also converted to Mustangs, although both units continued to operate from Japanese bases.

By August 11th, a total of six Fifth Air Force fighter-bomber squadrons had converted to Mustangs. These six squadrons were to bear the brunt of the close support air operations during the critical days to come, when both sides battled it out in the greatest test so far. The prize was Pusan, and with it the whole of Korea.

CHAPTER THREE

# The Battle for Pusan

However hard the Allies fought to establish some kind of order out of the chaos that accompanied the grim retreat during those last days of July, it seemed that the Communists were always one jump ahead. The principal enemy threat during the last days of the month came from the North Korean Sixth Division, which a few days earlier had crossed the Kum estuary at Kunsan before moving on to capture Chonju at about the time of the fall of Taejon. The Division, whose apparent aim was to outflank the whole of the United Nations' forces in Korea by a drive on Pusan from the west, pushed on at an average speed of two miles per hour by day and night, easily brushing aside the feeble resistance it encountered.

It was clear that one thing alone would enable General Walker's 8th US Army to establish a perimeter for the defence of Pusan, and that was the use of tactical air power on a massive scale. However, although the Allied capability for waging a round-the-clock tactical air offensive against the advancing enemy was growing steadily, the employment of tactical air power in Korea still suffered from a general lack of co-ordination. For example, although it was clearly understood that the Fifth Air Force was to be responsible for providing close air support for the Eighth Army, there was still no liaison between the latter and Task Force 77, whose carrier aircraft were playing a growing part in the battle. Nevertheless, even though at this stage there was no hope of exercising firm control over the naval air strikes from the ground, the rapid advance of the North Korean forces led General MacArthur to believe that the employment of naval aircraft was fully justified as an emergency measure, even though there might be a risk of friendly forces being attacked by mistake.

On July 25th, Task Force 77 was accordingly authorised to begin a two-day series of air strikes against Communist targets in South Western Korea. The Navy pilots were detailed to work over a precisely defined area where they would not conflict with Fifth Air Force fighter-bombers. That evening two naval officers from the aircraft carrier USS *Valley Forge* arrived at the Joint Operations Centre to analyse the results of the day's naval air operations. It was quickly realised that because of the lack of liaison with the ground these were far from satisfactory. A great deal more could have been achieved had the Navy pilots, operating under the strict control of the JOC, been permitted to range along the entire battle line. The naval liaison officers chewed over the problem with their Army and Air Force counterparts in the JOC and reached an informal agreement that, beginning at first light the following morning, carrier aircraft would join the Fifth Air Force's fighter-bombers in attacking targets along the whole front.

As a result of this understanding, which incidentally provoked some friction between General Walker and General Partridge because the request for Naval air support was not directed through proper channels —in other words Fifth Air Force HQ—Task Force 77 began a new three-day series of strikes on July 26th with the launching of some sixty sorties from the *Valley Forge*. As soon as they were in the combat area the Navy pilots, in common with their Fifth Air Force counterparts, reported to Airborne Tactical Air Co-ordinators, nicknamed Mosquitoes, whose task was to locate enemy ground targets and vector the Allied fighter-bombers on to them. Tactical Air Co-ordination in Korea dated from July 9th, when the Fifth Air Force established a TAC flight equipped with two L-5 liaison aircraft modified to carry VHF radios.

These two aircraft had some narrow escapes while co-ordinating air strikes in support of the 24th Division in mid-July, and it was soon realised that a faster aircraft would be more suited to the task. A request to this effect was quickly approved by Fifth Air Force and the Airborne Control Detachment operating out of Taejon under the command of Major Merril H. Carlton rapidly re-equipped with T-6 Texan aircraft, whose much higher speed gave their crews a far better chance of surviving in a hostile environment of enemy fighters and intense ground fire. By July 26th, however, the number of Mosquitoes operating in support of the various sectors of the Eighth Army was still relatively small and when the carrier pilots of Task Force 77 joined the Fifth Air Force in a co-ordinated ground attack effort the TAC crews found themselves seriously overworked. It was not an insurmountable problem, and the Navy quickly came up with a solution by detailing a flight of Skyraiders from the *Valley Forge* to act as control aircraft, working in conjunction with the Mosquitoes. The Skyraiders were able to stay over the front line for up to four hours, and the arrangement worked very well until Task Force 77 withdrew for replenishment at sea at the close of the three-day series of operations.

The success of the combined air offensive was a triumph for those who, since the beginning of the war, had advocated full co-operation between the US Naval and Air Forces in Korea. Maximum future co-operation seemed assured when, on August 3rd, senior Air Force and

Navy Officers met in conference to decide on the policy that would govern the future use of combined American air power. It was agreed that from now on Navy pilots would give first priority to close support work under the guidance of the Joint Operations Centre, second priority to interdiction strikes south of the 38th Parallel in co-operation with the Fifth Air Force, and third priority to interdiction strikes north of the 38th Parallel when requested to do so by Far East Air Forces Bomber Command.

Meanwhile, the continuing advance of the North Korean Forces had brought about a change in the plans governing the deployment of American air power in Korea. On August 4th General Partridge issued orders that no additional air units were to be sent to Korea for the time being and that some of those already on their way to front-line bases were to return to Japan. Airfield construction work at Taegu was also brought to a halt and all the personnel and heavy equipment not considered absolutely essential were evacuated to Pusan. Despite these precautions General Partridge was determined to hang on to Taegu and Pohang airfields at all costs, for if these fell into enemy hands the Allies would only have the unsatisfactory primitive airstrip at Pusan at their disposal.

By this time, in accordance with Eighth Army directives, all Allied forces were making a planned withdrawal behind the Naktong River to new defensive positions along the Pusan perimeter. By August 4th all bridges across the river had been destroyed and skirmishing had broken out along the perimeter itself. These early days of July were critical, for on July 31st the 6th North Korean Division, in a brilliant stroke, had captured Chinju and plunged on eastwards towards Masan, which lay only thirty miles from Pusan. The North Koreans were engaged by the 25th US Infantry Division—hastily moved to this sector by General Walker—and after two days of confused fighting they were brought to a halt. Both sides then withdrew slightly to lick their wounds and prepare themselves for the next round.

While the South Koreans and the Americans fought valiantly to stabilise the front more US reinforcements arrived through the vital port of Pusan. First of all on July 24th came the 29th Infantry Regiment from Okinawa. This was immediately sent to the Masan sector where it formed part of the 25th Division. Then on July 21st the 5th Regimental Combat Team arrived from Hawaii and was attached to the 24th Division. The last day of the month also saw the arrival of the 2nd Infantry Division: an important development, for these were the first ground troops to arrive in Korea from the United States. The 2nd Infantry was followed on August 2nd by the 1st Provisional Marine Brigade, also from the United States. Apart from replacements these were the last ground troops to reach Korea until the arrival of the

British 27th Infantry Brigade from Hong Kong on August 29th. However, the embattled Allied ground forces within the Pusan perimeter received a powerful boost during August with the arrival of 500 American tanks, which gave the allies a superiority of five to one in armour over their North Korean opponents.

The entry of the US Marines into the Korean conflict during the first week of August was not confined solely to infantry. On August 1st, Marine Aircraft Group 33, commanded by Brigadier-General Thomas J. Cushman, established itself at Itami in Japan. This was the vanguard of the 1st Marine Air Wing, which was the air component of the First Marine Division. Two of the Marine Air Squadrons, VMF-214 and VMF-323, both flying Corsair fighters, were immediately earmarked to support the First Provisional Marine Brigade. During the first week of August they embarked on the escort carriers *Sicily* and *Badoeng Strait*, and this force—known as Task Element 96.23—stationed itself off the south coast of Korea. During the days that followed the Marine pilots flew an average of 45 ground attack missions per day. Most of these were undertaken in support of the First Marine Brigade, but the Corsairs could be diverted to support Allied forces along the whole battlefront when necessary. The remainder of the Marine Air Wing, with no possibility of deployment in Korea for the foreseeable future, was placed under the temporary control of the Fifth Air Force in Japan. One of its Squadrons, VMF(N)-513, was a night-fighter unit operating F4U-5N Corsair all-weather fighters; this was attached to the 8th Fighter-Bomber Wing at Itazuke and immediately began night intruder operations over Korea as directed by Fifth Air Force.

About this time Allied air power in Korea received an additional bonus in the shape of the fast attack carrier, the USS *Philippine Sea*, which joined Task Force 77 on July 31st. The *Philippine Sea*'s aircraft arrived in the combat theatre just in time to take part in the air support operations that accompanied the United Nations offensive launched in the Masan sector on August 7th. On that date two regiments of the 25th Infantry Division, together with the First Provisional Marine Brigade and No 5 Regimental Combat Team, attacked westwards with the object of re-capturing Chinju. During the accompanying air support operations the Marine Air Wing scored heavily, destroying a large North Korean motorised column at Konsong. However, despite the continual weight of air attack the North Koreans strongly resisted the counter-offensive and the American units failed to reach their primary objectives. By August 12th they were pulling back towards Masan with men dropping like flies from heat exhaustion—it was over a hundred degrees F—and by the 14th they were back on their starting line. Nevertheless the counter-offensive had succeeded in bringing the North Korean 6th Division to a standstill, and for the remainder of August this dangerous enemy spearhead made no further serious advance.

Although the Allied counter-offensive had temporarily averted disaster at the south-western edge of the perimeter, the crisis now shifted to two other sectors of the front. The biggest threat of all materialised in the area defended by the 24th Division on the Naktong. Ten miles to the east lay the main road and rail link between Pusan and Taegu; if the 24th Division were to crumble in the face of a determined Communist attack in this sector and this vital link cut the perimeter would be sliced in two and the entire allied defence would collapse.

This was precisely the Communists' aim when, on the night of August 6th, the North Korean 4th Division began crossing the Naktong near Yongsan, forcing its way through thinly scattered units of the 24th Division and occupying strategic high ground to the east of the river. While the 1st Marine Brigade rushed over from Masan to help the 24th Division meet the Communist offensive, flare-dropping B-26s of the 3rd Bombardment Wing made night attacks on the enemy forces bringing artillery and other heavy equipment across the river. On August 15th General Walker ordered a counter-offensive. This was launched two days later and by the morning of the 18th the Marines and elements of the 24th Division had re-taken most of the high ground overlooking the enemy bridgehead. An all-out offensive against the latter was launched at first light of the 19th, and by the end of the day the North Korean 4th Division had been hurled back across the Naktong with massive casualties.

The biggest concentration of enemy troops, however, lay further north, where five North Korean divisions were deployed in a huge semi-circle around Taegu. By August 15th the enemy forces were only twenty miles from the vital town and the situation was so serious that the Republic of Korea Government moved its provisional headquarters to Pusan. The main enemy build-up was in the neighbourhood of Waegwan and on August 15th the Fifth Air Force's fighter-bombers launched a strong offensive against it. In the course of the day they knocked out several T-34 tanks and killed an estimated 300 enemy troops.

Meanwhile General MacArthur, who viewed the enemy threat with the greatest alarm, had discussed the possibility with General Stratemeyer of employing the entire B-29 force to carry out a massive bombing mission against the enemy troop concentration. General Emmett O'Donnell, the Commander of the Far East Air Forces Bomber Command, had mixed feelings about the operation but he thought that favourable results might be obtained if the troop concentrations attacked were sufficiently dense.

Accordingly, on the morning of August 16th, 98 B-29s took off from their respective bases and set course in several waves towards the strip

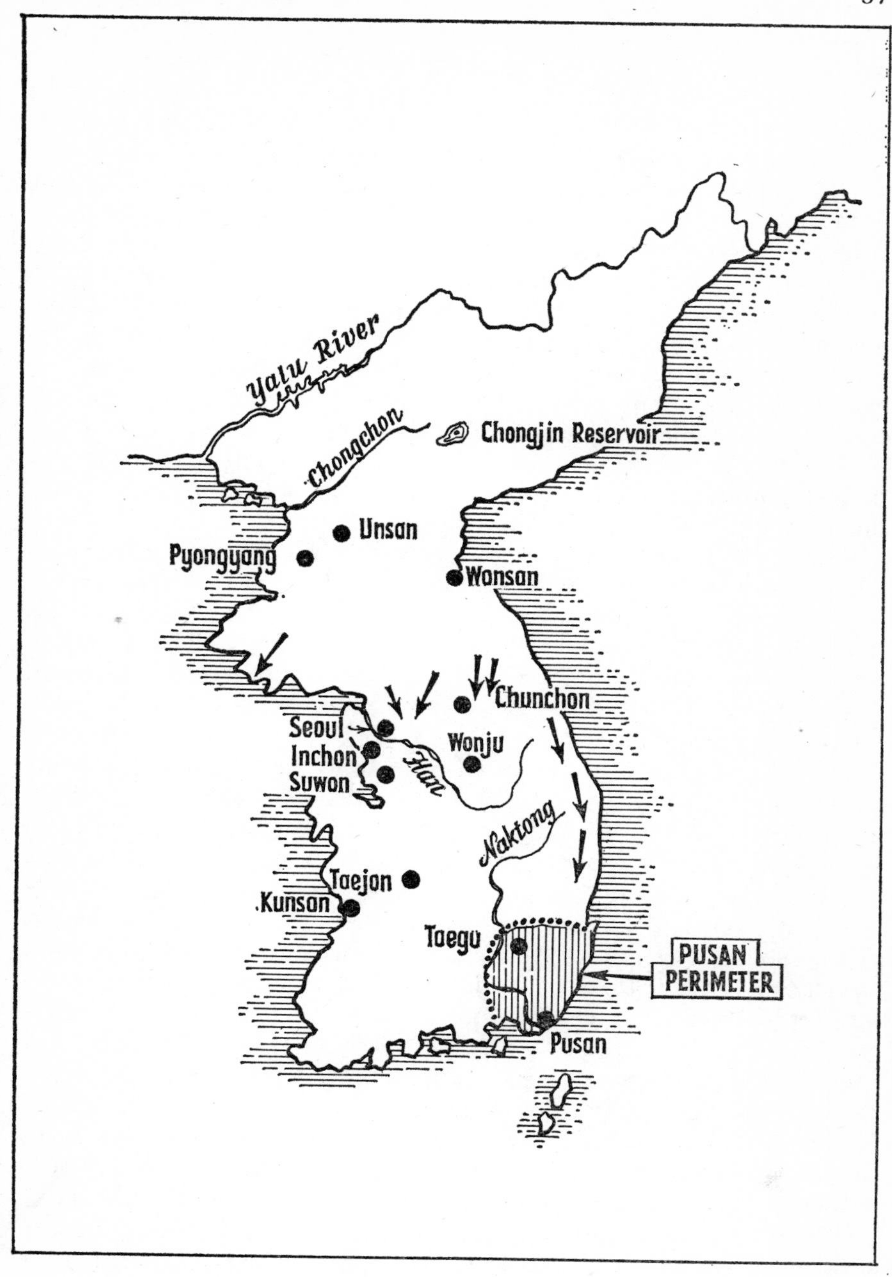


The North Korean offensive, June–Sept 1950.

of Korean territory 3½ miles wide by 7½ miles long running along the Naktong, north-west of Waegwan. It was in this sector that about 40,000 Communist troops were reported to be preparing for an all-out attack on the US First Cavalry Division. The B-29s were carrying 500lb general purpose bombs; fragmentation bombs would have been better but the mission had been planned at short notice and there had not been time to change the bomb loads.

In the space of 26 minutes the 98 bombers, attacking from altitudes of between 5,000 and 10,000 feet, pulverised the area with almost 1,000 tons of bombs. As the great pall of smoke and dust cleared RF-80 reconnaissance aircraft streaked across the Naktong to photograph the results. The pictures they brought back revealed nothing: no troops, no enemy vehicles of any kind. No evidence was ever produced that this mission—the biggest use of air power in direct support of ground troops since the Normandy invasion of 1944—had killed a single North Korean soldier, and there was certainly no let-up in the heavy Communist pressure against the Allied defences.

While the North Koreans grouped for their planned assault on Taegu other enemy forces had made considerable gains at the north-western end of the Pusan perimeter. At first the main threat in this sector appeared to come from the North Korean 5th division, which early in August had struck down the coast and driven the ROK 3rd Division out of the Yongdok area. Then came a new threat as elements of the North Korean 12th Division pushed southwards down a mountain corridor, which ran all the way to Pusan. Mustangs of the 35th Fighter-Interceptor Group, based on Pohang airfield, struck hard at the enemy as they advanced rapidly but on August 12th the North Koreans entered the port of Pohang and later in the day the 35th's ground crews found themselves engaged in a series of skirmishes with Communist guerillas on the perimeter of the airfield itself. The Americans had no choice but to destroy all the equipment they did not need and fly out their Mustangs to Japan. This meant that effective air support was no longer available for the hard-pressed troops of the ROK 3rd Division, now hopelessly trapped against the coast, and on August 17th they were evacuated and brought behind the Pusan perimeter. The situation in this sector only improved three days later when the Allies rallied and launched a counter-offensive that hit the North Korean 5th and 12th Divisions hard and drove them out of Pohang, bringing a halt to the dangerous thrust down the mountain corridor.

Back on the Taegu sector the expected Communist offensive finally developed on August 18th with a fast North Korean push against Taegu, driving a wedge through the ROK 1st and 6th Divisions. By the following morning the enemy spearheads had penetrated to within twelve miles of Taegu and it was now, during the bitter fighting that ensued, that the piston-engined Mustangs of the Fifth Air Force came into their own.

The initial Mustang strikes during this critical period were made from Japan, the fighter-bombers carrying maximum fuel and weapon loads. The Mustangs then landed at Taegu where sweating ground crews strove to refuel and re-arm them for a new series of strikes. The Mustang pilots, ready to drop from exhaustion and the terrible heat that turned the confines of their narrow cockpits into sweltering furnaces, operated virtually non-stop for 48 hours, taking a fearful toll of the enemy. The air attacks bought time for the hard-pressed ROK divisions—sufficient time to enable General Walker to shift a regiment of the US 25th Division northward to reinforce them.

The arrival of the American troops turned the tide of the battle. The North Koreans were pushed steadily back and by August 21st the Allies had re-captured most of the ground they had lost during the enemy onslaught. As the Allied troops moved forward once more they found fearful evidence of the efficiency of air support; in one place ROK troops found a stretch of road choked with the bodies of 700 enemy dead after a flight of Mustangs had made a concentrated attack with rockets, napalm and machine guns.

While the tide of battle along the Pusan perimeter swayed back and forth a considerable portion of the United Nations air power had been committed to interdiction work, with Air Force and Navy aircraft attacking selected targets far to the North. This programme, which was known simply as Interdiction Campaign No 1 and which was to last throughout the whole of August began officially on the 4th of that month when B-29s of the 19th, 22nd and 92nd Bombardment Groups hit the marshalling yards at Seoul on two successive days. Two days later aircraft of the 22nd, 92nd and 98th Groups hit the marshalling yards and ammunition factories at Pyongyang and on August 8th these targets were also bombed by B-29s of the 307th Group flying their first mission of the Korean war. Marshalling yards together with an oil refinery were again the targets selected on August 10th when the 22nd, 92nd and 98th Groups bombed Wonsan.

After these initial strikes, which wrought havoc with the North Korean logistic system at its principal sources, the main interdiction task was switched against bridge targets. For eight days beginning on August 12th three B-29 Groups attacked a total of 44 bridges north of the 37th Parallel. Subsequent photographic reconnaissance showed that the bombs had succeeded in completely destroying 37 of the bridges and that the remaining seven were so badly damaged as to be unusable by the Communists for some considerable time. It was no mean achievement, for most of the bridges were strong steel and concrete structures built by the Japanese during the war and it required very precise bombing in order to knock them out. Nevertheless the B-29 crews achieved it with 500 and 1000lb bombs—not exactly the ideal type of weapon to use against this kind of target.

Although most of the bridges were knocked out with comparative ease there was, of course, an exception. The exception was the big steel railway bridge west of Seoul, which during the early days of the offensive weathered a storm of 1000lb bombs without so much as buckling. The 19th Group, whose B-29s—unlike those of the other Groups—were equipped to carry 2,000 and 4,000lb bombs were assigned this bridge as their own special target. They bombed the bridge almost every day for three weeks, on one occasion dropping 54 tons of bombs on and around it, yet it still stood. General Stratemeyer quietly promised a case of best Scotch to the crew who succeeded in destroying it. The word must have got around for suddenly the Navy pilots of Task Force 77 decided to have a try. On August 19th, 37 Corsairs and Skyraiders from the *Philippine Sea* and *Valley Forge* scored eight direct hits on the bridge; they bent it a little but it still showed no signs of collapsing. The 19th Group, determined not to let the Navy walk off with the Scotch, came back the following day grimly determined to finish the job. They were too late. Two spans of the bridge, seriously weakened by the days of air bombardment, had fallen into the water during the night. The bomber crews dropped their loads on what was still standing and to their delight a third span collapsed into the water. A couple of days later the 19th Group received its case of Scotch and so did the crews of Navy Air Group 11, with General Stratemeyer's compliments. Honour was satisfied all round.

While the B-29s and carrier aircraft hit their targets to the north, the Fifth Air Force carried out a comprehensive interdiction programme against road and rail communications between the 27th and 38th Parallels. By the end of August the fighter-bombers, medium-bombers and carrier aircraft had made 140 bridges in this area unserviceable, including 93 totally destroyed. Nevertheless there was little appreciable check in the flow of supplies to the North Korean forces massing on the Pusan perimeter. As soon as an air strike knocked down a permanent bridge the North Koreans threw up a pontoon alongside it and continued to ferry their supplies across. Most of this activity went on at night time, the pontoons being dismantled during the hours of daylight and their sections cleverly camouflaged. Constant attempts to destroy the pontoons were made by flare-dropping B-26s of the 3rd Bombardment Wing, but no real success was achieved. All the Americans could do was saturate the area round the river crossings with delayed action bombs in the hope that these tactics would seriously hamper the North Koreans. They failed to do so.

Interdiction at night, in fact, was posing a whole spate of problems.

A long line of sleek F-80 Shooting Star jet fighters of the Fifth Air Force's 49th Fighter-Bomber Wing stand ready for action. They will soon be aiming their rockets, napalm and 0.50 calibre ammunition at Communist targets in close support of UN forces, or attacking rear area tactical targets. Another returns home.

A Communist flak burst ripped cowling and a large portion of the nose from this F-80 Shooting Star while it was making a low level attack on main rail lines in North Korea. The pilot, 2nd Lt Colin M. McCrary, Hickory Corners, Michigan appears happy over his safe return. Note hanging cowling, left, exposing ammunition magazines for the three guns.

*Top:* Loaded down with two 500 pound bombs and a full load of 50 calibre ammunition a Fifth Air Force F-80 Shooting Star jet of the 49th Fighter-Bomber Wing is helped off the runway by JATO (Jet assist take-off) as the pilot starts out for another strike against a Communist target beyond the battle line.

*Above:* Giant C-124 Globemaster dwarfs other representative types of the 315th Air Division at Ashiya air base, Japan.

*Below:* F-51D of the ROK Air Force running-up at a forward airstrip near Kongnung.

*Below:* 'He was coming in at eight o'clock', says S/Sgt Norman S. Greene, left, B-29 Gunner, North Sacramento, California while demonstrating to fellow crew members of the US Far East Air Forces' 19th Bomb Group how he shot down an enemy jet fighter over North Korea. Sgt Greene was also credited with one 'probable' during a 17-minute battle with 20 Russian-built MiG-15s of the type shown on the chart held by the Superfort commander, 1st Lt Leonard N. Rummel, Lincoln, Nebraska, Gunners who also furthered the UN cause by knocking down a MiG jet are T/Sgt Charles W. Summer, Eugene, Oregon and S/Sgt William E. Dages, Utica, New York.

*Foot:* MiG-15*bis* flown to a South Korean air base by defecting North Korean pilot.

Sabres of 4th Fighter-Interceptor Wing prepare to take off from Kimpo.

This series of four pictures taken from gun camera film show the beginning of the end for a Russian-built MiG-15 in an air battle high over North Korea. Monday, May 18th, 1953. The 'kill' was recorded by the camera in a US Air Force F-86 Sabre jet flown by 2nd Lt James L. Thompson of Monroe Park, Wilmington, Delaware, a member of the 51st Fighter-Interceptor Wing who was credited with the destruction. During a combat patrol in MiG Alley, two MiGs jumped Lt Thompson's element leader. The two Sabre pilots then lined up on the enemy pilot who, using his speed brakes to slow his flight, caused the Sabre jet leader to overshoot. Lt Thompson, in the meantime, lined up on his quarry and opened fire. These pictures tell what followed. In the first photo, the 0.50 calibre slugs have hit the MiG causing fiery explosions. In the second picture, smoke envelops the enemy plane while in the third photo fire has broken out. The fourth picture shows the MiG burning and helpless. The loss of power caused the MiG to go into a spin and the pilot baled out.

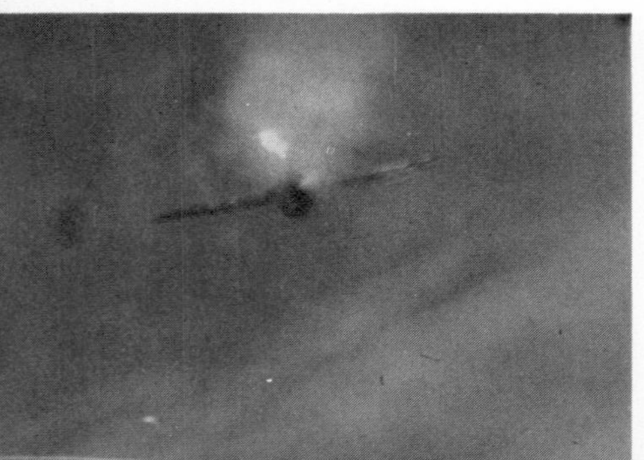

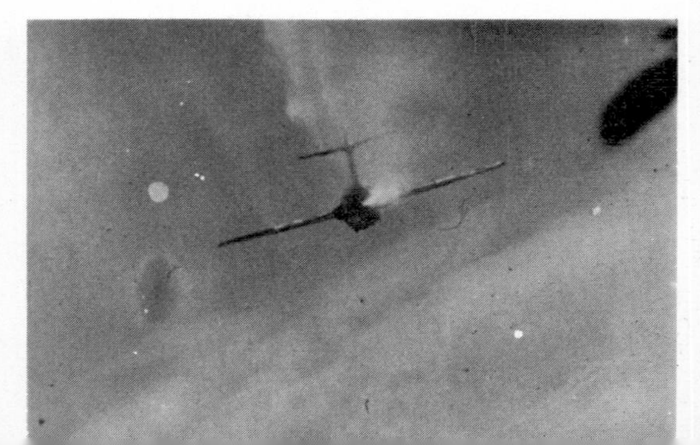

*Top:* Airman 1/C Donald Bedenstedd (left) of Carroll, Nebraska, crew chief of a F-94-B Starfire, takes a picture of 2nd Lt Sam Lyons (left) of Houston, Texas, radar operator and Capt Ben Fithian, pilot, of Kansas City, beside their Starfire at a Korean base. These officers are credited with the first enemy plane downed by a Starfire.

*Above:* B-29s of the 22nd BG attacking targets in north-western Korea.

*Above:* A Panther jet hits the Sea of Japan, with the pilot tightly strapped in and awaiting the impact. The carrier *Levte* had executed an 'Emergency turn to Port' ready to pick up the pilot.

*Left:* Lt Paul A. Hayek, USN, of Chicago, Illinois, surveys the 200 holes blown in the tail section of his Panther jet by a 37mm anti-aircraft shell while on a bombing run over North Korea. Flying from the carrier USS *Boxer* (CVA-21) in the closing days of the war, it was the third time his jet had been hit.

This Panther jet, flown by Lt (JG) Robert E. Rostine, of Henderson, Nevada had its fuel line shot away by Red anti-aircraft fire while on a mission over enemy territory in Korea. On landing, a spark turned the rear of the Panther into a blazing torch. Fire fighters are working on the blaze here.

A Panther jet aircraft from the aircraft carrier *Bon Homme Richard,* flying an interdiction mission over North Korea, is on its target. A bomb has just been dropped from its cradle while a second bomb which will follow is momentarily in position in its cradle beneath the other wing (right). Dropping the first bomb gave the jet an opportunity to use its 6in rockets. The puff of white smoke under the wing at left is the result of the plane firing the rockets.

*Top:* 'Miss Jacque II' the first US Air Force F-84 Thunderjet to fly 1,000 hours, taxis out to the runway to take off on her 364th combat mission against North Korean Communists. 'Miss Jacque' and other Thunderjets of the 136th Fighter-Bomber Wing flew daily interdiction missions against the Reds as part of the Fifth Air Force's all-out participation in 'Operation Strangle'.

*Above:* Armourers of the 49th Fighter-Bomber Wing, Fifth Air Force 'fire in' the 0.50 calibre machine guns on a Thunderjet at Taegu (K-2) airstrip in Korea. The guns are checked for accuracy and convergence on the target range at a given distance from the plane. Such jobs were accomplished at night leaving the aircraft tree during daylight hours for attacking Communist supply transportation and troop targets in North Korea.

Not the least of the problems was that the USAF had no units specifically trained for night intruder work, which meant that the Fifth Air Force's crews had to develop their own night interdiction tactics from experience as they went along. Mustangs and F-80s both tried their hand at night intruder work with an almost complete lack of result and up to the end of July the night interdiction task over Korea was carried out by B-26s and by three F-82 Twin Mustangs of the 68th Fighter all-weather Squadron. Even then successful attacks depended on visual contact and accurate target identification, for the B-26s carried no short-range navigation radar or blind bombing equipment. Early in August the all-weather F4U-5N Corsairs of Marine Squadron VMF(N)-513 joined the night offensive operating from Itazuke, but because of their short range their operations were restricted to attacks on enemy communications and artillery in the vicinity of the Pusan perimeter. Nevertheless the Corsairs accounted for up to ten of the 35 sorties per night carried out on average by the Fifth Air Force's intruders during August.

The great Communist offensive against the Pusan perimeter began on the night of August 31st. The enemy attacked in human waves, apparently heedless of the appalling casualties they suffered. Their tactics were born of desperation, for their commanders knew that if the offensive failed the North Korean People's Army—sadly depleted as it was by the battles of the previous weeks and by continual Allied air attack—could not withstand a strong Allied counter-offensive.

The main weight of the assault fell on the 25th Division's sector to the west of Masan. The sheer ferocity of the attack took the United Nations forces completely by surprise and the Communists raced on to capture Haman. At the same time two North Korean divisions supported by armour crossed the Naktong river and speared on to occupy Yongsan on September 1st, effectively cutting the 2nd Division in half. Another strong attack developed in the Waegwan sector, which was held by the First Cavalry, and by September 6th the North Koreans had advanced to within eight miles of Taegu, cutting the lateral Taegu road in two places. On September 5th elements of the British 27th Brigade, a battalion from the Middlesex Regiment and the Argyll and Sutherland Highlanders were hurled into the fighting on the Naktong river in the hills north of Taegu. While the line was held in this critical sector General Walker hastily sent his marines to Yongsan and on September 5th they successfully drove the North Koreans out of the area in the second battle of Naktong Bulge.

Right from the start of the Communist offensive the Fifth Air Force's fighter-bombers flew almost non-stop in direct support of the Allied ground forces. Over a hundred ground attack sorties were flown on September 1st in support of the hard-pressed 25th Division and sixty more were flown that same day in support of the 2nd Division. The Mustangs proved particularly effective; on more than one occasion they enabled pockets of American infantry encircled by the North Koreans to break out of the trap by dropping clusters of napalm on the enemy concentrations. Other groups of Americans, hopelessly surrounded in their positions, survived thanks to the efforts of the 21st Troop Carrier Squadron which air-dropped rations and ammunition to them. During the afternoon of September 1st the weight of the Fifth Air Force's fire-power was increased by the arrival of aircraft from Task Force 77, whose carriers had raced down the Korean coast at top speed from the position from which they had been launching interdiction sorties against targets in the North. The Navy pilots flew 85 sorties before dusk, most of them in support of the 2nd Division.

On September 2nd the Fifth Air Force and the Marine Corsair Squadron flew 200 close support missions and the Navy pilots of Task Force 77 flew 127, almost all of them in support of the 2nd and 25th Divisions. In addition 25 B-29s of the 307th Bombardment Group were despatched to attack North Korean supplies which were building up in Kumchon, Kochang and Chinju. On September 3rd Task Force 77 withdrew for replenishment at sea, but this did not prevent the carriers from launching a further 28 sorties in support of ground forces in the Yongsan sector.

After replenishment the Task Force then proceeded northwards once more to carry out further interdiction work. From September 3rd, therefore, it was once again left to the Fifth Air Force to bear the brunt of the ground attack operations. The results they achieved exceeded all expectations. On September 3rd alone the Fifth Air Force flew 249 close support and 89 interdiction missions. B-29s once again bombed troop concentrations and supplies in selected towns close to the battle-front. Thanks to this intense air activity Communist pressure on the Allied defences had lifted appreciably by the end of the day. On the 4th most of the tanks which were supporting the two North Korean divisions attacking in the Yongsan sector were knocked out in the course of 43 missions by Marine and Fifth Air Force fighter-bombers, and in the early hours of the following morning the North Koreans began to fall back in the face of determined counter-attacks by the 2nd Division.

The Fifth Air Force now turned its attention to supporting the ROK divisions fighting to the east of Taegu, flying 160 sorties on September 4th, 51 on September 5th and 183 on the 6th. Here too the air onslaught blunted the Communist attacks, and with the help of the US 24th Division the South Korean forces were soon launching a counter-offensive.

By September 7th the North Koreans were being held all along the line. The real turning point came on the 11th when the Fifth Air Force, the Marines and Bomber Command flew no fewer than 683 sorties against the enemy. On this day the fighter-bombers killed 1,500 soldiers and destroyed their equipment in the 2nd Division's sector alone. The following day the Eighth Army launched a general counter-offensive and the enemy began to fall back.

The North Koreans' gamble had failed and the immediate threat to the Pusan perimeter was over. The stage was now set for a brilliant Allied counter-stroke which had been in the making since the dark days of July, and which was designed to hurl the North Koreans back across the 38th Parallel.

CHAPTER FOUR

# On The Offensive

The story has it that General MacArthur first envisaged the masterstroke that would sweep the Communist aggressors from South Korea as early as June 29th 1950, when—in the days before the arrival of the first contingents of American combat troops—he stood on the hilltop overlooking the Han River and watched the shattered remnants of the ROK forces retreating in disorder before the rapid enemy advance.

His experiences as Allied Commander in the Pacific during the Second World War had taught MacArthur that a rapid advance by an enemy was almost always accompanied by a critical overstretching of his lines of supply and communication. This factor, coupled with the surprise of an amphibious landing on the Admiralty Islands in February 1944, had enabled his forces to bypass an entire Japanese army by leapfrogging 500 miles along the coast of New Guinea, a move that shortened the war by a month. This, on a smaller scale, was the strategy MacArthur planned to use to ensure an early Communist defeat in Korea. A seaborne force of the United States Marines, taking advantage of the full element of surprise, would land at Inchon far behind the enemy lines, at one blow slicing the North Koreans' vital supply lines in the Inchon-Seoul area in two and opening up a second front.

Operation Chromite, as the venture was named, was scheduled to begin on September 15th, by which time it was hoped that the whole of the 1st Marine Division would have arrived in Korea. There were four major objectives: the elimination of North Korean artillery batteries on Wolmi-Do, an island which controlled the approaches to Inchon harbour, a landing in the town of Inchon itself, the seizure of Kimpo airfield and the capture of Seoul. In addition to the Marine Division the Eighth Army's 7th Infantry Division—which had been held in reserve in Japan—was also to take part in the assault. The main thrust would be carried out by the Marines while the 7th Division covered the right flank and pushed on southwards towards Suwon. The invasion force would then hold on to the ground it had gained until the Eighth Army advanced north from the Pusan perimeter and linked up with it.

There was no denying that the Inchon landing would be one of the trickiest operations the US Marines had ever had to face. Not the least of the problems was the immense fluctuation of the spring tides. Only on two days, September 15th and October 11th, would the water be deep enough to allow the big landing craft with their draught of 29 feet to scrape through into the harbour, and even then the safety margin would be only three hours. Neither were there any beaches in the real sense of the word. Immediately on leaving their landing craft the Marines would have to scale 12 feet-high sea walls with the aid of ladders. These and other factors caused the US Chiefs of Staff to view Operation Chromite with grave concern, and attempts were made to persuade MacArthur to call off the whole undertaking.

The Operation and all the objections against it were debated at length at a high-level conference on August 23rd. MacArthur waited patiently while his colleagues had their say and then, in an impassioned speech lasting 45 minutes, he presented his own case. He pointed out that intuition alone, rather than any process of reasoned logic, had made him choose Inchon as the site of the amphibious landing. The enemy, he said, would not consider the Americans foolhardy enough to undertake an assault against such a difficult objective; therefore the Allied forces would have the fullest element of surprise. He compared Inchon with the assault on Quebec by General Wolfe nearly two centuries earlier. Wolfe's forces had scaled the heights of Abraham, taking the very route that the French Commander, General Montcalm, claimed was impossible. The result had been that the British had achieved complete surprise and Canada had been won for Britain in the subsequent battle on the 'Plains of Abraham'. "It is plainly apparent," the General went on, "that here in Asia is where the Communist conspirators have elected to make their play for global conquest. The test is not in Berlin or Vienna, London, Paris or Washington. It is here and now. It is along the Naktong River in South Korea." Forcefully, his words punctuated by short stabs of his corn-cob pipe, MacArthur said that elsewhere in the world the war against Communism was being fought with words—but there in Korea it was being fought with weapons. What they were fighting for was the prestige of the whole Western world. "I can almost hear the ticking of the second hand of destiny. We must act now or we will die. Inchon will succeed and it will save 100,000 lives. We shall land at Inchon and I shall crush them."

The objections against the Inchon landing had not been swept aside, but MacArthur's amazing oratory had turned the scales in his favour. On August 28th the Joint Chiefs of Staff approved the plans for Operation Chromite. MacArthur himself knew that the operation would be in the nature of a terrible gamble, yet he was conscious of the fact that the United Nations forces in Korea too were racing against time and that it was a race that amply justified the gamble however high the odds might be against it.

For weeks now, Intelligence reports had been coming in of Chinese Communist forces massing in strength in Manchuria beyond the Yalu River. There had already been several serious border incidents. Although United Nations aircrews had strict orders not to infringe Chinese air space, errors were inevitable. On August 27th, for example, two Fifth Air Force Mustang pilots strayed across the border as the result of a navigational error and attacked a Communist Chinese airstrip near Antung. There had also been several instances of RB-29 reconnaissance aircraft flying over North Korea being fired on by Chinese anti-aircraft batteries from across the border. MacArthur was convinced that the Red Chinese were planning a massive thrust across the Yalu in support of their North Korean allies and that the attack might come sooner than anyone anticipated. The inevitable result of such a move would be either a protracted war of attrition in Korea that might last for years, or an all-out confrontation between the United States and Red China. It was therefore vital to forestall such an eventuality by winning a rapid victory for the United Nations in Korea, and MacArthur saw Inchon as the best means of bringing this about.

It was realised at an early stage in the planning that the success of the Inchon operation would depend to a high degree on full co-ordination between the Naval and Air Forces. It was agreed that for three days prior to the invasion Naval aircraft would carry out a series of intensive sweeps of all enemy fighter airfields within a 150 mile radius of Inchon, and that the Navy pilots would then fly ground attack missions in support of the actual landing. Once the Marines were ashore close support operations would be taken over by aircraft of the 1st Marine Air Wing, and as soon as Kimpo airfield was recaptured and pronounced serviceable by a team of Air Force engineers Marine Aircraft Group 33 would transfer to this base from its escort carriers. The Fifth Air Force meanwhile was charged with continuing its primary task of maintaining overall air superiority while the B-29s of Far East Air Forces Bomber Command were to continue interdiction attacks against communications and industrial targets in the North. From D+1 three B-29 Groups were to stand by to carry out tactical bombing operations in support of the Eighth Army's breakout from the Pusan perimeter.

For two weeks prior to the scheduled date of the invasion—September 15th—the Inchon-Seoul area was photographed repeatedly by aircraft of the Far East Air Forces, primarily by RF-80 jets of the 8th Tactical Reconnaissance Squadron. The thousands of resultant photographs were at once turned over to the Navy planners, presenting them with accurate up-to-the-minute intelligence on enemy troop movements and defences. Meanwhile, Bomber Command continued to hit enemy communications in the Seoul area with the object of preventing the North Koreans from rushing reinforcements to Inchon, and between September 9th and 13th the B-29s cut 46 rail links. The biggest raid took place on the 13th when 60 B-29s drawn from four groups attacked marshalling yards and railway lines running southwards from Anju and Hungnam.

That evening, less than 36 hours before the Marines were due to hit the beaches, a sudden crisis developed when a typhoon swept over the Japanese Home Islands and threatened to ground the entire Fifth Air Force. Fortunately there had been adequate warning and two Mustang Groups, the 8th and 18th, were hastily flown to Taegu and the primitive K-9 airstrip near Pusan to continue operations in support of the Eighth Army.

The typhoon also made life difficult for the invasion forces, whose various components—consisting of 260 ships drawn from half a dozen different nations and carrying nearly 70,000 men—were then assembling off Sasebo. Despite all the difficulties, however, the transports succeeded in keeping station and after a few hours the typhoon wandered away. In the early hours of the 13th, shepherded by a screen of warship escorts that included the aircraft carrier HMS *Triumph*, the armada finally set course for Inchon.

At 06.33hrs on September 15th the 5th Marines went ashore on Wolmi-Do Island. They met only scattered resistance. For the previous three days the island had been subjected to an onslaught of bombs, rockets and napalm from Marine fighter-bombers and shells from American cruisers and destroyers, and just before the first assault wave went ashore the dazed defenders were pounded yet again by an intense bombardment from three rocket ships. By 06.55hrs the Island was in Allied hands and the way to Inchon harbour was open. Early in the afternoon the warships, joined by Navy and Marine fighter-bombers, turned the whole weight of their firepower on the buildings along the Inchon waterfront, softening up the area in readiness for the main landing, which was to be made with the high tide at 17.30hrs.

The assault went ahead on schedule, the Marines going ashore at two separate points. Air cover was provided throughout the operation by Navy Corsairs and Skyraiders from the *Valley Forge*, *Philippine Sea* and *Boxer*, which lately joined Task Force 77, and by the Seafires and Fireflies of HMS *Triumph*'s 800 and 827 Squadrons. By midnight the Marines had captured all their primary objectives for the cost of 196 casualties, including twenty killed in action. The first phase of Operation Chromite had succeeded and it seemed that MacArthur's gamble was being amply justified. Nevertheless it was apparent that luck had played a large part in the successful unfolding of the operation. The North Korean defences were strong, but they were found to be seriously undermanned. Had it been otherwise Operation Chromite might well have turned into a disaster on the scale of the tragic Dieppe operation of 1942.

At dawn the following morning, while South Korean Marines and No 5 Regimental Combat Team completed the mopping up operations in Inchon, the main forces began a two-pronged drive towards Seoul, 1st Marines advancing direct to the Han and the industrial suburbs of the city while 5th Marines headed towards Kimpo with the aim of capturing the airfield, crossing the Han from the north and striking into Seoul from the north-west. The North Koreans hastily assembled a scratch force known as the 1st Air Force Division to defend Kimpo, but after a confused night action the airfield fell to the Americans on September 17th.

The North Koreans appeared to have made very little use of Kimpo airfield. Only two Il-10s and one Yak-9 fighter fell into Allied hands and there was no evidence that the airfield had been fully occupied. The Americans were also surprised at the lack of North Korean air opposition to the landings at Inchon. Only on one occasion, at dawn on September 17th, did enemy aircraft put in an appearance, when two Yak-9s dropped down out of the clouds and released a few light bombs at the cruisers USS *Rochester* and HMS *Jamaica*. One of the fighters got away but the other was shot down by the British cruiser. It appeared that the North Koreans had hastily withdrawn most of the serviceable aircraft out of the area as soon as the Naval aircraft had begun their airfield strikes a few days earlier.

Kimpo airfield was captured with fairly little damage and the Marines lost no time in bringing up their air support. On September 19th the Corsairs of Marine Aircraft Group 33, consisting of Squadrons VMF(N)-542, VMF-212 and VMF-312 left the aircraft-carriers *Sicily* and *Badoeng Strait* and flew to Kimpo. Their place on board the carriers was taken by Marine Air Group 12, whose Corsairs were brought up from their transit base at Itami. The Kimpo-based Corsairs were in action almost immediately, covering the crossing of the Han by the 5th Marines on September 20th.

By this time Kimpo airfield—in terms of air traffic movements—had assumed the proportions of an international airport. From the afternoon of September 19th, in addition to the continual fighter-bomber sorties, a constant stream of C-54 and C-119 transports flew into the base carrying supplies for the ground forces and spare parts, fuel and ammunition for the Marine Corsairs. The non-stop airlift brought a daily average of 226 tons of supplies into Kimpo and on the return journeys the C-54s carried casualties to hospitals in Japan. On September 21st several C-54s were diverted to the newly captured airfield at Suwon, where they landed 65 tons of rations and ammunition, while nine C-119s dropped more food and ammunition to troops in the front line.

Meanwhile, preparations for the Eighth Army's breakout from the Pusan perimeter had been completed by September 16th. However, plans were held up by adverse weather, which prevented a force of 82 B-29s from bombing enemy troop concentrations near Waegwan early that morning. There were some sporadic ground attack missions in the course of the morning by F-80s and F-51s, but by mid-afternoon the weather had brought all air operations around the perimeter to a complete standstill. It was not until the following day—September 17th—that the ground offensive finally got under way and not until noon that the Fifth Air Force's fighter-bombers were able to operate. When they eventually did get off the ground, however, the Mustangs and F-80s dealt out considerable punishment to the enemy, attacking at low level just under the cloud base with napalm. In the sector covered by the advance of the US 2nd Division alone concentrated air attacks with napalm killed over 1,000 enemy soldiers as they were attempting to retreat across the Naktong River.

At last, on the night of September 17th/18th, the weather cleared sufficiently to allow the B-29s to operate in support of the ground forces. At dawn 42 B-29s of the 92nd and 98th Bombardment Groups placed 1,600 500lb bombs with beautiful precision in a strip of land a mile long by 500 yards wide as the North Koreans were trying to cross the Naktong by means of two bridges. Unlike the B-29 carpet bombing mission of August 16th this one was highly successful and the approaches to the two bridges were completely pulverised, effectively bottling up the retreating North Korean infantry and what remained of their motor transport.

Now, once again, it was the turn of the fighter-bombers. On September 18th the Fifth Air Force pilots carried out 286 ground attack missions and on the 19th this figure was stepped up to 361. It was on this day that the Eighth Army, spearheaded by troops of the 24th Division, began to cross the Nakton in force near Waegwan. With the river crossing successfully accomplished it was now up to the Allies to exploit their numerical superiority in armour. Spearheaded by tanks the Eighth Army's columns could thrust deep and rapidly into enemy territory, sweeping aside crumbling North Korean resistance. Ahead of the columns, scouting the way, flew the little Mosquitoes ready to call down floods of ground attack aircraft the moment anything suspicious was sighted. On September 21st, for example, the Mosquito pilots spotted a force of thirty enemy tanks moving up to attack the forward elements of the 24th Division. The T-34s were immediately pounced on by flights of rocket-firing Shooting Stars and Mustangs and half their number were left burning in the wake of the whirlwind air strike.

By September 24th the Fifth Air Force estimated that its fighter-bombers had killed nearly 8,000 enemy soldiers since the breakout began, and the Allied pilots were finding it increasingly difficult to locate worthwile targets as the North Korean armies broke up and scattered in confusion. On numerous occasions pilots returned to base with their bombs and rockets still on board rather than take the risk of hitting their own forces by mistake. This danger had been highlighted on the 23rd, when a flight of Mustangs mistakenly attacked a unit of the Argyll and Sutherland Highlanders, causing a considerable number of casualties.

As North Korean resistance crumbled the drive northwards by United Nations forces gathered momentum steadily. On September 26th 1st Cavalry joined up with 7th infantry at Osan, cutting off large numbers of North Korean troops. Meanwhile the Marines were advancing into Seoûl from the south, north and west, fighting every inch of the way. Corsairs of Marine Aircraft Group 33 whined over the shattered buildings, dropping napalm on pockets of enemy resistance in the streets and the surrounding hills. Finally, on the afternoon of the 27th the Stars and Stripes at last fluttered over the smoke of the devastated South Korean capital.

The virtual annihilation of the North Korean People's Army in the days that preceded the capture of Seoul, followed by the mopping up of isolated groups of North Korean soldiers who still fought on in the south, meant that the Fifth Air Force was now free to move its tactical air support units back to South Korea. By September 25th Headquarters Fifth Air Force in Korea had been re-established in Taegu city, while engineers re-serviced and reinforced the runways at Taegu airstrip to receive jet aircraft. The F-80 Shooting Stars of the 49th Fighter-Bomber Group were in position at Taegu by the end of the month, and a few days later the three Squadrons of the 49th Group were joined at Taegu by RF-80As of the 8th Tactical Reconnaissance Squadron and the RB-26s of the 162nd Tactical Reconnaissance Squadron. Meanwhile, Air Force engineers had also been hard at work on improving K-3 Airstrip at Pohang, and by October 12th this base was the home of three Mustang squadrons—the 39th and 40th Squadrons of the 35th Fighter-Interceptor Group and No 77 Squadron, Royal Australian Air Force. The Mustangs of the 18th Fighter-Bomber Group were based further south on K-9, Pusan East airfield.

Meanwhile, other engineer units had been hard at work restoring Kimpo and Suwon airfields to operational standard once more. Kimpo was in fairly good condition and the Marine Air Wing's Corsairs continued to operate from there quite satisfactorily, but Suwon's runways had taken a beating from Allied bombing and the tracks of American tanks which had churned up their surfaces. An engineer battalion patched up the field as best they could and laid down steel plank taxiways, and on October 7th the Mustangs of the 35th Squadron of the 8th Fighter-Bomber Group flew in. Only half of Suwon's runway, however, was still usable and operating heavily laden Mustangs from it was a dangerous business. Eventually, at the end of the month, the 35th Squadron was authorised to move to Kimpo, where it was joined a few days later by another of the 8th Group's units, the 36th Squadron. By this time the 51st Fighter-Interceptor Group had also established itself at Kimpo with three Squadrons, the 16th and 25th Fighter-Interceptor and the 80th Fighter-Bomber.

Operating combat aircraft, particularly F-80s, from the newly repaired Korean airstrips was not without its problems. At Taegu for example the steel plant runway subsided in places and became irregular, with the result that the 49th Group's F-80s frequently burst their tyres on landing. On one occasion an RB-26 burst a tyre on landing and slewed off the runway into a line of parked Shooting Stars, destroying four of them in the resulting collision. Excessive dust blown up by taxiing jets and sucked into air intakes was another problem, necessitating frequent engine overhauls. Nevertheless the F-80s showed up well even under these trying conditions, earning the unstinting praise of both air and ground crews.

The question that now faced the United Nations was whether the retreating enemy should be pursued across the 38th Parallel, and if so where the pursuit should stop. After some hesitation—there was a very real fear of Chinese or Russian intervention as a result of such a step—the United States Government authorised the Eighth Army to march into North Korea. On September 27th MacArthur was ordered by the Joint Chiefs of Staff to destroy the North Korean Army totally and form a united Korea under President Rhee. However, extreme caution was to be exercised; only South Korean forces were to be used in the vicinity of the Chinese and Russian frontiers and infinite pains were to be taken to ensure that no Allied units crossed the borders. MacArthur objected to this directive; he wanted his own forces to have complete freedom to advance as far as was necessary to ensure the complete surrender of the enemy. A demand for surrender had already been issued to the Korean Commander-in-Chief, and an immediate reaction had been threatening murmers from Communist China. On October 1st Premier Chou En-Lai warned the United Nations that China would come to the aid of the North Koreans if the latter's territory were invaded. There followed ten days of argument in the United Nations, with the Russian delegate pressing for a ceasefire and the immediate withdrawal of all foreign troops from Korean soil. Then on October 10th North Korean Premier Kim il Sung rejected MacAurthur's surrender demand outright. There was no alternative now but to proceed with the plan to occupy the whole of the North. Once again, it was a race against time; Chinese Communist forces were massing in Manchuria and Allied Intelligence indicated that by the middle of November the Chinese would have the ability to throw nine field armies into the action across the Yalu. What the Allies did not know was that by October 14th, only a fortnight after the first South Korean troops had crossed the 38th Parallel, Chinese Communist forces had already begun to cross the Yalu into North Korean territory. The crossings were made at night, undetected by allied air reconnaissance, over two large bridges at Antung and Manpojin.

General MacArthur's plan for the rapid conquest of North Korea involved yet another amphibious landing, this time at Wonsan on the east coast, by the Marine units which had carried out the Inchon invasion. The landing was to take place in conjunction with a push towards the North Korean capital, Pyongyang, by the Eighth Army. The scheme was opposed by both General Walker and Admiral Turner Joy, both of whom felt that it would be quicker to capture Wonsan following an overland march than by a cumbersome amphibious operation. Besides, South Korean forces were pushing rapidly along the east coast and they would probably capture the city first. Nevertheless the plan went ahead. On October 7th the Marines re-embarked on their armada of ships and sailed round the coast in readiness for the landing, which was scheduled to take place on the 20th. But they were too late; on October 10th the South Koreans were already fighting in the streets of Wonsan and the Marines found themselves in the embarassing position of being unable to go ashore because the harbour was sown with an uncharted forest of mines. All the 50,000 men could do was sit offshore in their transports and wait for further orders, with all hope of an overland drive to link up with the Eighth Army abandoned for the time being.

In fact the Eighth Army seemed to have little need of Marine support in its drive towards Pyongyang. On October 9th, supported all the way by Fifth Air Force fighter-bombers, American troops captured Kaesong and pushed on across the 38th Parallel, and on the 15th armoured columns of the 1st Cavalry Division began a headlong race towards the North Korean capital. The only serious opposition was encountered some ten miles south of the city when the Americans ran into a North Korean force supported by about 35 tanks and self-propelled guns. The enemy force was smashed by air strikes and artillery fire and on October 19th the 1st Cavalry Division, together with advance elements of the 27th Commonwealth Brigade, entered the outskirts of Pyongyang.

It was at this point that General MacArthur put another phase of his plan into operation. For two weeks the 187th Airborne Regimental Combat Team had been standing by to carry out an air drop behind

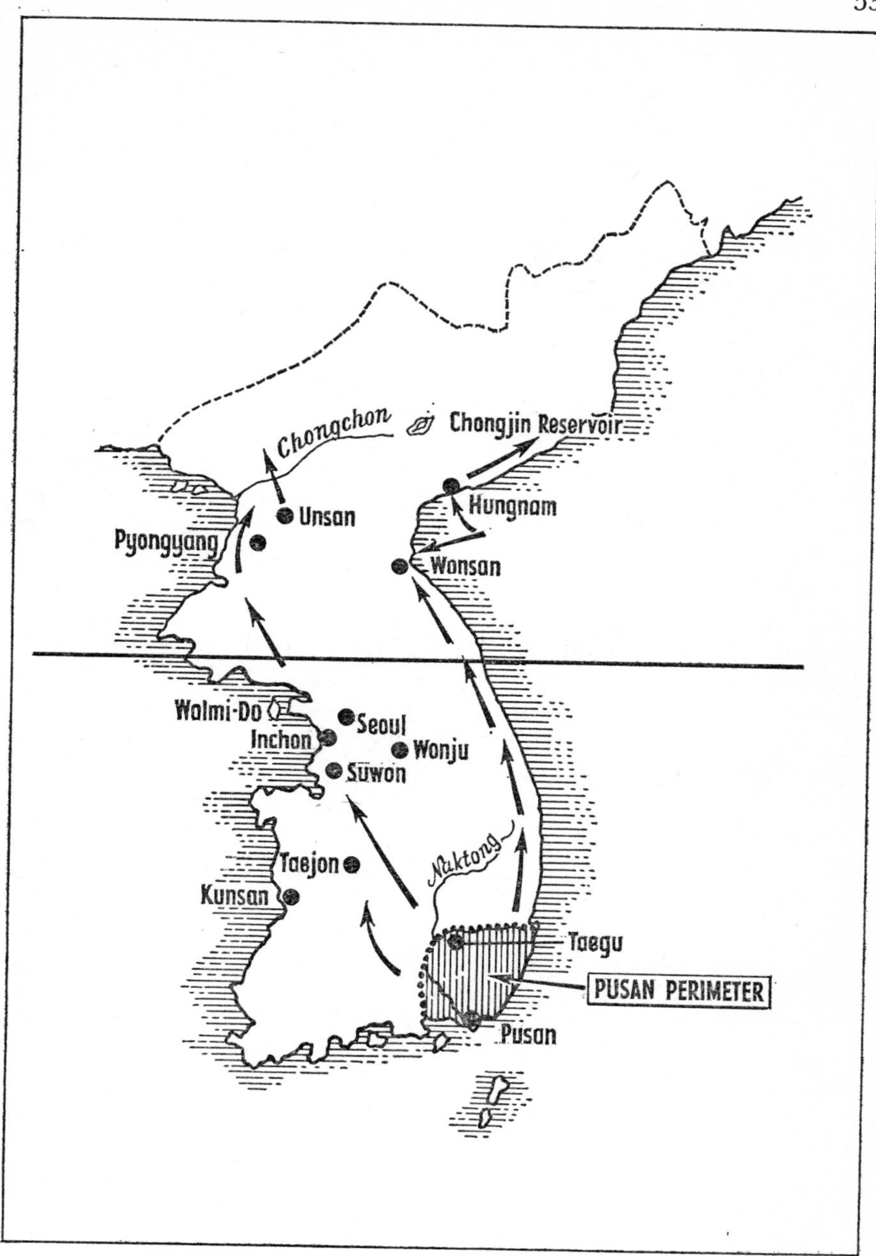


**UN** breakout, attack and pursuit, Sept–Oct 1950.

the enemy lines wherever it was considered necessary. It was now decided that the 187th should be dropped near the towns of Sukchon and Sunchon, about thirty miles north of Pyongyang astride an important road and rail complex leading to the city. The drop was scheduled for October 20th and an armada of 71 C-119s and 40 C-47s flew into Kimpo to take on the paratroops. From noon on the designated day 75 F-51s, 62 F-80s and 5 B-26s of the Fifth Air Force carried out intensive operations in and around the dropping zone, softening up enemy opposition in preparation for the airborne landings. Apart from a short delay caused by bad weather everything went as planned and 2,860 paratroops together with over 300 tons of equipment were unloaded from the transports during the afternoon. There were 37 casualties, including only one fatality. The paratroops quickly captured strategic high ground overlooking the drop zones and during the next three days fourteen C-119s dropped an additional 1,000 paratroops and 190 tons of supplies. On October 23rd, by which time the 187th had killed an estimated 2,700 enemy troops and taken 3,000 prisoners, the 1st Cavalry Division linked up with the Paratroops after pushing on from Pyongyang.

On the east coast the Marines were still waiting to go ashore at Wonsan. It was not until October 26th that the first units were able to carry out the landing, after Naval minesweepers had spent a week clearing the approaches to the port. On the 29th the US 7th Division also went ashore at Iwon about 90 miles to the north-east of Wonsan. Meanwhile, supported principally by the Corsairs of the 1st Marine Air Wing, South Korean forces had been pushing steadily up the coast towards the Yalu River. Then came a new development; on October 25th a South Korean division approaching the Yalu ran into strong enemy opposition. Within 48 hours the opposing troops had been identified as belonging to two Chinese Communist Divisions. By the end of the month it was apparent that Chinese intervention in North Korea was getting under way on a massive scale.

There had already been signs that the Red Chinese Air Force was also getting ready to take part in the battle. From October 15th onwards all the United Nations aircraft patrolling immediately south of the Yalu River were fired on by Chinese anti-aircraft batteries and one Mustang was shot down on the 16th. Then, on the 18th, the crew of an RB-29 of the 31st Strategic Reconnaissance Squadron reported that up to 75 Red Chinese fighters were massing on the airfield at Antung.

On the morning of November 1st a B-26 of the 730th Bombardment Squadron was attacked by three Yak-9 fighters bearing Chinese Communist markings near Sinuiju. One of the Yaks was shot down by the B-26's gunners and the remainder fled northwards when two Mustangs of the 18th Group appeared on the scene. Later that day, an

RF-80 reported that fifteen Yaks were drawn up on Sinuiju airfield and six F-80s were detailed to carry out an attack. One Yak was destroyed and six more damaged but one of the F-80s was shot down by heavy anti-aircraft fire from across the Yalu. The second F-80 strike was laid on at noon but the American pilots found the enemy airfield deserted. The Communists had apparently evacuated all their airworthy machines north of the river, leaving a few damaged aircraft behind.

At 14.00hrs that same day, four 18th Group Mustangs were patrolling south of the Yalu when they were attacked by six swept-wing jet aircraft. The jets made one firing pass without doing any damage, then flew back across the river. They were MiG-15 fighters. From now on it was going to be no picnic. It was grimly apparent to the United Nations pilots that the air war over Korea was only just beginning.

CHAPTER FIVE

# Strategic Bombing of North Korea, July-September 1950

The big drive northward by United Nations Forces during the autumn of 1950 was supported to the full by B-29s of the Far East Air Forces Bomber Command. This was made possible not so much because direct tactical support operations were accorded priority over any other type of mission flown by the medium bombers, but because by the end of August General O'Donnell's crews had simply run out of worthwhile strategic targets in North Korea. Early in July, when the decision had first been taken to launch a strategic bombing campaign against the North, Strategic Air Command Intelligence had selected five major industrial centres to receive the attention of Bomber Command. These were Pyongyang, which in addition to being the centre of the North Korean aircraft and armaments industry possessed extensive marshalling yards and railway repair shops; Wonsan, with its modern sea port and acres of oil refineries; Hungnam, with its chemical and light metal industries; the harbour town of Chongjin, with its iron foundries and railway yards; and the naval base, oil storage tanks and rail complex at Rashin, which lay only sixty miles from Vladivostok. All these targets, with the exception of Pyongyang, lay on the north east coast of Korea. Other targets of secondary strategic importance were the harbour of Chinnampo at the mouth of the Taedong River on the west coast, whose factories produced aluminium, magnesium, copper and zinc, and five east coast hydro-electric power complexes originally built by the Japanese during World War II at Fusen, Chosin, Kyosen, Funei and Kongosan. A sixth hydro-electric plant, also of Japanese construction, lay at Sui-Ho on the Yalu River. This was held to be of particular importance because half its output of electricity was channelled to the Chinese Communist industries in Manchuria.

Once these targets had been established, Strategic Air Command's planners had quickly worked out a list of priorities. Following a careful study of the five major target systems selected for attack it was quickly realised that since the industries and communications complexes within these areas were grouped so closely together, little advantage would be derived from a programme of precision bombing of the kind brought to a fine art by the Eighth and Ninth US Air Forces in Europe during World War II. Area bombing with widespread use of incendiary bombs was thought to present a far more effective solution. A similar policy had caused incalculable damage to the Japanese war effort during 1944–45, when massive and repeated incendiary attacks against selected Japanese cities had razed whole industrial areas to the ground. In the words of General O'Donnell, "It was my intention and hope that we would be able to get out there and to cash in on our psychological advantage in having gotten into the theatre and into the war so fast by putting a very severe blow on the North Koreans, with an advance warning, perhaps, telling them that they had gone too far in what we all recognise as being an act of aggression, and then go to work burning five major cities in North Korea to the ground, and to destroy completely every one of about 18 major strategic targets."

After the initial and isolated attack against the rail complex of Wonsan on July 13th by the 22nd and 92nd Bombardment Groups, the execution of the plan for a large scale strategic air offensive against North Korea had been delayed because of the urgent need for the medium bomber groups to fly tactical support missions at the request of the retreat Allied ground forces during the critical weeks that followed. It was not until the end of July that authority for the offensive to begin was given, and even then MacArthur was to reserve priority for the use of Bomber Command in direct support of his ground forces whenever it was considered necessary.

The first target selected for a large scale strike was Hungnam, or more specifically the factories of the Chosen nitrogen fertiliser company, the Chosen Nitrogen Explosives Factory and the Bogun Chemical Plant, all of which lay in the area of the town. Following intensive photographic coverage of the target by the RB-29s of the 31st Strategic Reconnaissance Squadron, the operation was scheduled to begin on the morning of July 30th. The first phase, code-named Operation Nannie Able, called for an attack on the Chosen Nitrogen Explosives Factory. Beginning at 09.50hrs 47 B-29s of the 22nd and 92nd Bombardment Groups unloaded their bombs through thin cloud on the plant and when the last of them droned away 70 per cent of the installations had been either destroyed or damaged. The second phase, Operation Nannie Baker, was directed against the Chosen Nitrogen Fertiliser Factory and took place on August 1st when 46 B-29s of the same Groups attacked the target visually with 500lb bombs from 16,000 feet. The crews reported observing large explosions with extensive smoke and flames in the target area. The third phase, Nannie Charlie, was carried out on the 3rd when 39 B-29s attacked the Bogun Chemical Plant with good results. All three raids had involved precision attacks with high explosives, for authority to use incendiaries on a large scale had not yet been received by General O'Donnell. Nevertheless in the space of three days Bomber Command had succeeded in inflicting appalling damage on the biggest explosives and chemical centre in Asia.

At a very early stage in the strategic bombing campaign General O'Donnell had stated that he did not intend adverse weather conditions to interfere with the efforts of his crews. It was no idle promise. Between July 13th and October 31st Bomber Command dropped more than 30,000 tons of bombs on North Korean targets, bettering the record of the Far East Air Forces B-29s operating out of the Marianas against Japanese targets during the Second World War. Although formation attacks were naturally desirable against industrial complexes, when these were precluded by bad weather the bombers made their runs across the target area in a long stream, each aircraft bombing singly by radar. Every effort was also made to maintain a high degree of efficiency in ground control approach techniques at the bomber bases, and the fact that there were no major bad weather landing accidents during this initial phase of the strategic bombing campaign was ample testimony of the skill of the GCA controllers.

By the end of the second week in August all five of the industrial complexes designated by the Strategic Air Command planners had been visited by General O'Donnell's bombers. The last target to be attacked was Rashin, which was bombed on August 12th by radar. Most of the bombs, however, fell in open country and no damage was inflicted on the target itself. A second attempt to bomb this target on August 27th was frustrated by bad weather and 64 B-29s bombed secondary targets at Chongjin.

The fact that the bombers had failed to hit Rashin at all on their first attack, coupled with the target's close proximity to the Soviet border, had given rise to serious anxieties in the US State Department and something of a battle now developed between the politicians and the Joint Chiefs of Staff. The latter reasoned that large quantities of war supplies were continuing to flow into North Korea through the port and therefore Bomber Command was justified in attacking it, no matter how close it lay to Soviet territory. Nevertheless, the politicians won the day and on September 1st the Joint Chiefs of Staff instructed General Stratemeyer to call off any future plans for attacks on this objective.

At the beginning of September FEAF strategists found themselves confronted with a dilemma. Although MacArthur's plans for an amphibious landing at Inchon and a breakout from the Pusan perimeter were well advanced it had not yet been decided whether Allied forces would push on beyond the 38th Parallel to occupy the whole of North Korea or come to a halt when the invaders had been cleared from the South.

In the latter case FEAF's planners were determined to complete the destruction of a wide cross-section of North Korea's industrial potential, including the hydro-electrical plants which were supplying power to Red China. The problem was that despite repeated requests to Washington for approval to attack the hydro-electrical complexes, no advice at all was forthcoming from that quarter. In the end the Far East Command Target Selection Committee, with General MacArthur's approval, directed Bomber Command to carry out attacks on North Korea's hydro-electric power sources as planned and on September 26th B-29s of the 92nd Bombardment Group destroyed the Fusen hydro-electric plant near Hungnam. It was the last attack in this phase of the strategic bombing campaign. Even as the B-29s were unloading their bombs on the target a signal reached General MacArthur from Washington informing him that his troops were authorised to cross the 38th Parallel. During the days that followed the Allied forces made rapid progress northwards, and since the early occupation of the whole of North Korea now seemed assured it was decided at a high level conference in Tokyo that further strategic bombing attacks on the North would serve no useful purpose.

With the exception of the solitary attack on Rashin the strategic bombing offensive against North Korea had been characterised throughout by an unparalled degree of accuracy. Although industrial targets in the selected North Korean cities had been almost completely wiped out the urban areas surrounding them had emerged virtually unscathed. Also, in the majority of cases, loss of life among the North Korean workers had been relatively small, for each raid had been preceded by a leaflet dropping mission stating the time and place selected for the attack. Nevertheless, the personnel of Bomber Command —from General O'Donnell down to the last B-29 rear-gunner—were under no illusions. They were aware that their success had been attributable in the main to one fact: the lack of enemy opposition. The ideal conditions were not to last. They ended on November 1st with the dramatic appearance of the first MiG-15 over North Korea. From now on the sky south of the Yalu River would be a dangerous place.

CHAPTER SIX

# Battle Over the Yalu

During the last week of October 1950, advance units of the ROK 3rd Division began to run into stiff resistance in their advance northwards from Hungnam. The hard-pressed South Koreans sent out a call for reinforcements and on November 1st the 7th US Marine Regiment moved up to their assistance. Within 24 hours the Marines had also begun to run into trouble and during the next four days they were locked in a fierce battle with strong enemy forces astride the road north in the Sudong area. It was the same story in the west where the ROK 1st Division, the 8th Cavalry Regiment and units of the Commonwealth Brigade all encountered superior enemy forces. Some of the fiercest fighting in this sector took place on November 5th when the Commonwealth Brigade and waves of Communist troops fought a bitter engagement for possession of the river-crossing at Pakchon. Then, suddenly, the fighting died down. Cautiously, the badly mauled Allied forces pushed ahead once more, to find that the enemy had inexplicably melted away all along the front, leaving behind a handful of prisoners. The latter, in their drab quilted uniforms decorated with a plain red star, told their own story. There was no longer any doubt that the Chinese Communist intervention in North Korea had begun.

The prospect of massive attacks by Chinese Communist forces in the days ahead presented General Walker, commander of the Eighth US Army, with a serious problem. Because of the rapid drive northwards his own forces were already badly overstretched, with supplies of food and ammunition for only two or three days. On November 3rd he therefore ordered the Eighth Army to fall back to the line of the Chongchon River where it could re-group and build up its supplies in preparation for a renewed offensive. The withdrawal, which was effectively covered by the fighter-bombers of the Fifth Air Force, was completed by November 7th. Almost as soon as the Allies were in position along the Chongchon the Communists attacked in strength, but they were shrivelled up by intense and accurate artillery fire.

At this stage there was no clear picture of the extent of the Chinese Communist intervention in Korea. As yet, United Nations commanders in the field did not know whether the enemy forces they were encountering were regular Chinese units or bands of 'volunteers' sent to the assistance of the North Koreans. One thing, however, was certain: the new threat meant that the already overtaxed Allied Air Forces would now have an even greater burden to bear. Moreover, if Allied air power was to be exploited to its fullest effectiveness there would have to be a change in the policy that had hitherto prevented Allied air attacks on targets that lay close to the Manchurian and Soviet frontiers. On November 3rd representatives of the Far East Air Forces and the US 7th Fleet met in Tokyo to work out a new formula for waging a new stepped-up air offensive. Repeated requests by General Partridge to allow his fighter pilots to attack and destroy Communist aircraft on their airfields just over the Manchurian border met with equally repeated refusals, but General Stratemeyer did give authority for the Fifth Air Force's fighter-bombers to range over the whole of North Korea up to the banks of the Yalu River with the proviso that such missions were to be flown by highly experienced pilots with accurate details of the targets they were briefed to attack. At the same time General O'Donnell was authorised to send his B-29s to attack four North Korean cities which were key centres of munitions and communications. This time the kid gloves were off; there was to be no attempt at ultra-precise bombing to avoid high civilian casualties. The B-29s were to carry full loads of incendiaries and their task was to burn the selected cities from end to end. These decisions were ratified on November 5th, when General MacArthur issued a directive calling for a maximum air effort lasting two weeks.

MacArthur's directive in fact gave carte blanche for the beginning of an unrestricted bombing campaign against North Korea. Bomber Command, Fifth Air Force and the carrier aircraft of Task Force 77 were to destroy everything that might be useful to the Communists in their attempt to hurl back the United Nations forces. Targets listed included the Korean ends of several strategic bridges over the Yalu River, with particular reference to the twin 3,098ft bridges which linked Antung in Manchuria with Sinuiju in North Korea, and over which a steady flow of supplies was reaching Chinese combat troops fighting in the North.

By the time a copy of MacArthur's directive was received in Washington in the evening of November 5th the first incendiary attack had already been carried out. Earlier that day B-29s of the 19th Bombardment Group had unloaded 170 tons of fire bombs on the North Korean town of Kanggye, destroying more than half of the built-up area. This, together with the decision to attack the bridges across the Yalu, caused a political storm and a response was not long in coming. Before midnight that same day President Truman himself, through the Joint Chiefs of Staff, had sent a signal forbidding MacArthur to employ his bombers within five miles of the Manchurian border. MacArthur immediately countered with another signal in which he informed the Joint Chiefs of Staff that vast quantities of Chinese troops and material were pouring across the bridges. In fact, most of the damage had by this time been done; the majority of the Chinese combat troops, together with full supporting equipment, had already made the crossing during the preceding two weeks under cover of darkness. Nevertheless, this explanation was enough to convince the Joint Chiefs that MacArthur was right, if even only for the time being. On November 6th attacks on the bridges were authorised, though every precaution was to be taken to ensure that no United Nations aircraft strayed over the frontier into Manchuria. The Joint Chiefs also made it clear that the territory in the vicinity of the Soviet border was to remain strictly prohibited and that no attacks were to be made on targets in this area, no matter how promising they might appear.

At dawn on November 7th 70 B-29s stood ready to carry out the first mission of the two-week bombing campaign: a concentrated attack on the town of Sinuiju, with the object of blocking the approaches to the vital twin bridges across the Yalu. The operation, however, had to be postponed at the last minute because of bad weather, and it was not until the following day that the bombers were finally able to take off. Several minutes ahead of the massive B-29 formation, F-51 and F-80 fighter-bombers swarmed down on the south bank of the Yalu, hammering enemy anti-aircraft positions around Sinuiju with rockets, napalm and machine guns. High above, two flights of Shooting Stars of the 51st Fighter-Interceptor Wing circled watchfully, their pilots scanning the hostile sky to the north of the River. The Reds had been up in strength during the past week, and seven Yaks had been shot down in the course of several skirmishes. United Nations pilots had little to fear from the elderly piston-engined Communist fighters, but with the MiG-15 it was a different story. Only the day before, Fifth Air Force Mustangs operating in the area south of the river had been attacked by MiGs on five separate occasions and only the inexperience of the Communist jet pilots had prevented a massacre. Now, as they patrolled at 20,000 feet, the 51st Wing's F-80 pilots knew what frustration felt like as—powerless to intervene—they watched more MiGs taking off from Antung airfield just across the river. Unmolested, six MiGs went into a leisurely climb that took them to 30,000 feet on the Manchurian side of the river; then, in pairs, they came arrowing down towards the F-80s. The latter turned to meet them, a manoeuvre that seemed to confuse the Communist pilots who broke in all directions after making one wildly inaccurate firing pass. Five of the MiGs immediately turned away and climbed flat out towards sanctuary on the far side of the river, easily drawing away from the slower F-80s. The sixth, however, went into a shallow dive, and one of the Shooting Star pilots—Lieutenant Russell J. Brown—spotted his opportunity. The F-80 was heavier than the MiG and the distance gradually narrowed between the two aircraft as they plummeted earthwards. The MiG pilot realised his mistake and began to climb, but it was too late. Clinging like a leech to the enemy fighter's tail Brown held his thumb down on the gun button and loosed off a five-second burst with his 0·5 machine guns. Pieces flew off the MiG and it went down vertically, burning fiercely and trailing a long banner of white smoke, to explode on the banks of the river. So ended the first jet versus jet battle in history.

Half an hour later 70 B-29s arrived over Sinuiju and dropped over 580 tons of incendiary bombs on the town. Communist anti-aircraft batteries put up a heavy barrage from across the river but none of the bombers, attacking from 18,000 feet, was hit. As the main B-29 force droned away nine more medium bombers flew over the great pall of smoke that spread over the sky from the shattered town and unloaded 1,000lb bombs on the North Korean end of the bridges. The nine B-29s were aircraft of the 19th Bombardment Group, but on this occasion 'the bridge specialists' failed to live up to their reputation. Although the 1,000-pounders severely damaged the approaches to the bridges the structures themselves still stood.

The next day, November 9th, it was the Navy's turn. For three consecutive days Corsairs and Skyraiders from the carriers *Valley Forge*, *Philippine Sea* and *Leyte* pounded the bridges at Sinuiju and two other bridges further up the river at Hyesanjin. The Navy pilots succeeded in knocking out the two latter bridges and the road bridge at Sinuiju, but the vital railway bridge still stood.

From now on Allied aircraft engaged in attacking bridge targets along the Yalu began to run into increasingly determined opposition from enemy jet fighters. On November 10th MiG-15s shot down a B-29 of the 307th Group over Uiju and on the 12th a 98th Group B-29 just managed to limp into Kimpo after being badly mauled by MiGs several miles south of the river. Other 98th Group B-29s which attacked the bridges at Sinuiju two days later sighted no enemy interceptors, but the next day two bombers of the 19th and 307th Groups were badly damaged by MiGs while attacking the same target. Further medium bomber operations along the Yalu were curtailed for a week because of bad weather, but on November 25th and 26th B-29s of the 19th and 307th Groups destroyed two more bridges across the river, one at Manpojin and the other at Chongsonjin.

By the last week in November a combined Navy and Air Force effort had destroyed or damaged some 65 per cent of North Korea's strategic bridges. Subsequent air reconnaissance, however, revealed that much of the effort had been wasted. As fast as the bombers knocked down a bridge Chinese engineers threw up pontoons alongside it and the flow of men and equipment continued unhindered across the river. Moreover, by mid-November the Yalu had begun to freeze over rapidly and it would not be long before the ice was thick enough to support heavy equipment. Attacks by B-29s and by B-26s of the 3rd and 452nd Bombardment Groups on nine major supply and communications centres in North Korea, although they caused considerable devastation, did little to hinder the steady Chinese build-up.

American Intelligence sources in fact had gravely underestimated the actual number of Chinese troops in North Korea at the beginning of November. Eighth Army G-2, Far East Command Intelligence and the Central Intelligence Agency all agreed that the number of Chinese present in North Korea at the beginning of November did not exceed 60,000, but by that time more than 180,000 Chinese troops had already crossed the Yalu. It was only when Allied combat troops in the front line began to suffer heavy and repeated setbacks at the hands of vastly superior Communist forces that the serious nature of the error was appreciated.

The reason for the failure to realise the true gravity of the situation was twofold. First of all there was the utmost stealth and secrecy with which the Chinese field armies, split into small components, moved across the countryside at night-time to their assembly positions, and then there was the almost complete lack of any kind of effective Allied spy network in North Korea. Such a network had in fact flourished when the Americans had occupied the South prior to 1949, but it had subsequently become disorganised and many of the remaining agents had been captured and killed following the invasion of South Korea by the North in June 1950. The only real tool at the disposal of the Intelligence experts, therefore, remained air reconnaissance, and even this suffered from a critical shortage of aircraft and crews and from the fact that there were no accurate detailed maps of North Korea—a serious omission when it came to interpreting aerial photographs.

The plain fact was that the USAF's reconnaissance units in FEAF and elsewhere had suffered particularly heavily under the post-war economy drive. The result was that American reconnaissance aircraft and systems had simply not kept pace with other fields of aviation technology. On the outbreak of hostilities in Korea, in fact, FEAF did not have an air reconnaissance system as such at all. The sole reconnaissance capability—if one discounted the two ancient RB-17s of the 6204th photo-mapping flight at Clark Air Force base—lay with the RB-29s of the 31st Strategic Reconnaissance Squadron at Kadena and the RF-80As of the 8th Tactical Reconnaissance Squadron at Yakota, but no real plan existed for their operational use, and their effectiveness suffered as a consequence. All this meant that FEAF had to build up a reconnaissance system from scratch, and it was a slow process. A third reconnaissance unit—the 167th Tactical Reconnaissance Squadron (Night Photography) with RB-26s—reached Itazuke towards the end of August 1950, but the next unit to arrive, the 45th Tactical Reconnaissance Squadron operating RF-51s, was not able to begin operations from Itazuke until November because of a shortage of aircraft. The 45th Squadron's task was visual reconnaissance and until it began operations this task was carried out on behalf of the Eighth Army almost entirely by elderly T-6 Texans, their pilots running incredible risks.

The first really effective step towards organising an air reconnaissance capability came in September, when the 543rd Tactical Support Group was established at Itazuke. Now at least Far East Air Forces Reconnaissance had a headquarters, if only a makeshift one. This led to the formation in February 1951 of the 67th Tactical Reconnaissance Wing which grouped all existing Fifth Air Force Reconnaissance Units under its command. The designations of some of the latter were changed. The 543rd Group became the 67th, while the 8th and 162nd Tactical Reconnaissance Squadrons became the 15th and 12th respectively. Only the 45th Tactical Reconnaissance Squadron retained its original designation. The 31st Strategic Reconnaissance Squadron, which remained under the orders of Strategic Air Command, had already been re-designated the 91st Squadron on November 16th. It was the crews of the latter Squadron who, during the early days or reorganisation, paid with their lives for the lack of foresight and planning of the previous years. In fact the RB-29s began to suffer so heavily from flak and hostile fighters over the Yalu that in mid-November their task in this sector was taken over by the RF-80As of the 8th Squadron.

November also saw the re-deployment of some of the Fifth Air Force's Mustang units from their bases around Pusan to newly-captured airfields further north, closer to the battle areas. Among the units involved were the 35th Fighter-Interceptor Group and No 77 Squadron RAAF, which flew into Yonpo on November 19th, and the 18th Fighter-Bomber Group and No 2 Squadron South African Air Force, which established themselves at Pyongyang East airfield on the 22nd. Both these airfields had been badly hit by Allied bombing and conditions were primitive, but pilots were more than willing to put up with them in exchange for fewer fatiguing hours spent in the air during each sortie.

No 2 'Cheetah' Squadron, South African Air Force, was the latest Commonwealth air unit to arrive in Korea, having sailed for Japan in September, a matter of days after the Union Government had agreed to place a Squadron at the disposal of the United Nations Organisation. There was another Commonwealth detachment at Iwakuni in Japan, comprising Nos 88 and 209 Squadrons RAF. These two units, which formed the RAF's Far East Flying Boat Wing, had been based on

Iwakuni since August 1950. Operating Short Sunderland flying boats their task was to provide reconnaissance cover and a ferry service between Iwakuni and the Korean coast. On one occasion, in September 1950, a Sunderland of 209 Squadron reconnoitred for mines and submarines as far as the approaches to Vladivostok. Although both Squadrons were subsequently sent to Singapore in 1951 to take part in the campaign against the Malayan terrorists, each left a detachment at Iwakuni and these carried out patrol duties along the Korean coast for the duration of the war.

The biggest single Commonwealth commitment, of course, continued to rest with the Fleet Air Arm. Early in October HMS *Triumph* had returned to Hong Kong after three months of operations in Korean waters, during which her aircraft had flown 895 sorties mainly in the ground attack role. She was replaced by HMS *Theseus*, which together with her 17th Carrier Air Group—No 807 Squadron with Sea Furies and No 810 with Fireflies—had been in the UK when the carrier was warned for duty in Korean waters. After six weeks of intensive training in the UK and en route to the Far East she eventually went to action stations off Korea on October 9th, having embarked one Sikorsky S-51 plane guard helicopter at Hong Kong.

The *Theseus* formed part of a Task Force under Rear Admiral Andrews. Her Air Group began operations on the day of her arrival in the Yellow Sea, and between then and the 22nd October her aircraft attacked targets at Chinnampo, Haeju in Hwanghai Province and at Pakchon and Chongju. Several strikes were flown against Chinnampo, which the UN forces—then beginning to drive the North Koreans back—hoped to capture and use as a supply port. During this period 807 Squadron flew 264 sorties and the Fireflies of 810 flew 120. On the 22nd the carrier withdrew for a short rest at Iwakuni, returning early in November to cover minesweeping operations in the Chinnampo estuary. She then returned to Hong Kong to take part in another exercise, having temporarily disembarked six of her Fireflies for bombardment spotting duties.

The next series of strikes was mounted between December 6th and 26th, the aircraft this time concentrating on roads, bridges, airfields and rolling stock—any target whose destruction might help to impede the advance of the Chinese field armies which were now pouring into the country, and give the UN forces a badly needed respite. So far no enemy aircraft had been encountered by the Fleet Air Arm pilots; in fact none were to be met at all by the *Theseus*'s aircraft during her period of operations, and the only damage was caused by anti-aircraft fire and technical troubles. The latter gave one of 807 Squadron's pilots, Lieutenant D. P. W. Kelly, a few nasty moments on Christmas Day 1950 shortly after he had set off on a strike in his heavily laden Sea

Fury. The engine began to bang and cough alarmingly and there was nothing for it but to ditch in the icy waters of the Yellow Sea. Kelly was not encouraged by the rumour currently doing the rounds that it was impossible to ditch a Sea Fury successfully—but he brought it off all right and the aircraft stayed afloat long enough to allow him to scramble out of the cockpit. Fortunately the ditching had been seen by the crew of the Canadian destroyer *Sioux*, which picked him up minutes later. He was flying again the next day.

During the December series of strikes the 17th Carrier Air Group flew 630 sorties. Throughout the period, Fireflies equipped with long-range tanks maintained anti-submarine patrols. It was known that the small North Korean Navy had two Russian-built submarines and they were believed to be in the Yellow Sea, but they were not sighted. A combat air patrol was also maintained during daylight and a staggering total of 3,900 interceptions and visual identifications were made by the Fireflies and Sea Furies. All the aircraft intercepted turned out to be Allied types, mainly B-29s, Neptunes and Sunderlands.

Top cover—up to 40,000 feet—for all strikes launched by the *Theseus* and subsequent carriers operating off Korea was provided by the United States Air Force, with Mustangs, F-80s and later F-84s and Sabres. The strikes were direct by T-6 or L-4 Mosquito aircraft. Armed reconnaissance was the task of 810 Squadron's Fireflies, flying at 1,500 feet or less over enemy territory—often a risky business because of intense small arms fire. The information they and other UN recce aircraft brought back was co-ordinated by the Joint Operations Centre at Taegu, where two US Navy officers and one Royal Navy liaison officers analysed potential targets for assignment to the carrier aircraft. The high quality of the reconnaissance, resulting in very accurate and devastating strikes, soon made enemy movements in daylight extremely hazardous. Bridges were among the main objectives. Following the early strikes, however, reconnaissance showed that the enemy was rebuilding these almost as quickly as the FAA knocked them down, so from then on delayed action bombs were used to make this task more difficult. Because of the shallow waters off the Korean coast the *Theseus* had to stand off at a distance of up to seventy miles—a long haul over water in an aircraft suffering from battle damage. It was here that the plane guard S-51 helicopters proved their worth. They rescued four ditched pilots and also snatched another four from behind enemy lines.

In January and February 1951 aircraft from the *Theseus* were engaged in spotting for the Allied naval forces bombarding Inchon. Afterwards the carrier moved from her station on the west coast into the Sea of Japan, where between April 9th and 19th—in company with the US carrier *Bataan*—her aircraft spotted for warships shelling Wonsan and Songjin. It was the British carrier's final operation in Korean waters, where she had spent a total of 6½ months. During that time her aircraft had made 3,489 operational sorties, dropping 92 1000lb and 1,474 500lb bombs, launching 7,317 rocket projectiles and firing over half a million rounds of 20 mm ammunition. Many of the operational sorties had been flown in bad weather particularly in December and January when snowstorms often swept across the country without warning. The *Theseus* was eventually relieved by HMS *Glory*, whose aircraft carried on in the pattern laid down by the preceding carrier.

In November 1950, despite continuing reports of growing numbers of Chinese troops south of the Yalu, hopes for a rapid and successful final Allied drive to the Manchurian border were still high. Combat patrols pushed out along the front by the Eighth Army and the ROK forces reported only weak enemy resistance. United Nations commanders, however, seemed unaware that their forces, like a great cumbersome bear, were plunging headlong towards a deadly trap. The Chinese were faithfully obeying the tactics formulated by Mao Tse Tung's guerillas in the mountains of China twenty years earlier. The tactics were simple enough. The enemy would be allowed to advance, the Communists falling back before him and offering only minimal resistance; then, when the enemy's lines were overstretched the full fury of the Communist armies would be turned upon him. The United Nations in Korea, like Chiang Kai-Shek's Chinese Nationalists before them, were soon to learn this elementary military lesson the hard way.

Across the border China's leaders were under no illusions. They knew that the coming offensive by their armies in Korea would bring with it the strong possibility of an all-out war against the United States. It was a risk they were prepared to accept, including the awesome threat of an atomic strike against Chinese targets by Strategic Air Command. By the beginning of November 1950, in preparation for this eventuality, the whole of North-east China was placed on a war footing. Air raid drill was being carried out in every town and village and deep air raid shelters were being built in and around major targets. These activities were accompanied by a rapid expansion of the Chinese Communist air defence system, which was being brought up to date with Soviet help.

The United Nations Command still had no clear picture of Chinese preparations and intentions on November 23rd, when plans for the final Allied drive to the Yalu were finalised. The battle order envisaged an advance to the battle area in the Sinuiju–Suiho area by 24th Division and the ROK 1st Division, with the Commonwealth Brigade in reserve on the Eighth Army's left flank. Simultaneously in the centre the 2nd and 25th Divisions would advance north and north-eastwards along the Kuryong and Chingchon valleys to the border, while on the right covering the mountains around Tokchon was the ROK 2nd Corps,

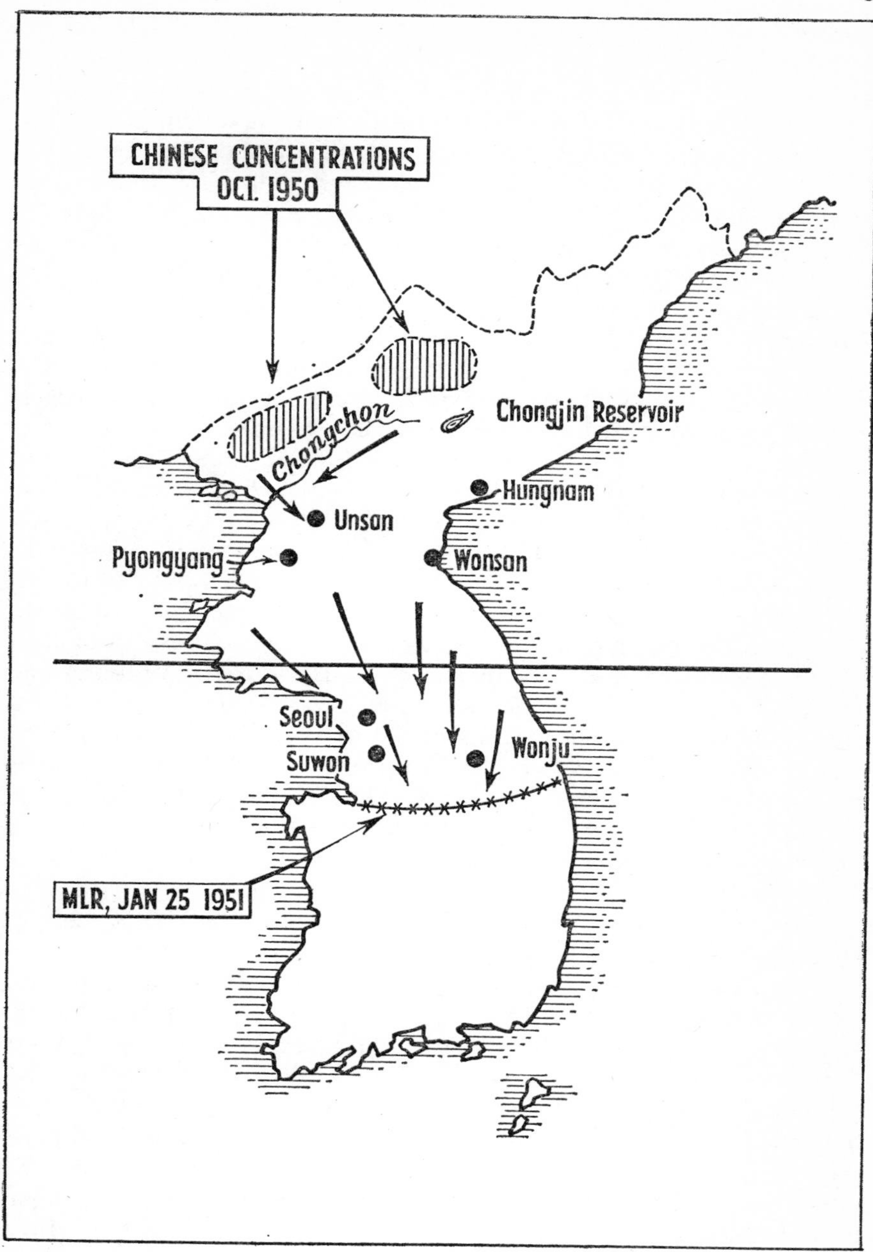


Chinese/North Korean winter offensive, Oct 1950–Jan 1951.

with the 1st Cavalry Division in reserve at Sunchon. In addition two US Marine Regiments, the 5th and 7th, were already advanced as far as Yudam-Ni at the eastern end of the Chosin reservoir. Their orders were to remain there for four days before advancing to join up with the Eighth Army at Mupyong, after which the combined force was to press on to Manpojin on the Manchurian border. On the eastern side of the reservoir three battalions of the 7th Division were to move northwards to the frontier, while the remainder of the division was eventually to join up with the ROK 1st Corps advancing towards Chongjin and from there to the Soviet border. The whole gave the United Nations a front-line fighting strength of 100,000 troops facing an as yet indeterminate number of Communist Chinese and North Koreans. It was perhaps as well that the UN combat troops were as yet unaware that they were already outnumbered by something like two to one.

At 10.00hrs on November 24th the Allied line rolled forward once again. By nightfall, the long mechanised columns had pushed on up to eight miles inside enemy territory, meeting almost no opposition. There was little work for the Fifth Air Force and few calls were made on its fighter-bombers. Then, soon after dawn on November 25th, a Company of the 9th Infantry Regiment, 2nd Infantry Division, ran into heavy mortar and machine gun fire from Hill 219 guarding the east bank of the Chongchon. The American Infantry quickly went to ground and began to slog it out with the enemy, who were quickly identified as Chinese. Two hours later wave after wave of screaming Chinese infantry made a suicidal charge across the river from the north-west, only to be beaten back with terrific losses by Allied artillery fire. That afternoon however, a second charge smashed through the 2nd Division's line two miles upriver and forced an Allied withdrawal. By the evening of the following day the 2nd Division had been thrown back two more miles down the Chongchon, while on the left in the Kuryong Valley the 25th Division was desperately withstanding heavy Chinese attacks.

Then came the big punch: the springing of the trap so carefully laid during the preceding weeks by the Communist Commander, General Lin Piao. At dusk on the 26th the Fourth Red Chinese Field Army flooded down the central mountain passes and collided headlong with the ROK 2nd Corps at Tokchon. Within 24 hours ROK 2nd Corps had been shattered and dislocated under the onslaught and with it crumbled the Eighth Army's right flank. The Fifth Air Force flew 345 ground attack sorties in two days but there was nothing they could do to stem the enemy tide. The Turkish Brigade, hurrying to the assistance of the South Koreans, met the remnants of the ROK infantry streaming southwards in disorderly retreat, totally demoralised. By daybreak on November 27th the United Nations commanders had at last begun to realise the full terrifying extent of the Chinese Communist involvement.

Ranged against the Allied forces were no fewer than six Chinese Armies, comprising 18 Divisions of the Chinese Communist Thirteenth Army Group. On the 28th MacArthur informed the United Nations in a special communiqué that "Enemy reactions developed in the course of our assault operations of the past four days disclose that a major segment of the Chinese continental forces in Army, Corps and Divisional organisation of an aggregate strength of over 200,000 men is now arrayed against the United Nations forces in North Korea. Consequently, we face an entirely new war."

By the time the communiqué was being read in Washington, Allied forces were in full retreat from the Chongchon. The chaos was appalling. Everywhere the Chinese had infiltrated behind the Allied lines in strength. On the 30th the 2nd Division, retreating southwards along the Kunuri–Sunchon road was ambushed by an entire Chinese division, dug in along a six mile stretch of the river. The Chinese knocked out the leading vehicles of the mechanised column with a storm of mortar and machine gun fire and from then on it was a massacre. In two hours the Division suffered 3,000 casualties, some of them the victims of machine-gun fire from Allied fighter-bombers attempting to knock out Chinese positions only a few yards away from the friendly infantry. The survivors managed to fight their way out in small groups during the night, eventually staggering exhausted and broken into the lines of the Commonwealth 27th Brigade and the 1st Cavalry to the south. It was the same tragedy all over again in the area of the Chosin reservoir, where elements of the 1st Marine and 7th Infantry Division were cut off and decimated by General Chen Yi's Third Field Army.

On December 7th the United Nations Commission for the Unification and Rehabilitation of Korea reported to the United Nations that "On the basis of existing evidence the Commission had come to the conclusion that Chinese forces in great strength are attacking the United Nations forces in North Korea and that these Chinese forces form part of the Armed Forces of the People's Republic of China."

The conclusion was somewhat belated. By the time it was reached the Allied retreat had turned into a rout. Pyongyang had been evacuated on the 5th and the roads were jammed solid as a disorganised mass of men and equipment streamed southwards towards the 38th Parallel. They would not be coming back.

CHAPTER SEVEN

# The Winter of Defeat

As the Communist offensive gathered momentum during the early days of December 1950, United Nations pilots engaged in attacking targets in the narrow strip of territory bordering the Yalu River reported a corresponding increase in activity on the part of the Red Chinese MiG squadrons. The Chinese pilots were becoming more aggressive, and as their experience grew it was grimly apparent that the Russian-built fighter hopelessly outclassed every type of aircraft used by the United Nations in Korea. Not only was the MiG-15 a good 100 miles an hour faster than the two types of American jet aircraft then deployed in the Far East—the F-80 Shooting Star and the Navy's Grummar F9F Panther—but, more serious still from the point of view of air to air combat, it could outclimb, outdive and outturn them. The Panther's limitations in this respect became apparent on November 10th, when a flight of the Navy jets of Squadron VF-111 received a bad mauling during their first encounter with the MiG-15s over Sinuiju. Nevertheless, the superior experience of the Navy pilots paid dividends on this occasion, and before they broke off the engagement VF-111's CO, Lt-Cdr W. T. Amen, managed to get in a lucky burst that sent an MiG down in flames. Although the Shooting Star and Panther pilots usually elected to engage the MiGs during these early days of jet combat over Korea, banking on their opponent's general lack of experience to give them a chance of survival, the only escape routes open to the pilots of piston-engined Allied types such as the Mustang if they were unlucky enough to be trapped by MiGs was to keep on turning tightly as possible and wait for their opportunity to dive away and head southwards at top speed on the deck. These tactics usually worked because the MiG pilots rarely made more than two firing passes before breaking off the attack.

The USAF, to its credit, lost little time in taking steps to meet the enemy jet fighter menace. The initiative came from General Hoyt S. Vandenburg, who on November 8th—just a week after the MiGs first appeared in Korean skies—offered to release a wing each of F-86A Sabres and F-84E Thunderjets for duty in Korea. Generals Partridge and Stratemeyer accepted the offer immediately, and on that same day the Sabres of the 4th Fighter-Interceptor Wing and the Thunderjets of the 27th Fighter Escort Wing were placed on readiness for immediate overseas deployment. Embarkation of the aircraft aboard carriers began at San Diego, California, on November 14th, and within two weeks the bulk of the machines had arrived in Japan. Assembly work at Itazuke was delayed for several days because some of the aircraft, lacking adequate waterproofing, had suffered corrosion during their journey across the Pacific, but on December 5th the first elements of the 27th Wing were established at Taegu and the Thunderjets flew their first combat mission—an armed reconnaissance sortie—the following day. A week later the first Sabres of the 4th Wing arrived at Kimpo and on December 15th began operations with a familiarisation flight over North Korea.

Two days later, on the 17th, the 4th Wing mounted its first offensive sweep of the war when four Sabres of the 336th Fighter-Interceptor Squadron took off from Kimpo and headed north towards the Yalu. A few minutes after entering the combat area at 27,000 feet the Sabre leader, Lieutenant-Colonel Bruce H. Hinton—the 336th Squadron's Commander—spotted a flight of four MiG-15s climbing rapidly to intercept. The Communist pilots apparently failed to realise that they were dealing with a new and deadly adversary, otherwise they would almost certainly have climbed for altitude on their own side of the Yalu. They realised their mistake only when the Sabres came arrowing down towards them and broke away, diving for the safety of the river. They were too late. Colonel Hinton got a MiG squarely in his sights and fired three four-second bursts with his six 0·5 machine guns. The MiG began to burn and went into a spin, racked by explosions as it fell. The pilot did not bail out. It was the first of 792 MiG-15s which were to be claimed as destroyed by Sabre pilots during the 2½ years of air combat that followed.

There were several more skirmishes between MiGs and Sabres during the next few days, but these were inconclusive and no casualties were suffered by either side. By this time both sides were quickly catching on to the other's tactics and rapidly taking steps to counter them. The Sabre's main drawback was its lack of endurance; patrolling at speeds of Mach 0·85 and higher the Sabre pilots could afford to spend only 20 minutes in the vicinity of the Yalu before being forced to head for home with a safe margin of fuel. The Red pilots quickly realised this limitation and exploited it to the fullest advantage, climbing to altitude north of the Yalu and then diving across at high speed to make their attack as the Sabres were withdrawing towards the end of their patrols. The Americans in turn began to mount patrols of sixteen aircraft, operating in four flights of four, which arrived in the patrol area at various altitudes at intervals of five minutes. In this way the withdrawal of all but the last Sabre flight was adequately covered.

On December 22nd, eight Sabres on an offensive patrol at 30,000 feet, south of the Yalu, found the MiGs up in strength. Sixteen enemy fighters sped across the river and a whirling dog-fight developed, the swept-wing MiGs and Sabres chasing one another down to ground level. One Sabre, piloted by Captain L. V. Bach, was shot down almost as soon as the fight began, but in the next ten minutes six MiGs were destroyed. After this mauling the MiGs disappeared from the sky for a week, and the next time they showed up—on December 30th—their pilots showed extreme caution in tangling with the Sabres. On this occasion 36 MiGs crossed the Yalu and engaged 16 F-86s, but the enemy quickly broke off the action and headed for home. The Sabre pilots claimed two MiG-15s damaged.

In all the 4th Wing's Sabres carried out 234 offensive sorties during December 1950, claiming the destruction of eight MiGs together with two more probably destroyed and seven damaged in exchange for the loss of one of their own number. These early encounters left the Sabre pilots with the conviction that the two fighter types were more or less evenly matched; the slight advantages enjoyed by one over the other in various respects could almost be dismissed. What counted was the comparative skill of the pilots, and it was quickly apparent that in this respect the Americans enjoyed overwhelming superiority. Time and again superior tactics combined with superior training were to pay dividends for the United Nations in the air war over Korea.

Meanwhile, the crucifixion of the Allied ground forces continued during the early days of September. A fair proportion of the Fifth Air Force's striking power was directed in support of the hard pressed 2nd US Infantry Division, and it was heavy and accurate air attacks that enabled the Division to fight its way through miles of Communist ambushes along the Sunchon road.

Air power, too, blunted the attacks by twelve divisions of the CCF Ninth Army Group on the Marine Division at Udam-ni and its supply route leading south. In this case most of the air support was provided by the 1st Marine Air Wing and the aircraft of Task Force 77, with the assistance of the Fifth Air Force's 35th Fighter-Interceptor Group at Yonpo. As well as tactical support, air supply also played a vital part in sustaining the men of the embattled Marine Division, fighting as they were in sub-zero temperatures against vastly superior numbers of enemy troops.

During the Marines' advance northwards in November air supply had been provided by a detachment of four C-47s of the 21st Troop Carrier Squadron operating out of Wonsan. The detachment's peak effort had been on the morning of November 28th, the day after the Chinese began their offensive, when the C-47s dropped ten tons of ammunition to the 5th and 7th Marines at Udam-ni and sixteen tons to the 31st Infantry at Sinhung-ni. The following day, however, the Marines were frantically requesting the immediate air drop of over 400 tons of rations, medical supplies and ammunition, and since the whole of the FEAF Combat Cargo Command was only equipped to air drop 70 tons of supplies a day this obviously gave rise to a problem of gigantic proportions. Drastic measures were taken to improve the position, including the recruitment of large numbers of Japanese civilians to help pack supplies at Ashiya air base, and within two days—using all its available C-46s, C-47s and C-119s in support of the Marines—Combat Cargo Command was able to air drop a daily total of 250 tons. The burden eased a little on December 7th when troops of the 1st Marine Regiment completed the preparation of two primitive airstrips at Hagaru-ri and Koto-ri. Both strips were just big enough to accommodate a C-47, albeit with a certain element of risk, and in three days—by December 10th—the 21st Troop Carrier Squadron had flown 240 sorties into the rocky landing grounds, bringing in 274 tons of supplies and flying out 4,689 casualties. The task was shared by three C-47s of the Royal Hellenic Air Force which—newly arrived in Korea—flew an additional thirty sorties.

The transport aircraft did not return empty to Yongpo after carrying out the airdrops. During December 1st and 2nd a steady flow of casualties arrived at Hagaru-ri; many of them were troops of the 7th Infantry Division, three battalions of which had been virtually destroyed east of the Chosin reservoir. Of an original force of 2,500 men only a thousand survivors had managed to reach Hagaru by the 2nd December and only 385 of these were able-bodied. In all, the transports—mainly C-47s—evacuated more than 3,500 casualties from Hagaru airstrip, many of them frostbite cases.

On December 6th, 10,000 men and 1,000 vehicles began the breakout from Hagaru to Koto-ri, eleven miles further south, where infiltrating Chinese forces had completely surrounded a garrison of 4,000 marines and infantry. The breakout took 38 hours, the Allied columns fighting their way through heavy snowfalls and periodic Chinese ambushes.

As though the weather and the enemy were not enough the next stage of the breakout—over the ten-mile distance from Koto-ri to Chinhung-ni—posed yet another problem. About four miles south of Koto-ri the Chinese had destroyed a bridge over a 1500ft deep gorge. The Marines would be able to negotiate the gorge on foot with difficulty, but unless the bridge could be repaired they would have to abandon all their vehicles, tanks and artillery. To overcome the obstacle the Marines asked if Combat Cargo Command could drop eight sections of an M2 pre-fabricated bridge. Four sections were enough to span the gorge but the bulky two-ton structures had never been air dropped before and there was a good chance that about 50 per per cent would be damaged on landing or else fall into enemy hands. In fact the actual drop went off far more smoothly than anyone had expected. After one test drop eight C-119s, each carrying a bridge section, took off from Yonpo and headed for Koto-ri, where they dropped their loads at 800 feet among the mountains. One bridge section was captured by the Chinese and another was damaged when one of its big G5 parachutes failed to open, but the other six fell right on the drop zone and the marines soon set to work erecting them.

In the afternoon of December 9th the first of the 14,000 men from Koto-ri began crossing the newly-repaired bridge, followed by their heavy equipment. The leading echelon of the long column entered Chinhung-ni early the following morning and by nightfall on the 11th the marine division had begun to assemble in the Hungnam area in preparation for evacuation by sea. Since the beginning of the Chinese offensive the Division had suffered 4,400 battle casualties, including 718 killed, and 7,000 casualties from other causes, mostly frostbite.

The survival of the division during its 14-day ordeal had been attributable almost entirely to air supply. In two weeks of continual operations 313 C-119s and 37 C-47s had dropped 1,580 tons of supplies and ammunition, the majority of which—despite incredibly difficult operating conditions caused by the bad weather and the rapid Chinese advance—had fallen into Allied hands. For the part they played in sustaining the ground forces during the breakout the 314th Troop Carrier Group, the 21st Troop Carrier Squadron and the 801st Medical Air Evacuation Squadron were later awarded Distinguished Unit Citations.

There was to be no rest yet for the Combat Cargo crews, many of whom were suffering severely from tension and lack of sleep. Because of the possibility that the Chinese might break through the Hungnam defensive perimeter at any time it was decided to airlift anything that could be moved from Yonpo airfield to an emergency airstrip on the evacuation beach itself. During a four-day period beginning on December 14th, Combat Cargo Command—in 393 sorties—airlifted 228 casualties, 3,891 passengers and 2,088 tons of cargo out of Yonpo. When the evacuation was completed just about the only piece of equipment left on Yonpo was a C-119 which was grounded with engine trouble and which could not be repaired in time.

The final evacuation from Hungnam was completed on Christmas Eve 1950, by which time 100 ships—grouped together under the designation of Task Force 90—had lifted off 105,000 troops and 91,000 Korean refugees, some of whom had struggled through the snows from Chosin in the wake of the Marines. From Hungnam the Marines were evacuated to Pusan, followed by the bulk of the 7th Division which had retreated from the Yalu more or less intact. The last to leave were the defenders of the Hungnam perimeter, the 3rd ROK Division. Throughout the evacuation carrier aircraft and B-26s of the Fifth Air Force had carried out heavy and effective strikes by day and night against the Chinese forces confronting the perimeter. Most of the Naval air strikes were carried out by the Corsairs of Marine Fighter Squadrons 212 and 214, operating from the carriers USS *Sicily* and *Bataan*. The latter had been rushed to the area after delivering replacement aircraft to Japan.

While the Eighth Army, the Marines and the ROK forces strove to re-organise themselves and form a new defensive line the Allied air forces remained the only hope of slowing down the Chinese advance. During the first week of December the emphasis was on strikes in the vicinity of the front line, but after that General Partridge ordered the Fifth Air Force to devote its main effort to interdiction and armed reconnaissance sorties in the enemy rear. On December 15th, the Far East Air Forces launched Interdiction Campaign No 4, which called for sustained attacks by the Fifth Air Force and FEAF Bomber Command on targets in 11 separate zones north of the 37th Parallel. Once again the aim was to devastate the enemy's communications, 45 railway bridges, 12 highway bridges, 13 tunnels, 39 marshalling yards and 63 supply centres being slated for attack. Three of the interdiction zones—on the east coast, running from Wonsan to the Siberian border—were to be the responsibility of Naval Forces Far East.

Just as the North Koreans had done in the early days of the war the Chinese, in their headlong pursuit of the United Nations forces, cast aside all pretence of stealth and now began to move across country in large concentrations in daylight, which made them particularly vulnerable to air attack. The main roads leading south were packed with masses of troops and equipment, and the Fifth Air Force's fighter-bombers inflicted fearful casualties on the enemy with concentrated machine gun, rocket and napalm attacks. By December 16th FEAF Intelligence estimated that air attack had caused 33,000 enemy casualties. This figure was probably greatly exaggerated, but the fact that the Chinese were suffering heavily became apparent when on December 17th the Chinese armies suddenly went to ground again, either moving at night or in small camouflaged groups during daytime.

Meanwhile, Bomber Command's B-29s had been active in carrying out the tasks allotted to them under Interdiction Campaign No 4. On December 21st and 22nd, following sporadic attacks on supply centres and troop concentrations in various North Korean towns and on the airfield at Pyongyang, the whole of Bomber Command was airborne in attacks against four principal North Korean bridges. The following day the interdiction order was changed, and during the remainder of December most of the B-29s' effort was directed against towns and villages where there were reported to be enemy troop concentrations.

The Red Chinese onslaught in North Korea, unprecedented as it was in size and fury, had made necessary the hasty reorganisation of some of the Fifth Air Force combat units deployed on forward airfields. The Mustangs of the 8th and 18th Fighter-Bomber Wings, for example, had exactly four days to get out of Pyongyang and pull back to new bases at Seoul and Suwon, and it was to the credit of pilots and ground crews alike that during the withdrawal the Mustangs continued to operate at maximum effort. However, much of the two Wings' supporting equipment and considerable quantities of supplies had to be abandoned. The 35th Fighter-Interceptor Wing—which had been operating from Yonpo on the east coast in support of the Marines—had a much more orderly withdrawal, the Mustangs pulling back to Pusan East airfield without incident and the ground personnel and equipment being evacuated by sea. On December 10th the first Marine air squadron to operate jets in combat—VMF-311, flying F9F Panthers—arrived at Yonpo and carried out interdiction missions for four days before joining the 35th Fighter-Interceptor Wing at Pusan East. The land-based Corsair squadrons of the Marine Air Wing flew back to their escort carriers, some of them subsequently returning to Pohang late in December and the remainder to Itami Air Base in Japan.

The Eighth Army's plan was to hang on for as long as possible to its defensive lines around Seoul before withdrawing further south to the old Pusan perimeter. It could therefore only be a question of time before the United Nations airfields at Seoul, Kimpo and Suwon also fell into enemy hands, and in the middle of December the 18th Fighter-Bomber Wing underwent a further move, this time to the old Japanese airfield at Chinhae on the southern coast of Korea. The main bulk of the 51st Fighter-Interceptor Wing also moved back to Itazuke in Japan, leaving behind only a detachment at Kimpo. The 8th Wing also moved back to Itazuke to re-equip with F-80C Shooting Stars, its serviceable Mustangs being re-allocated to other units.

This redeployment meant an additional strain on the already overtaxed resources of Combat Cargo Command, more than a third of whose effort was directed in support of the Fifth Air Force, and the arrival of reinforcements in the shape of two squadrons of the 61st Troop Carrier Group at Ashiya in mid-December was greeted with considerable relief. The 61st Group's first operation in Korea was a mission of mercy; on December 20th twelve of its C-54s flew to Kimpo in a blinding snowstorm and airlifted nearly 1,000 Korean orphan children—a tiny fraction of the pitiful stream of refugees struggling southwards before the terror of the Chinese invasion—to a safe refuge on Cheju-do Island off the southern coast of Korea. The mission—known as Operation Christmas Kidlift—was flown at the request of two Fifth Air Force Chaplains, Colonel Wallace I. Wolverton and Lieutenant-Colonel Russell L. Blaisdell, who had been preoccupied with the terrible hardships endured by the refugee children since the Chinese offensive began.

By the middle of December morale among the American ground and air forces in Korea was at a low ebb. A 'what the hell are we doing here —let's get out quickly' philosophy was spreading rapidly, particularly through the ranks of the Eighth Army, even though the latter had been preserved more or less intact and the 13,000 United Nations Command casualties were far less than those suffered in most major American actions of the Second World War. Then, on December 23rd, came another blow; General Walton Walker, the Eighth Army's well-liked Commander, was tragically killed when his jeep was hit by a ROK Army truck and overturned in a paddy field. With the United Nations Command already in a state of confusion and a massive Chinese offensive expected momentarily, Walker's death was in the nature of a disaster. It was fortunate that General MacArthur had had the foresight to name his successor some time before, should one be needed. The chosen successor was General Matthew B. Ridgway, then the Deputy Chief of Staff.

Ridgway reached Tokyo on Christmas Day, and on December 26th he was in close conference with MacArthur. The Commander-in-Chief told him that all proposals for an attack on China had been rejected by Washington and the objective was now to fight a war of containment in South Korea. Ridgway also noted that, surprisingly, MacArthur appeared to have become disillusioned with the effectiveness of tactical air power. His main objection was that tactical air power had not so far been able to isolate the battlefield or stop the flow of hostile troops and supplies, nor did there seem to be any prospect of its doing so with any degree of success in the future.

Within 24 hours General Ridgway was stepping out of a transport aircraft on to the frozen earth of Taegu airstrip, still clad in the uniform he had been wearing in the Pentagon two days earlier. He was appalled at what he found. The Americans were in low spirits and there was a dearth of good leadership. Moreover, there was almost complete lack of accurate Intelligence. "All Intelligence could show me," he wrote later, "was a big red goose egg out in front of us with 174,000 scrawled in the middle of it." He quickly realised that his first task was to carry out a lightning tour of the battlefield, telling his troops that they were going to stay in Korea and fight, and, most important of all, why they were going to do it. Only when the rot had been stopped could he hope for a successful course of action to repel the coming Chinese thrust.

The basis of such action had already been laid by the late General Walker, who had drawn four defensive lines designed to hold the enemy as long as possible in their drive southwards. The first of these lines—'Able', to the north of Pyongyang—had been pierced by the Chinese before Walker's troops had been able to take up their positions, and when Ridgway took over, the Eighth Army was establishing itself on the 135 mile long second line of defence; 'Baker', which ran along the Imjin River and the 38th Parallel. The third line of defence was 'Charlie', stretching around Seoul in a crescent-shaped bridgehead and from there via Hongchon to the east coast; and the fourth line, 'Dog', cut across the Korean peninsula through Pyongtaek, Wonju and Samchok. Theoretically, Ridgway had at his disposal some 350,000 men to defend these lines, but it was soon apparent that this was nothing more than a paper figure, for on Christmas Day 1950 less than half the total were combat ready. It must have been one of the gloomiest situations ever to face a Commander in the field, yet Ridgway was undeterred by it. His priorities were simple: first of all to check the headlong rush southwards, and then to launch an early counter-offensive designed to secure all of Korea south of the 38th Parallel from the threat of Communist aggression.

In an effort to fill the intelligence gap Ridgway ordered the Eighth Army to step up its patrol activities by 100 per cent. This had the desired result, and within a very few days Far East Command Intelligence officers were able to form a fairly accurate picture of the size and composition of the enemy forces poised for a renewal of their offensive. The main threat came from the Chinese Fourth Field Army, which—numbering some 177,000 men—stood directly opposed to the US Eighth Army. Also confronting the United Nations forces were units of the North Korean Army, which had been reorganised and re-equipped with Chinese help. The North Korean 1st Corps with about 15,000 men lay on the left flank of the Chinese Fourth Field Army, while the North Korean 2nd and 5th Corps with just over 24,000 men between them confronted the ROK forces in the central highlands. On November 27th the North Korean 2nd Corps made a serious mistake when it launched a series of probing attacks against the ROK positions. From these activities it did not take UN Intelligence officers long to work out that the enemy plan involved a drive southwards from central Korea by the North Koreans with the object of diverting a large proportion of the Eighth Army preparatory to a large scale assault on Seoul by the Chinese Fourth Field Army. In addition UN Intelligence indicated the possibility that the Chinese Third Field Army, then held in reserve at Hungnam with 100,000 men, might also be committed to the battle early in January soon after the enemy offensive began.

Although the employment of the enemy's ground forces in the immediate future was now more or less clear, there still remained one big question mark. In Manchuria and China the Communists had some

*Above:* **Sikorsky H-19s of the US Army's 6th Transportation Helicopter Company in Korea.**

*Left:* **H-19 of the 3rd Air Rescue Squadron.**

*Below:* **Sikorsky H03S-1 of Marine Observation Squadron VMO-6.**

*Top:* Against a backdrop of rugged Korean terrain, a Marine Corps OY-1 observation plane of VMO-6 piloted by Major Vincent J. Gottschalk, of Pontiac, Michigan spots concentrations of Communists for Marine Corsair fighter-bombers to sear with napalm bombs.

*Above:* F3D Skynight of VMF(N)-513.

*Below:* Stencilled bombs on its fuselage denote long combat record of this F9F of VMF-311.

Deck crew gaze ruefully at temporary paint job on Corsair of VF-64, USS *Boxer* after the aircraft landed on the wrong carrier by mistake; and . . .

Set about clearing up the mess!

*Above:* F2H Banshees of VF-172, USS *Essex*.

*Right:* Corsairs of Composite Squadron VC-3 on USS *Boxer*.

*Right:* Condensation from propeller tips spirals round fuselage of F4U-5N taking off from USS *Boxer*.

Arming an F4U-4 for a rocket strike, USS *Boxer.*

F4U-4 about to hook the wire on USS *Boxer.*

Corsair climbs away after dropping napalm on Chinese positions.

Replenishment at sea for USS *Princeton*, with Corsairs and Skyraiders ranged on deck.

*Top:* Flak damage to an F-80C of the 8th Fighter-Bomber Wing.

*Above:* F-80 Shooting Star and its extensive weapons load.

Flak-damaged B-26C of the 3rd BW makes a belly landing at a South Korean airfield.

Framed beneath the wingtip and feathered propeller of the dead number 4 engine of a 19th Bomb Group B-29, an F-80 jet fighter is shown escorting the bomber home from a mission over enemy territory in Korea. The fighter sticks close to the B-29, prepared for combat in the event that Communist planes attempt an attack on the crippled bomber.

700 combat aircraft, and another 500 Russian first line types based on airfields around Vladivostok just across the border might conceivably be added to this total. What Allied Intelligence desperately needed to know was whether the Communists intended to use a substantial proportion of this air power in support of the coming offensive. If they did it would mean not only that the Allied Air Forces would be diverted from their all-important primary task of battlefield support, but also that there would be a continual air threat to the sea and air supply routes to the Allies in Korea. Looking towards even gloomier horizons, there was also the possibility that the Russians might step in with attacks on strategic ports and airfields in Japan, possibly with atomic weapons. However, the United Nations Command could not afford to stake its future strategic and tactical plans in Korea on vague possibilities. If a major Communist air offensive did develop then it would be countered with every available means. In the meantime the crews of the Fifth Air Force and Task Force 77 would continue to fulfil their triple role of air superiority, interdiction and close support.

On December 29th the North Korean 2nd Corps launched an attack on the ROK forces holding the line in central Korea. Two days later, on New Year's Eve, the Chinese Communists opened up with mortar fire along the whole of the Eighth Army's front and at daybreak the shock troops of the Fourth Field Army charged into action. The offensive opened in bitter cold and pitch darkness, with icy crystals of snow lashing across the land from low-hanging clouds. The weather conditions were near ideal for the Chinese; as long as they lasted the advancing hordes would be immune from air attack.

Then the miracle happened. At daybreak on January 1st the clouds broke, leaving a gin-clear sky. Fifth Air Force pilots flying armed reconnaissance near the front line found the roads leading to Seoul jammed solid with long columns of Chinese infantry. From then on it was a massacre. Between New Year's Day and January 5th, the Fifth Air Force's fighter-bombers flew 2,596 sorties. By nightfall on January 5th the aircrews estimated that they had killed approximately 8,000 Communist troops; the Eighth Army, counting the enemy dead on the battlefield, place the total number of enemy casualties at nearer 15,000. Neither did the air onslaught cease with the onset of darkness. Night attacks were carried out by the B-26s of the 3rd Bombardment Wing, the crews seeking out enemy troop concentrations by the light of flares dropped by C-47s. The latter—nicknamed 'Lightning Bugs'—could carry 130 Mark 8 flares of the type used by US Navy flying boat crews. Igniting at 5,500 feet they turned night into day for about five minutes, giving the B-26s ample time to locate and hit their targets with devastating effect before the Communists could scatter for cover.

Fearful though the slaughter inflicted on the Chinese Communists by the Allied fighter-bombers may have been, it was not enough to check the enemy advance. On January 2nd the Eighth Army began to break contact and the following day—with masses of Chinese infantry crossing the ice-covered Han River—the evacuation of Seoul began. On the 4th the Sabres of the 4th Fight-Interceptor Wing left Korea for Johnson Air Base in Japan, while aviation engineers set fire to everything that would burn on Kimpo airfield. Suwon airfield was also evacuated by the 18th Fighter-Bomber Wing on January 5th, the Mustangs pulling back to Chinhae.

Meanwhile, in Central Korea, the US 2nd Infantry Division had been ordered northwards to Wonju, where the ROK 3rd Corps and the US Marines were coming under heavy pressure from the North Korean 2nd and 5th Corps. Air support in this sector was the responsibility of carrier aircraft from the *Valley Forge*, *Philippine Sea* and *Leyte*, but on January 6th a return of severe bad weather brought a halt to all air operations from the carriers for three days. In the meantime the defenders of Wonju were kept going by the C-47s of the 21st Troop Carrier Group, which landed or air dropped 115 and 460 tons of supplies respectively. However, the enemy drive could not be contained, and by January 10th Wonju was in North Korean hands. The Allied ground forces withdrew to a new defensive line three miles further south, which they held with the renewed assistance of tactical air support. On the 11th the weather cleared sufficiently to allow the Fifth Air Force to hammer Communist troop concentrations attempting to move round the flanks of the 2nd Division, while the following day ten B-29s of the 98th Group attacked Wonju with 500lb general purpose bombs timed to burst in the air.

As the Communist advance swept away United Nations control of one Korean airfield after another, the crews of Combat Cargo Command found themselves once more working overtime to keep up the flow of supplies to the ground forces. Anything that remotely resembled an airstrip was knocked into rough shape by the troops. With the help of these improvisations the transport crews flew in 12,486 tons of supplies during the first three weeks of January, simultaneously evacuating 10,489 casualties. C-46s and C-47s bore the brunt of these operations, although a further 2,000 tons of supplies were airdropped during the same period by C-119s.

By the end of the third week in January it was estimated that the Communists had suffered 38,000 casualties, about half of them inflicted by air attack. Not even the bottomless well of manpower could sustain losses of this kind, and on January 15th it was reported that the Reds were pulling back in several sectors to rest and re-group. Had they enjoyed the benefit of air support the Communists would undoubtedly have been able to keep up a sustained pressure, but the Communists had evidently decided not to commit their air power to the battle.

MiG-15s appeared only once in January when 15 of them crossed the Yalu to attack a solitary B-29 near Sinanju; they broke off the attack after only a minute or so and the bomber got away unharmed. Apart from an abortive attack on a B-26 of the 452nd Wing by a North Korean Yak-9 fighter on January 15th, the only other Red air activity took the form of several nuisance raids on Allied troops at night by elderly Po-2 biplanes, but the psychological effect of these attacks was far greater than the damage they actually caused.

By the end of January the Allied front was stabilised south of Wonju, and it became apparent that the Chinese Communist New Year Offensive had petered out. The war that developed now was to be unlike any other conflict in history. It was to be a fearful war of attrition, a war with no clearly defined aims, in which thousands of men on either side would die for possession of a useless hill or ridge or valley. It was a trial of strength between two power blocs which neither side could win—and which neither side dared lose.

CHAPTER EIGHT

# The Red Air Offensive, January—July 1951

Although the Chinese Communist Air Force had failed to intervene during the New Year Offensive of 1951, there were indications that it intended to do so in support of further offensives planned for the coming Spring. Interrogation of Chinese officers captured in Korea revealed that at least one officer from each Chinese regiment had been through a recent and intensive ground/air liaison course, while other reports indicated that Chinese Communist ground attack units equipped with Ilyushin Il-10s were training just across the border in Manchuria.

The onus of working out a battle plan for the future participation of Communist air power in Korea fell on the shoulders of General Liu Ya-Lou, the C-in-C of the Chinese People's Air Force. What Allied Intelligence did not know at this stage was that Liu, in addition to the numerous operational problems that confronted him, was also engaged in a political battle with his superiors, many of whom feared that direct air support of the Chinese ground forces in Korea would lead to immediate and massive American retaliation, particularly if ground attack operations were carried out from Manchurian bases.

Liu's battlefield support plans, however, did not envisage the use of the Manchurian bases at all—but the factors involved in reaching this decision were technical rather than political. For a start, it was probable that most of the close support work would have to be carried out at distances of 250 miles or more from China's Manchurian bases, and the only ground attack type on the CPAF's inventory with sufficient endurance to carry out missions at such a range was the Il-10 Sturmovik —but the Il-10 was hopelessly obsolescent and had little hope of survival in an environment where hostile jet fighters ruled the sky. Although the Chinese Communists were fully prepared to commit their Il-10 units, it was all too clear that most of the missions would be one way trips.

The only Chinese Communist aircraft which did have a fighting chance of survival in Allied-dominated air space was the MiG-15, but the combat radius of early model MiG-15s of the type used by the CPAF was little more than 100 miles. Quite apart from that, the Russian jet fighter had been designed as an interceptor and its suitability or otherwise as a ground attack aircraft was as yet untested.

What the Chinese Communists could do with the aid of the MiG-15 was endeavour to establish a definite margin of air superiority over north-western Korea. Once this had been established the Chinese could begin to go ahead with the rehabilitation of several key airfields in North Korea, turning them into heavily defended bases for future ground attack operations south of the 38th Parallel. Runways would be lengthened and strengthened to accommodate jet fighters as well as piston-engined types, and well-camouflaged satellite strips would be constructed in the vicinity of the Parallel itself. The idea was that combat aircraft would be flown into the latter to refuel and re-arm only a matter of hours before the launching of an air strike in the south, after which—if sufficient fuel remained—they could then fly direct to the permanent bases further north to avoid the possibility of being caught on the ground by Allied fighter-bombers.

Such, in broad outline, was General Liu's plan, and he lost no time in putting the first phase into effect. Late in January the MiGs suddenly appeared over the Yalu once more in larger formations than ever before. On January 21st two formations of MiG-15s—12 and 16 aircraft respectively—crossed the river to attack United Nations aircraft. The first formation trapped four F-80s near Sinuiju and destroyed one of them; the remainder managed to escape. Meanwhile the other 16 headed southwards to the Chongchon River, where they bounced eight F-84 Thunderjets which were attacking bridge targets. One Thunderjet went down in flames but Lieutenant-Colonel William E. Bertram, the Commander of the 523rd Squadron, evened up the score by shooting a MiG down into the river.

Meanwhile, in accordance with the second phase of General Liu's plan, the Communists had begun to repair the airfields at Sinuiju and Pyongyang. Sinuiju was the better placed of the two from the point of view of defence, for it was protected both by the MiG air umbrella from Antung and by heavy anti-aircraft emplacements on both sides of the Yalu. The anti-aircraft defences at Pyongyang, which was out of range of the MiGs, were steadily increased until the Reds had over 100 guns circling the airfield. On January 20th General Partridge, who was particularly worried about the heavy defensive screen around Pyongyang, asked Brigadier-General James E. Briggs—who had taken over command of FEAF Bomber Command from General O'Donnell a few days earlier—to lay on a B-29 strike against the airfield. Briggs agreed, although he stressed that it would first be necessary for the Fifth Air Force's fighter-bombers to go in low and fast to knock out the enemy anti-aircraft batteries.

While plans for this raid were being discussed Colonel Ashley B.

Packard, Commander of the 27th Fighter Escort Wing, came up with a proposal for a concentrated strafing attack on Sinuiju airfield by a large force of Thunderjets. The idea was approved and on January 23rd 33 Thunderjets took off from Taegu and headed towards their objective. While 25 F-84s flew top cover at altitudes of up to 20,000 feet the remaining eight Thunderjets swept like a whirlwind over Sinuiju and raked the airfield with machine-gun fire before the startled Communists had time to fire a shot. The strafers then climbed hard and fast to join their comrades higher up just as dust clouds across the river betrayed the take off of MiG-15s. The Thunderjets turned to meet the swept-wing enemy fighters as they raced across the river and a whirling dogfight spread out across the sky. The American pilots did their utmost to stay below 20,000 feet where the Thunderjet was able to turn tighter than the MiG, and these tactics paid dividends when Lieutenant Jacob Kratt destroyed two MiGs in the first two minutes of the combat. In the next 20 minutes, before the Communist pilots broke off the action, two more MiGs went down before the guns of Captains Alan McGuire and William W. Slaughter. In addition to these four confirmed victories other pilots of the 27th Wing claimed three more MiGs probably destroyed and four damaged. It was a superb victory for the Thunderjet pilots over aircraft which were superior to their own in most respects.

Half an hour later, as the wheels of the 27th Wing's F-84s were once again hitting the runways at Taegu, 46 F-80s of the 49th Fighter-Bomber Wing screamed down on Pyongyang and pounded the surrounding flak emplacements with guns, bombs and rockets. As they streaked away 21 B-29s of the 19th and 307th Bombardment Group, bombing through the pall of smoke and dust, cratered the newly repaired runways from end to end. There was sporadic light anti-aircraft fire from the few emplacements which had escaped the strafing attack unscathed, but none of the bombers was damaged. Both these actions had shown that the Communists still had a long way to go before they could hope to challenge United Nations air superiority over Korea with any real prospect of success, but a few days later their position became easier when both the 27th Wing and the 49th Wing withdrew from Taegu to airfields in southern Japan, leaving behind only detachments to service and re-arm F-80s and F-84s on combat missions over Korea. The move meant that until further notice the Fifth Air Force would not be able to guarantee jet fighter escort for medium bombers and reconnaissance aircraft operating over the north-western sector of the country.

This meant that Fifth Air Force operations in north-western Korea during February 1951 were mainly confined to fast photo reconnaissance sorties by RF-80s. The latter were attacked by MiGs several times

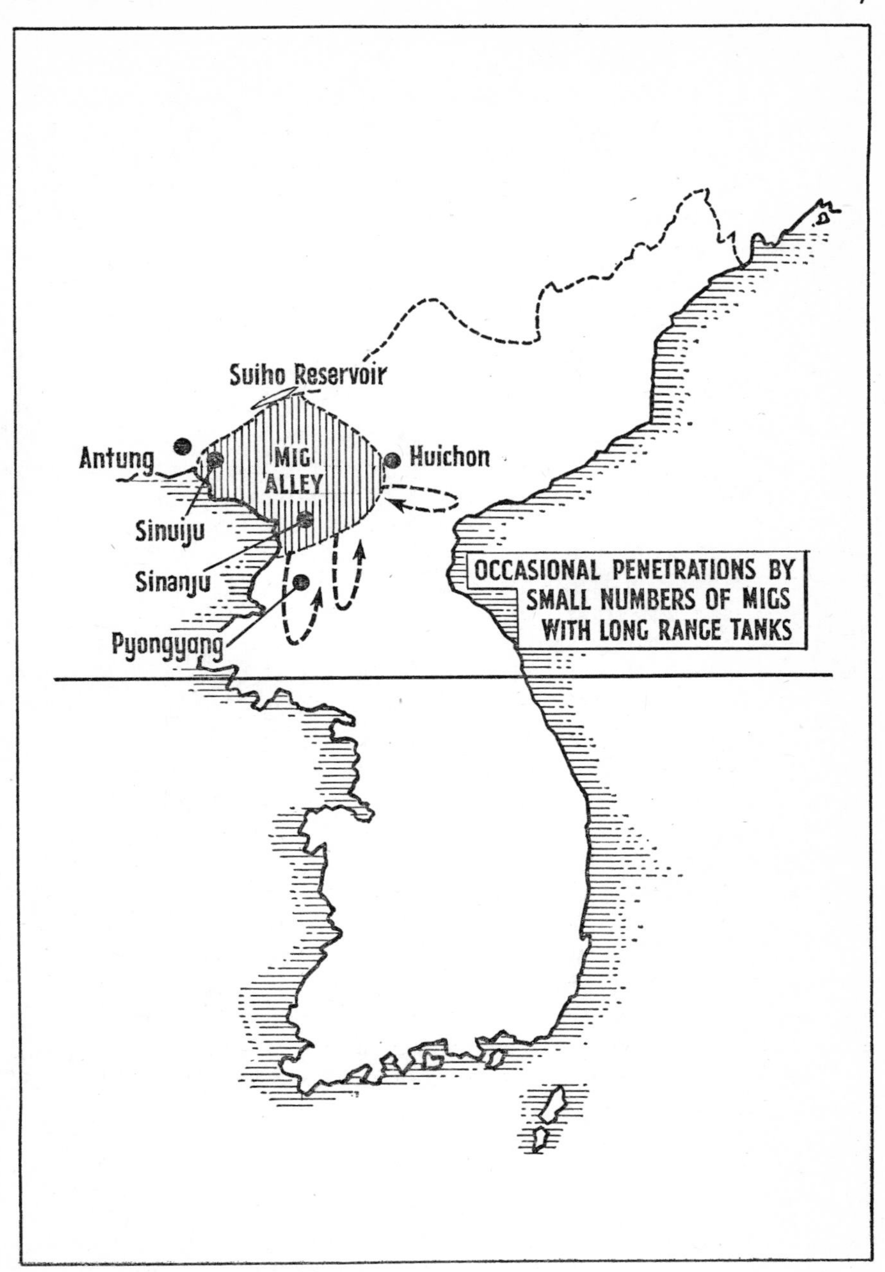


Areas of MiG-15 operations.

in the vicinity of the Yalu but all managed to get away. The only decisive air combat of the month occurred on February 5th when Major Arnold Mullins of the 67th Fighter-Bomber Squadron, attacking an airstrip near Pyongyang in his Mustang, surprised a Yak-9 with its wheels and flaps down on the approach and shot it down in flames.

The lack of a sustained Allied interdiction effort meant that the Reds were able to carry out repairs to at least ten North Korean airfields virtually unmolested, a fact that seriously alarmed United Nations Command. However, the state of affairs was not to last for long. On January 25th the Eighth Army launched its counter-offensive—code-named Operation Thunderbolt—with a twofold objective of reaching the Han River and destroying as many of the enemy forces as possible. Suwon and Inchon were quickly recaptured and in a secondary action, known as Operation Punch, a task force of the 25th Division took the strategic complex of Hill 440 north of Suwon on February 5th. When the operation ended on February 9th the United Nations forces counted over 4,200 Chinese dead on the battlefield. The United Nations lost 70 men killed. By the 10th the UN 1st Corps—consisting of the US 25th and 3rd Divisions, a Turkish Brigade, the 29th British Brigade and the ROK 1st Division—had reached the Han River, retaking Seoul and Kimpo on the way. General Partridge immediately gave orders for the re-habilitiation of Suwon, Kimpo and Seoul airfields, although it was obvious that it would be some time before the aviation engineers could get them fit for use by jet fighters. Nevertheless the engineers reported that Suwon could be made serviceable enough to operate jet fighters in an emergency, and General Partridge was sufficiently encouraged by this news to authorise the return of the 4th Wing's 334th Fighter-Interceptor Squadron to Taegu on February 22nd.

Towards the end of February, Bomber Command—working on the assumption that the Sabres would be able to stage through Suwon and provide escort all the way to the Yalu—embarked on another interdiction programme over north-western Korea. In fact the assumption was false. Suwon had taken such a battering during the fighting that it would take months to get it serviceable once more, and operating out of Taegu the Sabres had just enough range to take them as far as Pyongyang. Nevertheless it was decided to go ahead with the interdiction programme, escorting the B-29s with F-80s.

The first such interdiction mission on March 1st was a disaster. The Shooting Star pilots reached the rendezvous on time but there was no sign of the B-29s. The F-80s orbited, their thirsty turbines gulping up precious fuel minute by minute. Eventually, after 15 minutes, the B-29s—18 aircraft of the 98th Bombardment Group—came into sight after battling their way from Japan through unexpectedly severe headwinds. The combined formation turned towards the target—a bridge near Chongju—but by this time the F-80s were critically low on fuel and they were forced to abandon the escort while still some miles away from the objective. As the B-29s unloaded their bombs nine MiGs swept across the river to attack. The fast interceptors harried the medium bombers for several minutes as they headed homewards in tight defensive formation, and although no B-29s were shot down, ten of them were badly damaged by cannon fire. Three of the bombers barely managed to stagger in for an emergency landing at Taegu, with engines smoking, controls shot away and great holes ripped in wings and fuselage by shell splinters.

On March 10th, following days and nights of non-stop work by the aviation engineers, Suwon airstrip was declared serviceable enough for use by Sabres albeit with a certain element of risk. The 334th Squadron accordingly moved up from Taegu, its place at the latter base being taken by another Squadron of the 4th Wing, the 336th, fresh out from Japan. With minor exceptions the tactics used by the Sabres in their renewed patrols over north-western Korea were the same as those employed during December, the flights arriving in MiG Alley at intervals and quartering the sky like vultures ready to converge on any point in the patrol area where the MiGs appeared.

Nevertheless there were still considerable gaps in the Allied fighter screen. On March 12th, for example, while patrolling Sabres converged on a spot opposite where a formation of MiGs was reported to be assembling north of the Yalu, 12 more MiGs slipped across the river unnoticed and bounced a flight of four F-80s of the 8th Fighter-Bomber Group. Fortunately the Communist pilots appeared to be of low calibre; the Shooting Star pilots claimed four MiGs damaged and two more enemy fighters collided and spun into the ground, locked together. Five days later more 8th Group Shooting Stars were again attacked by three MiGs which managed to slip through the Sabre umbrella. A running battle ensued during which one MiG and one F-80 were destroyed when they collided head on with one another.

Meanwhile, following a pause after the 98th Bombardment Group's disastrous mission on March 1st, Bomber Command had once again intensified its attacks on bridge targets south of the Yalu. On March 23rd 22 B-29s of the 19th and 307th Groups encountered only light anti-aircraft fire during a successful attack on important rail bridges at Kogunyong and Chongju. The MiGs were airborne at the time but they found themselves engaged in a pitched battle with 45 Sabres of the 4th Wing several miles away and none of the Communist fighters succeeded in getting through to the bombers. This attack was followed on March 30th by a raid on the bridges at Chongsongjin, Manpojin and Namsan-ni by 36 B-29s of the 19th, 98th and 307th Groups, with Sabres of the 4th Wing flying top cover and F-80s of the 8th and 49th

Wings providing close escort. The usual cloud of dust just over the river at Antung signalled the presence of MiGs but most of them stayed over their own territory and only a few came across to attack B-29s of the 19th Group. The MiGs swept through the F-80 escort with almost contemptuous ease and inflicted severe damage on one B-29, although two MiGs were claimed as destroyed by the 19th Group's gunners.

After that, low cloud over the Yalu brought about a temporary lull in bomber operations, but on April 3rd and 4th both Sabres and MiGs were up in strength over the Yalu and the F-86 pilots claimed the destruction of four enemy jet fighters. The weather finally cleared on April 6th and the following day the B-29s of the 98th and 307th Groups were detailed to attack the railway bridges at Sinuiju and a road bridge at Uiju. The bombers were escorted by 48 F-84 Thunderjets of the 27th Wing, operating out of Itazuke, and these fought a hot engagement with 30 MiG-15s which crossed the Yalu to attack the B-29s as they were bombing their targets. The Thunderjet close escort proved so effective that only one MiG got through, but this destroyed a B-29 of the 307th Group. The F-84s claimed one MiG-15 destroyed for no loss to themselves.

It was a different story on April 12th when B-29s of the 19th, 98th and 307th Groups were once again ordered to attack the bridge at Sinuiju, which still stubbornly refused to collapse despite the battering it had received. Close escort was again provided by the 27th Wing, which put up 39 aircraft, while Sabres of the 4th Wing flew top cover. With the target still several minutes' flying time away the bomber formation was savagely attacked by about 50 MiG-15s which quickly destroyed one B-29 of the 19th Group and damaged five others. This attack had scarcely ended when another was launched by 20 more MiGs which sent the Thunderjets scattering in all directions as they dived vertically through them on to the bombers. This time it was the 307th Group's turn to be hit. One of its B-29s spun down to explode on the ground and a second was so severely damaged that it had to make a crash landing at Suwon. A small number of MiGs also attacked the 98th Group, which was bringing up the rear, but all its B-29s came through unscathed. On the credit side the Sabre pilots claimed four MiGs destroyed and six damaged, while the gunners of the B-29 formation claimed the destruction of ten enemy fighters, although the latter claim was in all probability greatly exaggerated. The Thunderjet pilots also claimed three MiGs probably destroyed. Nevertheless, the price of three B-29s destroyed—the one that crash-landed at Suwon was a complete write-off—and five more badly damaged was too high, and on General Stratemeyer's orders all further B-29 raids in the Sinuiju area were called off until some really effective means of escorting the bombers could be found.

It was clear that the F-86 was the only aircraft really suited to escort and air superiority duties, but by the third week in April even the Sabre pilots were finding it increasingly difficult to establish a clear margin of superiority over their Communist opponents. Flying discipline among the Red units had shown a marked improvement and as they gained combat experience the MiG pilots became more aggressive and determined. They appeared to have abandoned their large unwieldy formations of up to 50 aircraft, and instead were operating in squadron battle formations of 16 machines in four flights of four.

The growing prowess of the Red fighter pilots was disturbing, for it manifested itself at a time when FEAF Bomber Command was about to launch a new series of attacks on airfields in North Korea, which—as air reconnaissance showed—were now almost completely repaired. The attacks began on April 17th, and as it turned out fears that they would be contested by large numbers of MiGs proved to be unfounded. The MiGs were airborne all right, but they were successfully penned up near the Yalu by the 4th Wing's 334th and 336th Squadrons, which were now based side by side at Suwon. To counter the Communists' new tactics the Sabres now operated in flights of six aircraft and timed their arrival in the combat area at closer intervals. This policy apparently took the Red pilots completely by surprise, because when 36 MiGs came across the Yalu to attack 12 Sabres on April 22nd—no doubt believing that they could expect to enjoy complete numerical superiority for at least ten minutes—they were immediately bounced by a second formation of 12 Sabres coming along behind. Four MiGs were destroyed and four others damaged; the remainder fled back across the Yalu.

The airfield attacks, meanwhile, were going well. During the week preceding April 23rd Bomber Command repeatedly hit nine North Korean bases. The same targets were also attacked by Fifth Air Force fighter-bombers and by night-flying B-26s. By the 23rd, air reconnaissance indicated that the airfields had been sufficiently damaged to make them unusuable for several weeks to come, and Bomber Command was consequently ordered back to its more usual task of interdiction.

The next major airfield strike was carried out on May 9th against Sinuiju, which, with its protective umbrella of MiG-15s and its arsenal of anti-aircraft guns, was the best defended target in North Korea. The Reds had already deployed 38 combat aircraft there; these were all piston-engined types, but there were indications that the new concrete revetments sighted around the edge of the field would soon house jet fighters. Accordingly, in the early afternoon of the 9th, Shooting Stars of the 8th, 49th and 51st Wings, Mustangs of the 18th Wing and Corsairs of the 1st Marine Air Wing—a total of 312 aircraft—hammered Sinuiju for 45 minutes while 4th Wing Sabres, 27th Wing Thunderjets and

Panthers of the Marine Air Wing flew top cover overhead. Eighteen MiGs were sighted crossing the Yalu, but most of these avoided air combat and Allied pilots were credited with only two enemy fighters damaged. While these skirmishes went on the fighter-bomber pilots down below had a field day. The Shooting Stars went in first, blasting every flak emplacement with bombs and rockets. Then it was the turn of the Corsairs and Mustangs, each flight of which had been assigned a specific target within the perimeter of the airfield. Within minutes an enormous pall of smoke was rising thousands of feet into the sky from a big fuel dump and 26 ammunition and supply dumps destroyed by rockets and napalm. Over 106 buildings were also destroyed, as were all the enemy aircraft on the field. The Allied pilots observed enemy personnel milling about in the open like ants, apparently not knowing what to do or where to go, and mowed dozens of them down with machine gun fire. All the Allied aircraft returned safely to base.

It was the air battles of May 1951 that gave birth to the first jet ace in history. He was Captain James Jabara, a Sabre pilot with the 334th Squadron. On May 7th, when his own Squadron was rotated back to Japan, Jabara stayed on at Suwon to fly and fight with its replacement, the 335th Squadron. By that time his score stood at four MiGs destroyed and he needed just another enemy aircraft to his credit to earn the title of ace.

His chance came on May 20th, when 50 MiGs crossed the Yalu to attack 12 Sabres of the 334th. Two more flights of Sabres, one of which included Jabara, were quickly summoned by radio and hurled themselves into the fray. Jabara quickly got on the tail of one of the enemy fighters and saw his machine gun bullets registering strikes on the MiG's wing and fuselage. He followed it down to 10,000 feet and saw the pilot eject. He climbed back to 25,000 feet and within a couple of minutes was fighting it out with a second MiG which he set on fire. He had time to watch it spin down in flames before being forced to break violently as a third MiG fastened itself on to his own tail. He broke away hard and went into a long dive, losing the enemy fighter and returning to base. His two victories were made all the more noteworthy by the fact that one of his wing tanks had refused to jettison, a circumstance that would have compelled most pilots to go home immediately. Other Sabre pilots claimed one MiG destroyed with one probable and five damaged. Jabara himself scored no further victories before the end of his current tour, but he returned to Korea later in the war and increased his score to 15—becoming an ace three times over.

After the battle of May 20th the MiGs avoided combat for ten days until the 31st, when 12 of them crossed the Yalu to attack two B-29s of the 19th Group heading for Sinuiju. One MiG was destroyed by B-29 gunners and two more were shot down by a flight of Sabres which came up to the rescue. The MiGs tried again the following day, but this time they were more cautious; they waited until the Sabre escort turned for home, short of fuel, before crossing the river to attack four 98th Group B-29s which were bombing a bridge near Sinanju. One bomber went down, its wing torn off by a hail of cannon fire, and two more were badly damaged—but the gunners claimed the destruction of one MiG and two more were downed by more Sabres which came racing up from the south.

Despite the fact that they had failed to establish any kind of air superiority, the Communists still believed that they could overwhelm the Eighth Army by sheer weight of numbers in the course of their two major offensives of April and May 1951. By mid-April there were some 700,000 Communist troops deployed in North Korea, the majority of them Chinese. Command of the Chinese People's Volunteers now rested upon the shoulders of General Peng Teh-Huai, while the Chief of Staff of the Korean People's Army was General Nam Il—a former Soviet citizen of Korean parentage who had fought with the Red Army in the Second World War and who had only returned to Korea in 1945. Behind both men loomed an all-powerful nucleus of Soviet advisors led by Lieutenant-General Vladimir Razuvayev, who held undisputed control of all North Korean military operations.

The Communist forces were organised in 70 divisions, with 36 Chinese divisions on a line between the Imjin River and Hwachon Reservoir and a further 12 deployed eastwards between the reservoir and the Sea of Japan. To the west of the reservoir, four Chinese Communist Army groups were deployed along a 75-mile front between Hwachon and Munsan. Facing them was a front line strength of 230,000 United Nations troops under the command of Lieutenant-General James van Fleet, who had succeeded General Ridgway as commander of the Eighth Army on the 14th of April.

The great Communist Spring Offensive began on the night of April 22nd, the initial assault following the now familiar pattern of human wave attacks by masses of infantry all along the front. The Chinese scored an early success when, striking hard at the weakest part of the Allied line, they cut the ROK 6th Division to pieces, leaving a dangerous gap between the Marine Division on its right flank and the 24th Infantry on the left. It was now clear that the main Chinese aim was to isolate Seoul with an enveloping movement from the north and north-east, and General van Fleet was determined to hold on to the city at all costs. On April 26th the Chinese offensive was checked in the eastern sector by the 27th Commonwealth Brigade and the attention now switched to the west, where six Chinese Armies were flinging everything they had into a desperate bid to reach the South Korean capital. The main weight of the offensive here fell on the 29th British

Infantry Brigade, which—holding a 12,000 yard front with only 6,000 men—defended the vital river crossings over the Imjin.

The epic stand of the 29th Brigade—and particularly that of the 1st Battalion Gloucester Regiment on Hill 235 above the hamlet of Solma-ri—has gone down in history. General van Fleet later described it as the most outstanding example of unit bravery in modern warfare. The Brigade held on for three days against overwhelming odds before a general retreat was ordered to the north of Seoul. The holding action not only saved the left flank of the Eighth Army's 1st Corps, making possible an orderly withdrawal down the road to Seoul; it also disrupted the entire timetable of the Chinese offensive, robbing it of its momentum. Apart from that, during three days of savage fighting the 29th Brigade had destroyed a complete Chinese division.

By April 29th the Eighth Army had established a new defensive line running across the Korean penisula from Seoul to Sabangu and then on to Taepo-ri on the east coast. That same day the Communists made a last desperate attempt to reach Seoul along the Inchon road by ferrying 6,000 assault troops across the Han estuary but this was broken up by concentrated attacks. The following day the Chinese forces began to pull back. Their offensive had gained just 35 miles of ground and it had cost at least 70,000 casualties against the United Nations Command's loss of 7,000.

The battle, however, was by no means over. Van Fleet was grimly aware that the Communists had committed only half their forces to their first Spring offensive, and that a second major assault would soon be made on the new Allied defensive line. To meet it van Fleet assembled an enormous concentration of firepower, while vast areas of minefields were laid along the entire front. The Eighth Army's commander was determined to smash the Chinese offensive in no-man's-land. "We must expend steel and fire," he said, "not men. I want so many artillery holes that a man could step from one to the other."

Beginning on May 10th air reconnaissance reported a steady southward movement of large numbers of Chinese troops, and it soon became apparent from a concentration of five Chinese Communist Armies between Chunchon and Inje that the enemy was planning the weight of the offensive to fall on the eastern front. By the end of the second week in May the Communists had deployed 20 Chinese divisions east of Chunchon, together with six North Korean divisions.

On the night of May 15th/16th, 12 Chinese divisions struck along a 20-mile front against the ROK 5th and 7th Divisions, shattering them. This intial move was followed by a swing eastwards to attack the rear of the ROK 3rd Corps, precipitating a rapid 50 mile retreat down the east coast. The combined Chinese and North Korean forces exploited this by making a rapid drive for 30 miles, threatening the right flank of the Marine Division and the 2nd Infantry. Assessing the situation rapidly, General van Fleet decided to allow the enemy advance to continue in this sector while the 3rd Infantry Division and the 187th Airborne Regimental Combat Team made an emergency dash across the peninsula to the assistance of the Marines and the 2nd Infantry. A modified defensive line was quickly established with the help of overwhelming artillery support, and by the 19th it had become obvious that the Chinese offensive was rapidly collapsing. Weak enemy thrusts continued until the 23rd, then stopped altogether. In the space of just one week, between May 17th and 23rd, the Communists had suffered no fewer than 90,000 casualties, many of them victims of the Allied minefields which had been sown with electrically detonated 55-gallon drums of napalm and petrol.

Van Fleet fully intended that the reeling Chinese were to be given no respite. During the last two weeks of May the United Nations forces struck hard and fast, inflicting further casualties on the enemy and taking 17,000 prisoners. By the beginning of June the Communists had been driven out of the whole of South Korea with the exception of the sector west of the Imjin and south of the 38th Parallel. The myth of the invincible Chinese hordes had been smashed once and for all.

For the commanders of the Communist ground forces in Korea, the failure to win a smashing victory over the United Nations represented a not inconsiderable loss of face. It was natural that they should seek a scapegoat, and even more natural that they should place the blame for the failure of the offensive fairly and squarely on the shoulders of General Liu Ya-Lou and the inability of the Chinese Communist Air Force to establish superiority over Korea. Liu's counter-argument was that the offensive had been allowed to take place before the North Korean airfields had been made ready to accommodate his jet fighter and ground attack squadrons, and that his pilots in any event lacked sufficient combat experience. In an attempt to remedy the situation the organisation that governed the Red Chinese Air Force—The Red Chinese Aviation Inspection Group—put forward a revised air plan which called for the creation of an International Communist Volunteer Air Force composed of Soviet Bloc volunteer pilots as well as Chinese and North Koreans. While these renewed their efforts to wrest air superiority over North Western Korea from the United Nations, work on rehabilitating the North Korean airfields would continue as planned despite the continual threat of Allied air attack. Ultimately, it was hoped that the Communists would be able to fill in the bomb craters faster than the Allies could make them and that some, if not all, of the Il-10 ground attack units could be brought forward to support further Communist offensives. In the meantime, light aircraft flown by North Korean crews and operating from rough grass strips would carry out nightly nuisance raids against United Nations ground forces and installations. Although the Communists appreciated that such pinprick raids would be unlikely to cause serious damage they would certainly deprive Allied troops of sleep and possibly bring about a drop in morale. Similar tactics had been used by the Soviet Air Force on the Eastern Front during the Second World War with considerable success.

The first of these nuisance raids was carried out in the early hours of June 14th, 1951, when two little Polikarpov Po-2 biplane trainers took off from Sariwon airfield. Shortly after three o'clock one of the Po-2s dropped two bombs on Suwon airstrip, narrowly missing the runway, while the other dropped two more on an Eighth Army motor transport park at Inchon causing some splinter damage to several vehicles. The following night a third raider made a low strafing pass over Kimpo airfield, fortunately without doing any damage. This attack was carried out by what was probably the weirdest aircraft to make its appearance so far in Korea—an ancient Russian-built MBR-2 amphibian.

The third raid, carried out on the night of June 16th/17th, surpassed the Communists' wildest dreams. On this occasion two Po-2s led by Lieutenant La Woon Yung arrived over Suwon to find the airfield as brilliantly lit as a Christmas tree. In the glare of vehicle headlights the Communist pilots could clearly see the 4th Wing's Sabres parked in their dispersals. La Woon Yung's two bombs straddled a flight of 335th Squadron Sabres, completely destroying one aircraft and damaging eight others, four of them seriously. The other pilot dropped his bombs across the parked vehicles of the 802nd Engineer Aviation Battalion, severely damaging several of them. The Communists must have been well content with that night's work. In less than two minutes one rickety stick and canvas biplane had inflicted more damage on the Sabres of the 4th Fighter-Interceptor Wing than had the speedy MiG-15s in all their air combats so far.

The Sabres, however, were not to have it all their own way in air combat for much longer. On June 17th 25 MiG-15s came over the Yalu to attack two flights of 4th Wing Sabres on patrol. The Sabre pilots shot down one enemy fighter and damaged six others for no loss to themselves, but on their return to Suwon they reported that the MiG pilots had shown a high degree of skill and determination not previously encountered. The general opinion was that the enemy jets had been flown either by Russians or by extremely competent Red Chinese instructor pilots. The next day 40 MiG-15s that tangled with 32 Sabres over the Yalu showed the same high calibre, but that did not prevent them from losing five of their number to the more experienced Sabre pilots. Nevertheless, one Sabre failed to return from this encounter. There was a third fierce air fight on the 19th, and this time the MiG

*Right:* F-84s of the 27th Fighter-Escort Wing arriving in Japan aboard the escort carrier *Sitko Bay.* Many of the aircraft suffered badly from corrosion at the end of the voyage.

*Below:* Refuelling a 49th FBW F-84 at Taegu

Skyraider of VA-728 running-up before taking off on a strike.

With the North Korean coastline for a background, crew members of the USS *Boxer* (CVA-21) respot for the veteran carrier's final air strike against the Communists on the morning of July 27th, 1953.

*Top:* As the AD Skyraider (upper right) pulls away from his bombing run, three bombs from the cradles of the AD Skyraider in the foreground fall towards targets at Wonsan, North Korea. Smoke and debris can be seen erupting skyward from the first plane's bombs.

*Above:* Dramatic photograph of an F-84 strike on enemy communications in North Korea. *Republic Aviation Photo.*

Successful emergency landing by a Firefly of 812 Squadron. The propeller is still turning and the top blades appear to be undamaged. One underneath is bent by impact with the deck.

Firefly being loaded on board HMS *Theseus*, Iwakuni.

*Above:* Firefly of 825 Squadron, HMS *Ocean*, preparing for launch with a USN S-51 standing by watchfully.

*Below:* Flight deck of the light fleet carrier HMS *Theseus* covered with snow while operating off the Korean coast.

*Foot:* Three Sea Furies of 804 Squadron await their turn to be launched from *Glory's* flight deck on a strike against Communists in western Korea.

Sunderland of the Far East Flying Boat Wing at Iwakuni.

Dakota of No 30 Transport Unit, RAAF, at Iwakuni.

*Top:* Gaily coloured board proclaims K-2 (Taegu) is home of the 49th and 58th Fighter-Bomber Wings.

*Above:* C-47 of the Airways and Air Communications Service.

Meteors of No 77 Sqn in their revetments at Kimpo. Nearest the camera is P/O Ken Murray's aircraft, 'Black Murray'.

Auster and L-19 of 1913 Flight, RAF.

pilots came out on top when they shot down one Sabre for no loss to themselves, although the 4th Wing pilots claimed four enemy fighters damaged.

The Reds were evidently sufficiently encouraged by this limited success to make a cautious foray over the border with their Il-10 ground attack aircraft. On June 20th eight Il-10 fighter-bombers crossed the Yalu and set course for the island of Sinmi-do which lay just off the Korean coast about 75 miles south-east of Sinuiju, and which was being held by a small force of South Korean troops against repeated enemy attacks. Purely by chance the Ilyushins were spotted by Mustang pilots of the 18th Group, engaged on an offensive sweep over the road south of Sinuiji. The Allied pilots called up a second flight of Mustangs to provide top cover and then flung themselves on the Ilyushins, destroying two and damaging three more in a matter of minutes. The Reds had evidently called for reinforcements too, because as the 18th Group pilots continued to harry the Il-10s, a flight of six Yak-9s came racing up from the north-west. They were hotly engaged by the second Mustang flight which shot down one of the enemy fighters. Then a third Sabre flight arrived, with two flights of Sabres flying top cover—the latter reaching the scene just in time to intercept a dozen MiGs which also came streaking up from the direction of the Yalu. In the ensuing dogfight the Sabres damaged four MiGs, but one of them got through the screen and destroyed one Mustang. Both sides then broke off the action with the United Nations pilots the decided victors.

Meanwhile, steps were being taken to combat the nightly visits of the Bed Check Charlies—as the little Po-2 night raiders were nicknamed—to the Seoul area. The biplanes, cruising at 80 knots and at low level down the valleys on the approach to their targets, proved incredibly difficult to detect by radar and even when night fighters were sent up to intercept them the Po-2 pilots usually made full use of the low flying speed and high manoeuvrability to get away. Nevertheless, two Po-2s were in fact intercepted and destroyed during June—the first on the night of the 23rd by Captain Dick Heyman flying a B-26 of the 8th Squadron, and the second on the 30th over the Han river by Captain E. B. Long of Marine Squadron VMF-513, flying one of the unit's newly acquired F7F Tigercat night fighters.

The only real means of overcoming the threat of the nuisance raiders was to keep on hitting the North Korean airfields hard by day and night, and it was in opposing these attacks that Communist air activity over north-western Korea reached a new peak during the last days of June. On the 22nd, as Shooting Stars attacked Sinuiju airfield, Sabres and MiGs met in a hectic dogfight overhead that ended in the destruction of two MiGs and one F-86 of the 4th Wing. It was a measure of the MiG pilots' new-found confidence that they now penetrated on occasions, either singly or in pairs and fitted with wing tanks, almost as far as the 38th Parallel. They also appeared to be at last exploiting the advantages of their aircraft. During this period the United Nations pilots noted that the Communist appeared to be experimenting with various types of tactics, including one which the Sabre pilots nicknamed the Yo-yo. A large formation of MiGs would orbit over the battle area at maximum ceiling, breaking off in small sections to make high speed passes on the UN aircraft below and then zooming up to altitude again. Many American pilots observed that some of the Communist tactics seemed strangely familiar—and then they suddenly realised that they were exactly the same as those employed by the Luftwaffe's fighters against the big daylight bomber formations over Europe in 1944–45. The Russians had learnt a lot in the half decade since the war.

The MiG-15, however, was a high level interceptor and displayed most of its aerodynamic advantages at altitudes of 20,000 feet or more. At lower level these advantages were fewer—a fact that usually enabled slower F-80s and F-84s to hold their own when attacked by formations of enemy jet fighters. On June 24th, for example, F-80s of the 51st Wing came out on top when they were bounced by MiG-15s while strafing Sinanju airfield. The Shooting Star pilots claimed four MiGs damaged for no hurt to themselves. Two days later Thunderjets of the 136th Fighter-Bomber Wing—newly arrived in the combat theatre—destroyed one MiG-15 in a formation of six that swept down to attack four B-29s over Yongyu airfield and drove the remainder away, and on two further occasions before the end of the month MiG-15s attacking Mustangs near Sinanju and Songchon failed to score any victories at all over the slower piston-engined fighter-bombers.

July 1951 was a bad month for the Communist fighter pilots. On the 8th, 20 MiG pilots who crossed the river to attack Mustangs of the 18th Group strafing an airfield near Kangdong probably thought they had an easy engagement on their hands. Instead they ran into 35 Sabres of the 4th Wing which shot down three of the enemy fighters. The next day, six MiG-15s which took off to intercept six B-29s of the 19th Group over Sinanju airfield lost one of their number to the Superfortress gunners and another to the Sabre escort. On the 11th a fierce air battle developed south of Sinuiju when 30 MiGs attacked 21 F-80s. Thirty-four Sabres quickly swept up to join the fight, and in the ensuing mêlée three MiGs were destroyed.

Shortly after midnight on July 12th a Corsair night fighter of VMF-513 surprised a Po-2 night raider and shot it down in flames over Seoul. After that there were no more Bed Check Charlie raids in the Seoul area that year. The Red air offensive of the summer of 1951 was over, and it had failed.

CHAPTER NINE

# Battle of the Lifelines

During the early months of 1951, the presence of growing numbers of MiG-15s over north-western Korea brought about a complete revision of FEAF Bomber Command's bombing techniques. Up to the start of Interdiction Campaign No 4 in December 1950 the B-29 crews had been able to carry out their task in almost leisurely fashion, bombing from as low as 10,000 feet and making several runs over the target. The stiffening of Communist anti-aircraft defences around bridge and communications targets in the north-west, however, together with the constant threat of attack by MiG-15s, changed the situation entirely. From now on attacks usually had to be made at altitudes of 20,000 feet or more in order to escape the worst of the flak, and the constant threat of the MiG-15s meant that the bombers could make only one run across the target in relative safety.

The problem was that although the operational difficulties involved in taking out tricky targets such as bridges were increasing all the time, the precision of the average Bomber Command B-29 crew was not growing in proportion, nor was it likely to do so as long as the standard interdiction weapons continued to be free-falling 1000 and 2000lb bombs. In a bid to improve the overall standard of accuracy, the 19th Bombardment Group had made operational tests with 1000lb Razon radio-guided bombs in the autumn of 1950. These weapons, first developed during the Second World War, could be steered in flight to a limited degree by their remote-controlled tail fins, which responded to radio impulses sent out by a B-29 bombardier. After a lot of initial snags the 19th Group at last began to register some successes with the Razons, and in fact destroyed 15 bridges with them.

The trouble was that they were not big enough; although they could be dropped in the vicinity of a bridge with fair accuracy, about four of them were needed on average to destroy each target. In December 1950, however, the 19th Group tested another radio-guided weapon which showed far greater promise: the 12,000lb Tarzon bomb, with a destructive capacity similar to that of the 'Tallboys' dropped by the RAF's Lancasters during the Second World War.

As this was the biggest weapon ever handled operationally by a

United States Air Force unit it was hardly surprising that initial trials met with only limited success. In fact, out of ten Tarzons dropped during December 1960 only one scored a direct hit. On January 13th, 1951, however, the 19th Group scored a notable success when one of its B-29s dropped a Tarzon from 15,000 feet and destroyed a major railway bridge at Kanggye. Three more Tarzon attacks by the same Group during March, when a new consignment of the weapons arrived in Okinawa, resulted in the destruction of two more bridges and the damaging of a third.

The Tarzon missiles, however, were in very short supply, and most of Bomber Command's interdiction attacks continued to be carried out with more conventional bombs. Early in March 1951, because of the problem of providing effective fighter escort over north-western Korea, most of these attacks were directed against road, rail and bridge targets well clear of 'MiG Alley', but towards the end of the month—with the Sabres once again operating at full pitch from Korean bases—the B-29 Groups returned to the Yalu to carry out further strikes against the international bridges.

The first of these attacks, carried out on the 29th, was to have included a raid on the Sinuiju bridges by three Tarzon-carrying B-29s of the 19th Group, but this effort was dogged by bad luck right from the start. One B-29 was forced back to base with engine trouble; the second, flown by the 19th Group's commander, Colonel Payne Jennings, came down in the sea with the loss of all its crew; and the third—the only one to reach the Yalu—missed the target by a considerable margin.

A second raid the following day by the 19th, 98th and 307th Groups met with far greater success, the B-29s knocking out two spans of the Chongsonjin highway bridge and the Manpojin railway bridge, as well as destroying a poorly-camouflaged pontoon which the Chinese had erected further upriver.

By April 14th, 1951, Bomber Command's crews had destroyed a total of 48 out of 60 bridges and 27 out of 39 marshalling yards assigned to them under Interdiction Campaign No 4. Nevertheless, this success had not been achieved without its price; in the month preceding the 14th, eight B-29s and their crews had been lost on operations and a further 25 bombers had been temporarily put out of action with battle damage. At a time when strikes on North Korean airfields were assuming paramount importance and the Eighth Army needed all the medium bomber close support it could get, this was a dangerously higher rate of attrition. General Stratemeyer consequently ordered Bomber Command to cut back its effort to 12 sorties a day until further notice, although this was stepped up to 18 daily missions when the Communists began their new offensive on April 22nd.

This reduced sortie rate, with the emphasis on airfield attacks and close support, inevitably meant that few aircraft could be spared for interdiction work. The 19th Group still had a small stock of Tarzons, but any hopes that these could be effectively employed were dashed on April 20th, when a B-29 in difficulties jettisoned one over the sea. Although theoretically safe the missile exploded on contact with the water, and the subsequent investigation formed the opinion that a similar occurrence had been responsible for the loss of Colonel Jennings and his crew three weeks earlier. All existing Tarzons were withdrawn pending modifications, but further development of the weapon was finally abandoned on August 13th. During their brief operational career, 30 Tarzons had been dropped, destroying six bridges and damaging a seventh. Nineteen of the missiles had missed the target and three had failed to explode.

Towards the end of May 1951, following the collapse of the Communist offensive and the renewed push northwards by the Eighth Army, General Stratemeyer once again revised Interdiction Campaign No 4. As the Communists retreated it became apparent that they were relying heavily on supplies already stockpiled in North Korea, rather than on fresh consignments brought in from Manchuria, and Stratemeyer—with a strong nudge from General Vandenberg, who expressed his displeasure that small numbers of B-29s were still being used in costly attacks against heavily-defended targets—accordingly re-directed the main weight of Bomber Command's effort against marshalling yards and communications centres. Road and rail interdiction was now to be the primary responsibility of the Fifth Air Force, in conjunction with the 1st Marine Air Wing and Task Force 77. The object of this interdiction task, code-named Operation Strangle, was to cut off the main line of resistance (MLR) from the rest of North Korea by means of a concentrated air offensive against the enemy's lines of communication in a strip of territory stretching across Korea for a depth of one degree of latitude above 38°15'N. The road system was split up into eight main routes and all bridges, embankments, choke points, defiles and tunnels were slated as targets.

Operation Strangle began on May 31st, using every means of interdiction in a bid to paralyze the enemy's transportation in the zone between the 39th Parallel and the front line. In the western sector, Mustangs of the 18th Fighter-Bomber Wing repeatedly hit sections of roads and railways with 500lb bombs, many of them with delayed-action fuses, while B-26s of the 3rd Bombardment Wing concentrated on road junctions and choke points, saturating them with clusters of deadly 'butterfly bombs' which detonated when disturbed. While this was going on, Shooting Stars of the 49th and 51st Wings operated at maximum effort against railbridge targets in north-western Korea.

Road and rail bridges in the north-east were the primary targets of

Task Force 77, using almost 100 per cent of its offensive air potential. Since April 1951, the Navy's Corsairs and Skyraiders had been joined on ground attack missions by Grumman Panthers, the latter diverting from their more normal escort role; the first ground attack sortie by Navy jets had been flown on April 2nd, when two F9F-2B Panthers of VF-191, each loaded with four 250lb and two 100lb general purpose bombs, were launched from the USS *Princeton* for an attack on a rail bridge near Songjin.

Naval air attacks in the vicinity of the MLR within the scope of Operation Strangle were carried out by the Marine Air Wing and Task Force 95, the United Nations Blockading and Escort Force established in September 1950. TF 95 was split into two main elements, Task Group 95.1—under British command and including most of the British Commonwealth naval units—patrolling the west coast, and Task Group 95.2 patrolling the east coast from the MLR to the island of Yang-do. Operating with TG 95.1 the Sea Furies and Firefly-5s of HMS *Glory*'s 804 and 812 Squadrons were extremely active during Strangle; on one occasion in June the British carrier flew off 84 sorties in a single day, setting up a record that was only broken the following year by HMS *Ocean*'s 802 and 825 Squadrons.

The intial results of Operation Strangle were encouraging. It appeared that the sudden, ferocious air onslaught had taken the enemy by surprise, for as the UN forces pushed northwards they captured several large Communist supply dumps intact. A true assessment, however, could only be formed when Allied pressure on the enemy lifted following the capture of the primary United Nations objectives—and it proved beyond all doubt that Strangle had failed to isolate the MLR.

With hindsight, it is not difficult to pinpoint the reasons behind the operation's failure. First, and probably most important of all, the Communist sources of supply—the factories in Manchuria and the Soviet Union—remained unaffected by Allied bombing; secondly, bombing had the power to disrupt only supply routes and rolling stock: the great heart of the enemy logistics system, the stockpiles of material, were well concealed in mountain caves and tunnels and were virtually immune to air attack, as were the personnel who kept the roads and railways open; thirdly, Allied Intelligence had badly underestimated the amazing ingenuity of the North Korean Military Highway Administration and the Railway Recovery Bureau, whose bridging, track and road-laying techniques were so advanced that they were able to keep supplies moving continuously despite the bombing; and, lastly, the air interdiction campaign suffered from the outset because it was not co-ordinated with offensive action by the UN ground forces. Any advantages won by comprehensive interdiction in the MLR were consequently not exploited as they might have been.

The ability of the Communists to move men and supplies in secrecy at night underlined the importance of night intruder work. Since the autumn of 1950 this had been the primary responsibility of the 3rd Bombardment Wing and the 731st Bombardment Squadron, operating B-26s out of Iwakuni, and Marine Squadron VMF(N)-513, flying Corsairs from Itazuke, Wonsan and Yonpo—but neither of these aircraft types was really suited to intruder operations. Moreover, the 3rd Wing suffered from a shortage of aircraft and from the fact that the steel plank strip at Taegu—through which the B-26s staged on their intruder missions—ripped tyres to shreds. Nevertheless, at the critical time of the Communist offensive in April the Wing managed to fly up to 48 sorties nightly.

Most of the B-26 intruder sorties were carried out in conjunction with C-47 flare ships, a flight of which was usually on alert at Taegu. In the early days the C-47s worked as far north as Sinuiju, but with the stiffening of the enemy anti-aircraft defences in that sector they were later forbidden to go north of latitude 39°30′. Sometimes, as a variation from their more routine flare-dropping, the C-47s scattered loads of tacks over enemy roads to puncture the tyres of Red vehicles, which could then—hopefully—be knocked out at first light by the B-26s. About 30 vehicles were, in fact, destroyed in this way.

Since the C-47s could no longer be used far north of the MLR, most of the 3rd Wing's B-26s were adapted to carry flares on their rocket rails in March 1951. Fused to ignite at about 3,500 feet, the flares burned long enough to allow two or three strafing passes. Some of the Wing's most successful intruder crews, however, scorned the use of flares altogether, preferring to fix a convoy's position by noting its relation to ground shadows in the few seconds before the enemy vehicles switched off their lights and making a single pass with 100lb fire bombs and 260lb fragmentation bombs.

The Marine intruders of VMF(N)-513, flying out of Pusan's K-1 airstrip in their Corsairs and Tigercats against targets nearer the front line, were still able to make use of the C-47 flare-droppers. In the three-month period between April 1st and June 30th, the Marine crews reported attacks on 11,980 enemy vehicles and claimed the destruction of 1,420 of them. On average, 18 intruder missions were flown from K-1 nightly.

Further north, the B-26 crews of the 3rd Wing claimed the destruction of 21 locomotives and 856 vehicles during April and May 1951. At the beginning of June, to assist the 3rd Wing for the duration of Operation Strangle, the 452nd Bombardment Wing was moved up to Pusan East airfield (K-9) and its crews converted to night intruder duties, destroying 151 enemy vehicles and damaging 224 between June 11th and 20th. The 3rd Wing's tally of Communist transport during

June stood at 403 vehicles destroyed and 1,048 damaged. During Strangle the night intruders of VMF(N)-513 concentrated on four selected roads south of Pyongyang, the F4Us and F7Fs teaming up with C-47 flare ships and with a pair of PB4Y-2s of Patrol Squadron VP-772, which were transferred from Naval Air Station Atsugi, Japan, to Pusan on June 12th. These operations by the PB4Ys—initially conducted as an experiment—proved so successful that the practice of assigning specially equipped patrol aircraft for this purpose was continued for the duration of hostilities.

The work of the night intruders continued unabated during July, and although the overall effectiveness of Operation Strangle diminished steadily the B-26s of the 3rd and 452nd Wings continued to register successes. Throughout the month the 3rd Wing operated its B-26s in pairs, one aircraft to light up the target and the other to attack. In four weeks the Wing claimed 240 vehicles destroyed and 693 damaged. The 452nd Wing, on the other hand, preferred to send out its aircraft singly, and its claim for the month stood at 471 vehicles destroyed and 880 damaged. One of the 452nd's most spectacular successes was achieved shortly before dawn on July 14th, when a lone B-26 flown by Captain William L. Ford attacked two convoys in quick succession, destroying 38 trucks and damaging an estimated 30.

The element of surprise undoubtedly played a major part in the night intruders' success, as did the continual use of headlights by the enemy. Fighter-bombers operating in daylight had no such guide to the location of a convoy, and the time that could be spent by F-80s and F-84s in their search for the elusive, well-camouflaged enemy was strictly limited. Only on isolated occasions were the fighter-bombers able to catch large numbers of enemy transport out in the open; one such was on February 13th, 1951, when the Chinese—desperately short of supplies to support their flagging New Year offensive—threw caution to the winds and choked the roads with long columns of vehicles. In that one day alone Allied air power destroyed 236 enemy vehicles and damaged 80 more, most of them falling victim to the Mustangs and Corsairs of the 18th and 35th Groups and the Marine Air Wing.

The Fifth Air Force's Mustangs—and particularly the 18th Fighter-Bomber Wing—continued to be the top scorers in these daylight truck-busting operations. From March 1951 onwards, F-80 and F-84 scores of vehicles destroyed also began to climb following the development of new visual reconnaissance tactics by the RF-51s of the 45th Tactical Reconnaissance Squadron. Taking off before dawn, the RF-51 pilots would carry out an intensive first-light reconnaissance in a circle of ten miles radius around places where enemy convoys were thought to be hiding. Once a convoy had been pinpointed, jet fighter-bombers would be quickly called up to deal with it. The figures themselves speak for the success of these tactics; during February 1951 the Fifth Air Force claimed the destruction of 1,366 enemy vehicles (728 of them to the credit of the 18th Group), in March the figure rose to 2,261, and in April it was 2,336.

Nevertheless, by the end of the month the Allied fighter-bomber pilots were not having it all their own way. The Communists were now defending their convoys with a wide variety of automatic weapons, including Russian 12·7mm machine guns and 37mm cannon, the latter effective against aircraft from ground level up to 4,500 feet. The Mustangs, with their liquid-cooled engines, were particularly vulnerable. In all, hostile ground fire accounted for 81 Allied fighter-bombers and reconnaissance aircraft during April, May and June 1951, including 38 Mustangs.

The tactics developed by the Communists to counter the ever-present threat of the fighter-bombers were varied. Early in 1951 the Chinese began to organize volunteer anti-aircraft groups of infantry armed with light automatic weapons and heavy calibre machine guns. These groups would be deployed around cleverly-devised 'flak traps' such as dummy troops or vehicles. A highly efficient network of observers was also set up, with sentries trained in aircraft recognition positioned every 300 yards or so along the main supply routes.

By the beginning of July 1951, the Communists had a total of 900 anti-aircraft weapons of all types in position along their major supply routes in North Korea, and this figure was to increase steadily during the months that followed. Although the growing concentration of fire-power could not prevent the Allied Air Forces from hitting the enemy's lifelines again and again with devastating effect, it made interdiction a costly business; of the 3,200 Fifth Air Force, Bomber Command, Navy and Marine aircraft that were to be lost in action before the end of hostilities, about a third were the victims of intense ground fire.

CHAPTER TEN

# Battlefield Support, 1951

Of all the aircraft types operated by the United Nations in Korea, the honour of being those most hated and feared by the Communist troops —judging from prisoner interrogations—must surely fall to the little Mosquitoes, the T-6s, L-17s, L-19s and L-20s. The sudden appearance of one of these aircraft, popping up briefly from behind a hill or a wood, invariably heralded a storm of artillery fire or a whirlwind air strike. It was, therefore, hardly surprising that the Mosquito crews ran greater risks than most, for the enemy ground forces went to great efforts to bring them down.

Up to the beginning of 1951, the little Mosquito control aircraft had often penetrated up to 50 miles inside enemy territory in their search for worthwhile targets for the fighter-bombers, but as enemy ground fire intensified they were forced to restrict their operations to the front line areas.

From January 25th, 1951, the Mosquitoes operated at maximum effort in support of Operation Thunderbolt, the Eighth Army's large-scale reconnaissance drive towards the Han River. Throughout the operation the 6147th Tactical Air Control Squadron flew from the primitive forward airstrip at Taejon, which permitted its aircraft to patrol the battle area for up to three hours. In addition to its complement of T-6s the 6147th Squadron also had at its disposal two C-47s which—packed with VHF equipment and orbiting on station about 20 miles behind the front lines—relayed messages between the airborne controllers, flights of ground-attack aircraft and the TACC. For direct communication with ground forces, each Mosquito aircraft was equipped with an SCR-300 'Walkie-Talkie' type infantry radio. The air control tactics developed in the course of Thunderbolt proved so successful that they were adopted as standard procedure during the spring and summer campaigns of 1951.

Throughout the spring of 1951, having seen the effectiveness of Fifth Air Force, US Army and Marine Mosquitoes at first hand, the British Commonwealth Division in Korea made frequent requests for the establishment of its own flight of light observation aircraft. This demand was eventually met in June 1951, when No 1913 Light Liaison

Flight was formed at RAF Middle Wallop with Auster AOP 6s. The aircraft were shipped in crates to Iwakuni, where they were quickly assembled and delivered to forward Korean airstrips in No 1 Commonwealth Division's area. A second unit, No 1903 Independent Air OP Flight, also arrived in Korea in October 1951. Although Royal Air Force units—the only ones, in fact, to fly from Korean soil—the two Flights were manned almost exclusively by Army personnel.

Although No 1913 Flight's main task was liaison, its Austers undertook visual reconnaissance missions from the moment they arrived in Korea, penetrating up to four miles into enemy territory. Pilots normally flew with one ear uncovered so that they could hear the crackle of any bullets that passed dangerously close and take evasive action! The Flight also possessed one Cessna L-19, on loan from the Eighth Army for use by the GOC 1st Commonwealth Division; the British pilots pronounced the L-19 to be superior to the Auster in most respects.

The primary task of No 1903 Flight, which had seen service against the terrorists in Malaya before reaching Korea via Hong Kong, was counter bombardment—in other words, spotting enemy gun positions and assisting friendly artillery to zero in on them. For this dangerous job the Austers' cockpits were armour-plated and the pilots flew solo, carrying parachutes. A daily average of seven sorties was flown, with each pilot putting in about 45 hours' flying in the course of a good month. Most sorties were flown above 5,000 feet to escape the worst of the small-arms fire and light flak, as well as to avoid the trajectories of Allied shells.

The risks run by American and Commonwealth air observation pilots were probably surpassed only by the hazards that faced another valiant group of Allied airmen, the crews of the light aircraft and helicopters of the air rescue squadrons, flying deep behind the enemy lines to snatch shotdown pilots to safety. On the outbreak of war in Korea there were two search and rescue units at the disposal of the Far East Air Forces, the 2nd and 3rd Air Rescue Squadrons, the former serving the Thirteenth and Twentieth Air Forces and the latter under the operational control of the Fifth Air Force.

Naturally enough, it was the Japan-based 3rd Squadron that was to bear the brunt of air rescue operations in Korea. The Squadron's equipment at the outbreak of hostilities consisted of SB-17s and a handful of Sikorsky H-5 (S-51) helicopters, but on July 28th three Grumman SA-16 Albatross amphibians were added to the inventory. Along with the SB-17s, these maintained standing patrols over the Tsushima Straits.

On July 7th, 1950, the 3rd Squadron sent two L-5 liaison aircraft to Korea to carry out 'snatches' from inside enemy territory. Their rescue attempts, however, were severely hampered by the fact that they were totally unsuited to operating from the sodden paddy fields of the battle area. The situation changed for the better on July 22nd, with the arrival at Taegu airstrip of the first detachment of H-5s. Within a few days the helicopters were being used to evacuate badly-wounded soldiers of the Eighth Army from the mountainous or rice-paddy terrain of the front line to hospitals in Miryang and Pusan. These operations were so successful that General Partridge directed the 3rd Squadron to six of its nine H-5s in Korea. At the same time, General Stratemeyer asked the USAF to allocate 25 more H-5s to form a special duties and evacuation unit. Within a fortnight 14 H-5s—stripped from other commands—were on their way to Korea. By this time a second helicopter unit was also operational at the front; this was Marine Corps Observation Squadron VMO-6, equipped with a mixed bag of HO-3s helicopters and OY-1 light aircraft. The Marine helicopters began operations on August 3rd, 1950, in support of the 1st Marine Brigade in the Changwon area, delivering rations and water to troops in mountain positions and evacuating heat-stroke cases.

By the end of August, meanwhile, the 3rd Rescue Squadron's helicopters had flown 83 critically-wounded soldiers from the battle area. All of them would almost certainly have died had they been forced to make the journey to a field hospital by ambulance. The Squadron's operations were now co-ordinated by a Rescue Liaison Office, which had been set up in the United Nations Command Joint Operations Centre on August 27th, and it was while under the control of the Liaison Office that one of the unit's H-5s made history.

It happened on the morning of September 4th, 1950 when two flights of F-80 Shooting Stars of the 35th Fighter-Bomber Squadron swept over the 38th Parallel to attack targets at Hanggandong. During the attack, one of the F-80s was hit by anti-aircraft fire; the pilot, Captain Robert E. Wayne, baled out and landed safely. While two of the F-80s circled the area watchfully, on the lookout for North Korean ground forces, a third climbed and made radio contact with base. Half an hour later, while a flight of F-80s flew combat air patrol overhead to ward off any marauding North Korean fighters, Captain Wayne was on his way out of enemy territory aboard an H-5. It was flown by Lieutenant Paul W. Van Boven, who had just become the first-ever helicopter pilot to lift a shot-down airman to safety from behind enemy lines.

The H-5 unit, now designated Detachment F and Commanded by Captain Oscar N. Tibbetts, moved forward in the wake of the UN forces attacking northward from the Pusan Perimeter towards the end of September. During the first week of October the Detachment arrived at Seoul, and it was from this base that, on October 10th, the longest rescue mission to date was flown when an H-5 piloted by Lieut David

C. McDaniels made a 125 mile flight to Changjon to pick up the wounded pilot of a Sea Fury, shot down during a sortie from HMS *Theseus*. The British pilot was Lieut S. Leonard of 807 Squadron, who crashed while rocketing Communist troops ninety miles behind the lines. The fuselage of his aircraft buckled at the cockpit, trapping him with both legs and one arm broken. His flight, and a relief flight, shot up the enemy troops and prevented them from getting too near the crashed Sea Fury. Leonard came to, fired his revolver—with his broken arm—at the nearest adversaries, then passed out again. After about an hour the H-5 arrived and the pilot and a doctor hacked Leonard free, keeping the enemy at bay with bursts of fire from their automatic weapons. The Fleet Air Arm officer received a blood transfusion in the helicopter on the homeward flight, and subsequently made a full recovery.

Several more long-range rescue flights were made during November 1950 by H-5s operating from advanced bases at Kunu-ri and Sinanju. Then came a new development: the Chinese Communist flooded across the Yalu and before long the United Nations forces were in retreat. This forced Detachment F to withdraw its forward elements to Seoul, and as the Communist push southward continued, Seoul was evacuated in turn and the H-5s took up residence at Airstrip K-37, south of Taegu.

By the end of 1950 the H-5s had transported 618 medical cases, compared with 56 flown out by the L-5s. The Detachment's complement of 11 officers and 56 enlisted men worked miracles to keep the helicopters serviceable in the appalling weather conditions of the Korean winter. The aircrews often took tremendous risks to carry out their mercy missions, and on February 15th, 1951, they were called upon to undertake their most difficult and dangerous mission so far—supplying badly needed medical supplies to elements of the US 2nd Division, surrounded by Communist forces in a pocket at Chipyong-ni, some twenty miles east of Seoul.

The operation was carried out by six H-5s and continued until dark. During the afternoon, each helicopter made three sorties into the pocket; on the homeward run, they brought out a total of 30 wounded soldiers. At first light the following morning the operation got under way again, but with only four helicopters; the other two were unserviceable. As the morning wore on the weather grew steadily worse, with flurries of snow sweeping over the frozen rice-fields. By mid-afternoon the H-5s were battling their way through a blinding snowstorm and wind speeds of up to 40 knots; nevertheless they succeeded in evacuating another 22 casualties before nightfall, bringing the total for the two-day period to 52.

In March 1951, the handful of H-5s rescued six out of seven F-80 pilots of the 35th Fighter Group who were shot down over enemy territory. By this time, the Detachment was badly overworked; as the air war over Korea intensified the H-5s' primary task of rescuing shot-down pilots was becoming more and more demanding, and in addition the helicopter crews were heavily committed to casualty evacuation as well as a number of other sundry duties. Casualty evacuation was the biggest headache, for besides its two-man crew the little H-5 could carry only two passengers, and this often meant several sorties a day into the battle area.

The situation eased a little after March 23rd, when two experimental Sikorsky YH-19 (S-55) helicopters arrived in Korea to be evaluated under combat conditions. They did not have to wait long before going into action; less than 24 hours later they were assisting the H-5s to evacuate injured and wounded American paratroops from the dropping-zone at Munsan-ni, just south of the 38th Parallel, where the 187th Airborne RCT had been dropped in an attempt to surround Chinese forces falling back on Kaesong. The paradrop was part of Operation Ripper, the Allied drive northwards to the Han River, and was the second largest airborne operation of the Korean War, with 80 C-119s and 55 C-46s of the 314th Group and 437th Wing employed. Before the end of the day the C-119s had dropped 2,011 paratroops and 204 tons of supplies, while 1,436 paras and 16 tons of equipment went down from the C-46s.

The helicopters were clattering over the dropping zone just 15 minutes after the first airborne troops had hit the ground. The Chinese were beginning to rally, and before long the helicopters were carrying out their mission under heavy small-arms and mortar fire. Two H-5s were hit during their first sortie into the combat area, but the damage was not too serious and they did not have to be pulled out of the operation. By nightfall on March 25th, after two days of operations in daylight, the H-5s and YH-19s had together made a total of 77 sorties into the Munsan-ni sector and evacuated 148 paratroops, 48 of them jump casualties. Operations continued until the 29th, when the US 3rd Division linked up with the paras. By this time the number of helicopter sorties into the battle area had risen to 147.

In June 1951 the helicopter unit was re-designated Detachment 1, 3rd Air Rescue Squadron, and was split up into four separate flights—one serving the 8055th Mobile Army Surgical Hospital, another attached to the US 25th Division command post near the centre of the UN battleline, a third earmarked for use by the truce negotiators at Munsan-ni and the fourth on permanent alert at Seoul, once again in UN hands and the Detachment's headquarters. Later in the year two H-5s were moved to the islands of Paengyong-do and Cho-do, from where they made a number of highly effective rescues in enemy waters.

As stated previously, the US Marines had quickly followed the Air Force's lead in establishing a helicopter unit in Korea, and in fact it was the Marines who pioneered the use of the helicopter as an assault vehicle. On August 30th, 1951, Marine Helicopter Transport Squadron 161—equipped with 15 HRS-1s, as the S-55 was designated in Marine Corps service—arrived at Pusan. This unit was placed under the command of the 1st Marine Division, fighting in the savage mountain terrain of central Korea, and rapidly demonstrated its ability to carry troops and equipment into inaccessible areas of the battle zone when it airlifted an entire battalion into position on top of a strategically-important ridge. The airlift took place in the course of an exercise known as Windmill One, during which the helicopters made 28 sorties on September 13th into the mountains between Inje and the Punchbowl combat zone. The whole operation lasted 14 hours and was a complete success, the helicopters flying some nine tons of supplies to the Marine units in their positions over 2,000 feet above sea level and bringing out a total of 75 casualties. During a subsequent operation, Windmill Two, ten HRS-1s carried six tons of supplies to the same area.

The activities of the Marines' rotary-wing transport unit had been followed with great interest by General Ridgway, who succeeded MacArthur as the United Nations Commander in Korea in April 1951. He was impressed by the cargo-carrying performance of the HRS-1 under all kinds of conditions, and in November 1951 he asked the Army Department to provide four helicopter transport battalions, each with 28 helicopters. He pointed out that the events of the Korean War so far had proved conclusively that the Army vitally needed helicopters, and recommended that in the future each field army should be equipped with ten transport helicopter battalions. The Army Department agreed in principle to this recommendation, but was only willing to approve the assignment of four helicopter battalions to a field army.

For the first five months of the war there had been no Army helicopters of any kind in Korea. Patrol, observation and rescue was carried out by light aircraft, mostly Piper L-4s and Stinson L-5s. The pilots of these aircraft—many of which had been in service since the Second World War and were rapidly approaching the end of their useful lives—did a magnificent job under incredibly arduous conditions, but their task was hampered by a high unserviceability rate and by the inability of the light aircraft to land where they were most needed. Nevertheless, many Allied pilots had good reason to be grateful to them—including Lieutenant Tracy B. Mathewson of the 8th Fighter-Bomber Squadron, who featured in one of the war's more dramatic escapes on December 11th, 1950.

Mathewson was number two in a flight of four F-80s detailed to attack Pyongyang East. During the run-in to the target, his engine exploded without warning and the Shooting Star disintegrated. Mathewson was thrown clear, and his parachute had just begun to stream when he hit the ground in a rice paddy. Miraculously, apart from a few bruises, he was unhurt. Releasing his paracute, he scrambled to his feet and waved at the other F-80s, circling overhead—then bullets crackled around his ears and he dived for cover in a trench gouged by the remains of his aircraft's engine.

Nursing a flesh wound in his left leg, he dragged out his 0·45 revolver and prepared to shoot it out with the North Korean soldiers. The latter, however—with one eye no doubt on the F-80s circling watchfully overhead—showed no inclination to rush the shot-down pilot and contented themselves with sporadic sniping. When the F-80s flew away, short of fuel, their place was taken immediately by four Mustangs of No 77 Squadron RAAF.

The Australians kept the North Koreans' heads down for two hours. Finally, as it was getting dusk, a little Army L-5 appeared, skimming the rice-fields. Braving the storm of small-arms fire the pilot—Lieut John D. Michaelis—touched down on a relatively dry spot 50 yards from where Mathewson was hiding. Mathewson threw himself into a nearby drainage ditch and crawled through the slime, keeping his head well down, until he judged that he was near the little aircraft. Then he jumped out of the ditch—and charged straight through a bunch of North Korean infantry who had been advancing towards the L-5. Despite his injured leg he broke all records in that final sprint, and a few moments later the L-5 was lurching across the ground with Mathewson still hanging half out of the cockpit. Although riddled with holes the light aircraft got safely clear of enemy territory.

The first Army helicopters did not arrive in Korea until late in December 1950. They were Bell H-13s (Bell 47s), two-seat machines which, although destined for the liaison and artillery-spotting roles, had a limited casevac capability. Four H-13s equipped the 2nd Army Helicopter Detachment at Seoul and began operations in January 1951 under the Command of Captain Albert Seburn. By the end of the month, the Detachment had evacuated more than 500 casualties from the battle area—no mean achievement, since each H-13 could carry only one casualty at a time. In recognition of their work, the four helicopter pilots were each awarded the Distinguished Flying Cross. In February 1951 the H-13s were joined by a small number of two-seat Hiller H-23 Ravens, and in the months that followed both types were used increasingly for combat surveillance. By the end of the year the helicopters had proved their worth so many times that the arrival of the transport helicopters ordered by General Ridgway was awaited with great enthusiasm by the Eighth Army's commanders in the field. They were, however, in for a disappointment; it was to be more than a year before the Army in Korea received the first of the transport helicopters, and in the meantime the whole sphere of helicopter operations became a subject for heated argument between Army and Air Force.

Both sides were anxious to reach an agreement aimed at avoiding duplication of the tasks to be carried out by their respective rotorcraft. Air transport within the combat zone, for example, was the Air Force's province, and a much closer definition of the Army's aims in this respect was needed. In the end, it was agreed that the Army helicopter units would be responsible for transporting Army supplies, equipment and personnel within the combat zone—an area defined as extending 50–100 miles behind the front line—but the Air Force would continue to airlift supplies, equipment and personnel into the combat zone from points outside. In the event, the argument turned out to be mainly academic, because by the time the Army had begun to receive the transport helicopters ordered in 1951 the war was almost over. It was not until March 1953 that the first Army cargo helicopter unit—the 6th Transportation Company, equipped with 12 H-19Cs—arrived in Korea.

In January 1951, the Far East Air Forces' battlefield support organisation in Korea underwent considerable changes following the activation of the 315th Air Division, which assumed operational command or control of all Combat Cargo Command units in the Korean theatre. These were, at that time, the 374th Troop Carrier Wing, with two squadrons of C-54s at Tachikawa and a third—the 21st, with C-47s—at Itazuke; the 61st Troop Carrier Group, with three squadrons of C-54s at Ashiya; the 437th Troop Carrier Wing, with four squadrons of C-46s at Brady Air Base; the 314th Troop Carrier Group, with four squadrons of C-119s at Ashiya; and No 13 Flight, Royal Hellenic Air Force, with C-47s at Itazuke. This was to be joined later in the year by a transport detachment of the Royal Thai Air Force. British Commonwealth air transport units operated independently of USAF control.

The main purpose of the reorganisation was to ensure that the individual types of aircraft serving with the various units were used to their fullest advantage. The 314th Group's C-119s, which were best suited to airborne operations and dropping large loads, were located close to the main depot of the 187th Airborn Regimental Combat Team, while the 374th Wing's C-54s—situated near the Haneda International Airport—were well placed for hauling men and materials over long distances. The C-46s and C-47s—particularly the latter—were suitable for hauling cargo into Korea's smaller airstrips, and flights of the 437th Wing and the 21st Squadron were based on airfields near the main supply depots.

The reorganisation, however, only went a fraction of the way towards solving Combat Cargo Command's problems in the Far East. The diversification of aircraft types in itself gave rise to more than a few headaches, particularly when it came to getting hold of spares; the C-119s suffered most of all in this respect, and unserviceability was high—which meant that although the 314th Wing possessed four squadrons equipped with the C-119, there were never sufficient numbers serviceable at any one time to lift more than 60 per cent of the 187th Airborne Regiment.

What Combat Cargo Command clearly needed was a large, modern transport aircraft with long range and high load capacity—a machine that would do the work of two or three of the Command's older types, resulting in an economy of aircraft and crews and reducing congestion of the badly overcrowded airfields in the Far East. The one aircraft that might meet the requirement was the Douglas C-124A Globemaster II, then undergoing service trials, and at the request of the commander of Combat Cargo—General John P. Henebry—one of the giant machines was sent out to Japan in September 1951. During the weeks that followed it made 13 round trips to Korea, carrying double the maximum load that could be lifted by a C-54. The USAF was sufficiently impressed to authorise the re-equipment of two squadrons of the 374th Wing with C-124s beginning in May 1952, and by the end of July 13 were on the Wing's inventory—six of them used for conversion training and the remainder on a once-daily 'milk run' between Tachikawa and Korea with the 6th Troop Carrier Squadron. An additional 13 C-124s were received during August and September, permitting the rotation of the 61st Group's two squadrons of C-54s back to the United States.

The early operational career of the big Globemaster was attended by its share of problems. Because of the risk of damage to the Fifth Air Force's vital tactical airfields the big transports were authorised to land only at Kimpo, Taegu and Suwon, although a strengthened runway was laid down at Seoul Municipal Airport in October 1952. Even so, the Globemaster's payload had to be restricted to 36,000lb, and the transports could not be utilized enough even to make up for the loss of the C-54s. This meant that excess freight still had to be lifted to Korea by Combat Cargo's C-46s and ailing C-119s, and cargo delivered by the Globemasters to their principal Korean terminals still had to be flown to smaller tactical airstrips by C-46s and C-47s.

There were serious technical snags, too, with the aircraft themselves. In December 1952 several Globemasters developed fuel leaks and the entire fleet was grounded for modifications. Four months of relatively trouble-free operations followed, but in May 1953 two C-124s suffered engine fires in the air. While an investigation was in progress a third C-124 of the 22nd Squadron, taking off from Tachikawa, lost power suddenly in one engine and spun into the ground, killing all 129 passengers and crew. The cause of this—the worst air disaster in history up to that time—was diagnosed as generator failure, and the remaining Globemasters were once again grounded for several weeks pending more modifications. Some of them had still not been certified as airworthy when the war ended.

In terms of equipment, therefore, Combat Cargo Command ended the Korean war almost exactly as it had begun it—with C-47s, C-46s and C-119s carrying the burden of airlift operations. The C-119 continued to be a source of anxiety throughout, despite continual modifications, yet it had to be retained as it was the only aircraft capable of undertaking largescale paradrops and air supply operations. In the autumn of 1951 the C-119 units in Japan underwent some reorganisation with the transfer of the 403rd Troop Carrier Wing to Ashiya, bringing the number of C-119 Squadrons in the Korean theatre to six. One of the 314th Group's four squadrons was returned to the USA, but this was a paper transfer only as its aircraft were shared out among the other units.

In theory, the larger number of C-119s should have been capable of lifting the 187th Airborne in one go, but in practice this never worked out. By the middle of 1952 the serviceability situation was so bad that out of a total of 71 C-119s available on paper, only 28 were serviceable—and of those only about half a dozen were free from defects of some kind. Matters improved a little in July and August, when some of the older C-119s were returned to the USA for refurbishing and were replaced by newer models, but even then the average serviceability of the 403rd Wing in the autumn of 1952 was only about 60 per cent. More than half the Wing's C-119s were still aircraft that had arrived in Japan during 1950, and some of them had little more than scrap value. Following frequent undercarriage failures during 1952, all C-119s in the Far East were prohibited from carrying a payload in excess of six tons, and in March 1953—after a spate of in-flight propeller failures culminating in the loss of a C-119—the transports were forbidden to carry passengers. This state of affairs persisted until May, when the 403rd Wing was relieved by the 483rd Wing, equipped with newer machines.

Early in 1952, it had been decided to re-equip the 437th Wing's four C-46 squadrons with C-119s at the first available opportunity, activating a new transport Wing at the same time. But when the new 315th Wing was activated at Brady Air Base in June 1952, the aircraft handed over to it by the 437th were still C-46s—and the Korean War would be over before the twin-engined machines were finally retired. Time and again, the C-46s proved their ability to do almost anything, from paratroop dropping to casualty evacuation from primitive airstrips, and towards the end of 1952—with both the C-119s and the C-124s providing FEAF with continual headaches—they had been instrumental in sustaining the airlift.

In terms of reliability, the C-46 was unsurpassed by any other type, even the much-loved C-47—and the fact that the proposed re-equipment of the C-46 Wing was constantly postponed, even after the end of hostilities, was the finest tribute that could be paid to an aircraft that had been termed obsolete as much as four years earlier.

CHAPTER ELEVEN

# The New Communist Bid for Air Superiority

In June 1951, with the action in Korea settling down into a war of attrition and the ground being laid for what would turn out to be an apparently endless and fruitless series of Communist-dominated armistice talks, there were clear signs that the Chinese were planning a renewed air offensive against the United Nations. At this time the first-line strength of the Chinese People's Air Force stood at 1,050 combat aircraft, of which 690 were based in Manchuria, and several new airfields suitable for jet fighter operation were being built just across the Yalu in the Antung area.

This airfield complex would shortly house some 300 MiG-15s, controlled by a well-equipped operations centre at Antung. Fighter controllers here were either Chinese or North Korean, but they never made a move without the blessing of the teams of Russian advisers who were always in the background. Russian pilots were also very much in evidence on the combat units, where they usually assumed positions at flight- and squadron-commander level. Later, whole Soviet fighter regiments would be attached to Chinese Communist air divisions for a three-month tour of duty. The identity of the commander of the large Russian Air Force contingent in Manchuria has never been established with certainty, although it is known that the legendary Ivan Kozhedub—Russia's leading World War II ace, with 62 victories—took up a senior command in the Far East about this time following a ground tour at the Zhukovsky Military Academy.

A careful assessment of the CPAF's order of battle, coupled with the knowledge that highly experienced Soviet aircrew were arriving in Manchuria in large numbers, pointed to the possibility that the Reds might be planning a series of surprise attacks on Allied air bases in Korea—and possibly in Japan itself—as a prelude to a new bid for air superiority. On June 10th General Otto P. Weyland assumed command of the Far East Air Forces, and within a matter of hours—realising the potential seriousness of the situation—he sent an urgent request for four jet fighter wings to be sent out to the Far East, one pair to bolster

Japan's air defences and the other two for deployment in Korea. At the time of the request there were only 89 Sabres in the Far East, including 44 in Korea, facing over 400 MiG-15s; Weyland wanted not only more Sabres, but new F-86E models to replace the F-86As with which the 4th Wing was then equipped.

The USAF, however, did not share Weyland's sense of urgency, taking the view that the Communist air build-up was wholly defensive. Moreover, there were fears—fostered mainly by General Ridgway—that substantial United Nations air reinforcements in the Far East would be taken by the Reds as a clear sign that the Allies were about to engage in unrestricted air warfare against China destroying all hopes of early peace talks. Nevertheless, the USAF did authorise the deployment of one F-84 Wing—the 116th—to Japan; the 75 Thunderjets arrived on July 24th and the Wing settled in at Misawa and Chitose Air Bases.

The 116th Fighter-Bomber Wing formed part of the 314th Air Division, which—since May 18th, 1951—had been established as a separate FEAF Command responsible for the air defence of Japan. Also within the Division were the 68th and 339th Fighter-Interceptor Squadrons and the 35th Fighter-Interceptor Wing, which was transferred to Johnson Air Base from Korea on May 25th with the exception of the 39th Squadron. This unit, still flying Mustangs, was attached to the 18th Fighter-Bomber Wing and remained in Korea. The 35th Wing's 40th Squadron eventually went to Misawa for conversion to F-94 Starfire all-weather fighters.

By May 1951 the Fifth Air Force's F-80 and F-51 units in Korea were suffering a high rate of attrition, and before he relinquished command of FEAF General Stratemeyer made a strong plea for the re-equipment of all these units with F-84E Thunderjets at an early date. The USAF, however, could not agree; most of the F-84s rolling off the production line at that time were going to various NATO air forces in a top-priority equipment programme, and there were simply none to spare for the Far East. All the USAF was prepared to do was promise plentiful support to make good the F-51 and F-80 attrition for the duration of Korean hostilities, which it was hoped would end early in 1952.

In fact, the only unit under Fifth Air Force control slated for immediate re-equipment was No 77 Squadron RAAF, which had returned from Korea to Iwakuni at the end of April. Its new aircraft were Gloster Meteor Mk8s, 15 of which—together with two Mk7 trainers—had been shipped out to Japan in February aboard the aircraft carrier HMS *Warrior*. Twenty more Meteor 8s reached Iwakuni during April, accompanied by four RAF pilots with considerable Meteor experience to assist in the task of conversion; they were Flight Lieutenants Max Scannell, Frank Easley, Ian ("Joe") Blyth and Sergeant Lamb. All four volunteered to go to Pusan as soon as they arrived in Japan, rather than hang around at Iwakuni, and saw some operational flying before returning to Japan with the Squadron. By this time most of the Australian pilots had already been checked out on the Meteor, sandwiching the conversion course between operational commitments as the opportunity arose.

The Australians viewed the prospect of going into action in their Meteors with mixed feelings; they had been hoping to get Sabres, and there were some who believed the British fighter to be hopelessly outclassed. Others were reluctant to give up their faithful Mustangs. Also annoying for the Aussies was the big security clampdown to which everyone connected with the Meteor was subjected. The reason was one of diplomacy; at this stage Britain did not want to be associated too closely with the Korean War. Unfortunately, the security net had not closed quickly enough; the news that a British jet fighter was soon to receive its baptism of fire in Korea had already leaked out, causing the British Government some embarrassment.

The conversion went off fairly smoothly, although inevitably there were a number of accidents. The first aircraft casualty occurred on May 7th, when a Meteor 8 flown by Sergeant Bessel ditched in the sea eight miles south of Iwakuni after running out of fuel. The pilot paddled ashore safely and the aircraft was later salvaged. The first total aircraft loss occurred under curious circumstances on June 14th, when Sergeant Stoney—making a normal climb-out from Iwakuni—was suddenly shot through the canopy in his ejection seat. As Stoney descended in his parachute, the Meteor spiralled round him several times, frighteningly close, before crashing into a hillside.

Meanwhile, early in May, the Meteor had been tested in mock combat against a Sabre flown down from Johnson Air Base by Flt Lt Daniels, an RAF pilot attached to the 335th Fighter-Interceptor Squadron. The trials lasted two days and the entire personnel of Iwakuni, Commonwealth and American alike, turned out to watch them. Among the conclusions drawn was that the Sabre outclassed the Meteor in a steep dive or a long straight and level run, but the Meteor was superior in turning, zooming and in a sustained climb. This seemed to indicate that the Meteor would at least be able to hold its own against the MiG under most conditions, and the Australians were now looking forward to taking their jets into action for the first time.

Unfortunately, it was not to prove quite so simple. Acting on American advice, General Robertson, commanding the British Commonwealth forces in Japan, issued orders forbidding the Meteors to go to Korea until radio compasses had been installed in them. The first ARN-6 radio compass components arrived in June and installation work began at once. During this frustrating period of delay the Squadron's two Meteor 7s made frequent hops to Kimpo, their second seats usually occupied by signals officers whose task it was to work out joint communications procedures with their American counterparts.

Some of the Squadron's Meteors had still not been fitted with radio compasses when, towards the end of June, authority was finally given for the move to Kimpo to begin—on the understanding that the aircraft without radio compasses could only fly with a limited cloud base minimum of 1,000–1,500 feet. When the Squadron did move to Kimpo, it was as an interceptor unit; there had previously been a lot of uncertainty about how best to employ the Meteors, since they were inferior to the MiG-15 on most counts and were not approved for ground attack work, but No 77's CO—Squadron Leader Richard Cresswell—had managed to convince senior officers of both the RAAF and the Fifth Air Force that the Meteor could perform favourably as an interceptor if tactics were evolved enabling it to operate in conjunction with Sabres.

On June 30th the Squadron's supporting equipment was flown to Kimpo in 17 C-119s and seven C-54s, the personnel following in Dakotas of No 86 (Transport) Squadron, RAAF. After Iwakuni, Kimpo was a depressing sight; the summer rains and the continual comings and goings of heavy transport had churned most of the airfield into a foot-deep sea of mud.

During most of July No 77 was engaged in training and familiarisation flights, and it was not until the 30th of the month that the Squadron flew its first operational mission: a sweep by 16 Meteors south of the Yalu. The Meteors flew in finger fours between 30,000 and 35,000 feet, with 16 Sabres of the 4th Wing ten thousand feet lower down, but no contact was made with the enemy. Several more sweeps were flown during the first two weeks of August, with the same negative result. During one of them, on August 20th, two Meteors collided during a formation change and crashed north of the Han River. Both pilots—Sergeants Mitchell and Lamb, the latter one of the RAF instructors—were killed.

On four or five occasions during August the Meteors were detailed to escort B-29s and RF-80s to Sinanju, and it was while escorting a flight of Shooting Stars with two sections of four Meteors on the 25th that MiGs were sighted for the first time. Two enemy jets were spotted south of Sinanju and one of the Meteor flights gave chase; the leader, Flight Lieutenant Scannell, opened fire at extreme range but no hits were claimed.

The first real test came four days later, on the 29th, when eight Meteors were detailed to escort B-29s and another eight to carry out a diversionary sweep north of Sinanju. At 11.20hrs the latter flight, led by Squadron Leader Wilson, spotted six MiGs at 40,000 feet over

Chongju, 5,000 feet higher than themselves. Keeping the enemy in sight Wilson manoeuvred his formation up-sun, but as he did so two more MiGs suddenly appeared a few thousand feet below. Wilson decided to attack and went into a dive followed by his No 2, Flying Officer Woodroffe. As the two Meteors levelled out, however, Woodroffe's aircraft suddenly flicked into a spin and dropped away; the pilot managed to recover several thousand feet lower down, but now Wilson had no-one to cover his tail. As he went in to the attack, a MiG jumped him out of the sun, unnoticed in the 30-degree blind spot caused by the dural structure at the rear of the Meteor's cockpit. The first warning Wilson had of the danger was when cannon shells flickered over his wing; he immediately flung his aircraft into a maximum-rate turn in a bid to shake off his pursuer. He was rescued by Flight Lieutenant Cedric Wilson and Flying Officer Ken Blight, who spotted his predicament and drove the MiG away—but not before cannon shells had shot away Sqn Ldr Wilson's port aileron and blasted a three-foot hole in his wing, as well as puncturing his main fuel tank. Wilson nevertheless managed to reach base safely, touching down at 30 knots above normal landing speed.

Meanwhile, a fierce air battle had developed over Chongju. Thirty MiGs appeared from nowhere and the Meteor pilots were soon fighting for their lives. The weight of the attack fell on 'Dog' section, led by Flight Lieutenant Geoff Thornton; there was a short flurry of cannon fire and a Meteor went spinning down out of control. The pilot, Warrant Officer Don Guthrie, baled out safely and spent the rest of the war in a prison camp. It had not been an encouraging start to the Meteor's combat career.

By September 1st, 1951, the Communist Air Forces' order of battle included 525 MiG-15s, and the Reds judged that the time was ripe to launch their new air offensive. The MiGs began to appear in greater numbers than ever before, as many as 90 crossing the Yalu at one time. They were also better led, better organised and displayed superior tactics—clear evidence that the 'honchos', as the Soviet and Soviet-satellite pilots were nicknamed, were in full control.

Nevertheless, the MiGs got a severe mauling on September 2nd, when 40 of them crossed the river and tangled with 22 Sabres in a furious 30-minute air battle that spread over the sky from Sinuiju to Pyongyang; it ended with the destruction of four enemy fighters. Three days later, on the 5th, No 77 Squadron was once again on the receiving end when six Meteors—escorting RF-80s at 20,000 feet in the Antung area—were bounced by a dozen MiGs, attacking in pairs from astern. During the five-minute dog-fight that followed Warrant Officer W. Michelson was attacked by three MiGs which severely damaged his tail before he succeeded in shaking them off. All the Meteors returned safely to base;

three Meteor pilots—Blyth, Cannon and Dawson—had managed to get in the occasional burst at a MiG, but no hits were claimed.

There was another skirmish on the 26th, when 12 Meteors—once again escorting RF-80s—were attacked by more than 30 MiGs. One of the enemy fighters was headed off by Flt Lt Thomas, who chased it well south of Pyongyang before its superior speed enabled it to escape; Flt Lt Dawson managed to get in several good bursts at another MiG and pieces were seen to fly off it, but the cine film of the action was unfortunately over-exposed and this could not be confirmed.

In all, 14 MiGs were destroyed by the 4th Wing's Sabres during the air battles of September. In the course of one engagement, when 28 Sabres fought 70 MiGs on September 9th, two Sabre pilots—Captains Richard S. Becker and Ralph D. Gibson—each destroyed his fifth MiG to claim second and third places on the list of Korean aces after James Jabara.

The monopoly on knocking down MiGs, however, did not belong entirely to the Sabres. On September 19th, Captain Kenneth L. Skeen—a Thunderjet pilot with the 49th Group—neatly turned the tables on a MiG that tried to intercept him while he was attacking a ground target and shot it down in flames, while several more enemy fighters were claimed by B-29 gunners. Allied air losses for the month were three Sabres, a Shooting Star, a Mustang and a Thunderjet.

By the end of September the Communist Air Forces were seriously interfering with the activities of Allied fighter-bombers striking at targets in north-western Korea, and General Weyland once again stressed the urgent need to provide an additional Sabre wing—or, failing this, convert one of the existing F-80 wings to F-86s. The USAF's reply was blunt and to the point; supporting the existing Sabre wing in the Far East was difficult enough—supporting a second was out of the question. As soon as he received this news, General Frank F. Everest—commanding the Fifth Air Force since June 1st, 1951—immediately ordered a halt to all fighter-bomber attacks on targets in MiG Alley. Instead, the fighter-bombers were to concentrate on a zone between Pyongyang and the Chongchon River.

Necessary though this move was in the light of the growing Communist challenge to Allied air superiority, it had dangerous implications. It meant that the enemy's airfield construction and re-habilitation programme in North Korea—brought to a standstill by comprehensive interdiction attacks during the spring and early summer—could now get under way again, and it soon became apparent that the Reds were taking full advantage of the lull in Allied fighter-bomber activity. During late September and early October reconnaissance aircraft located three major enemy airfields under construction inside a 20-mile radius north of the Chongchon; each of these fields could be defended

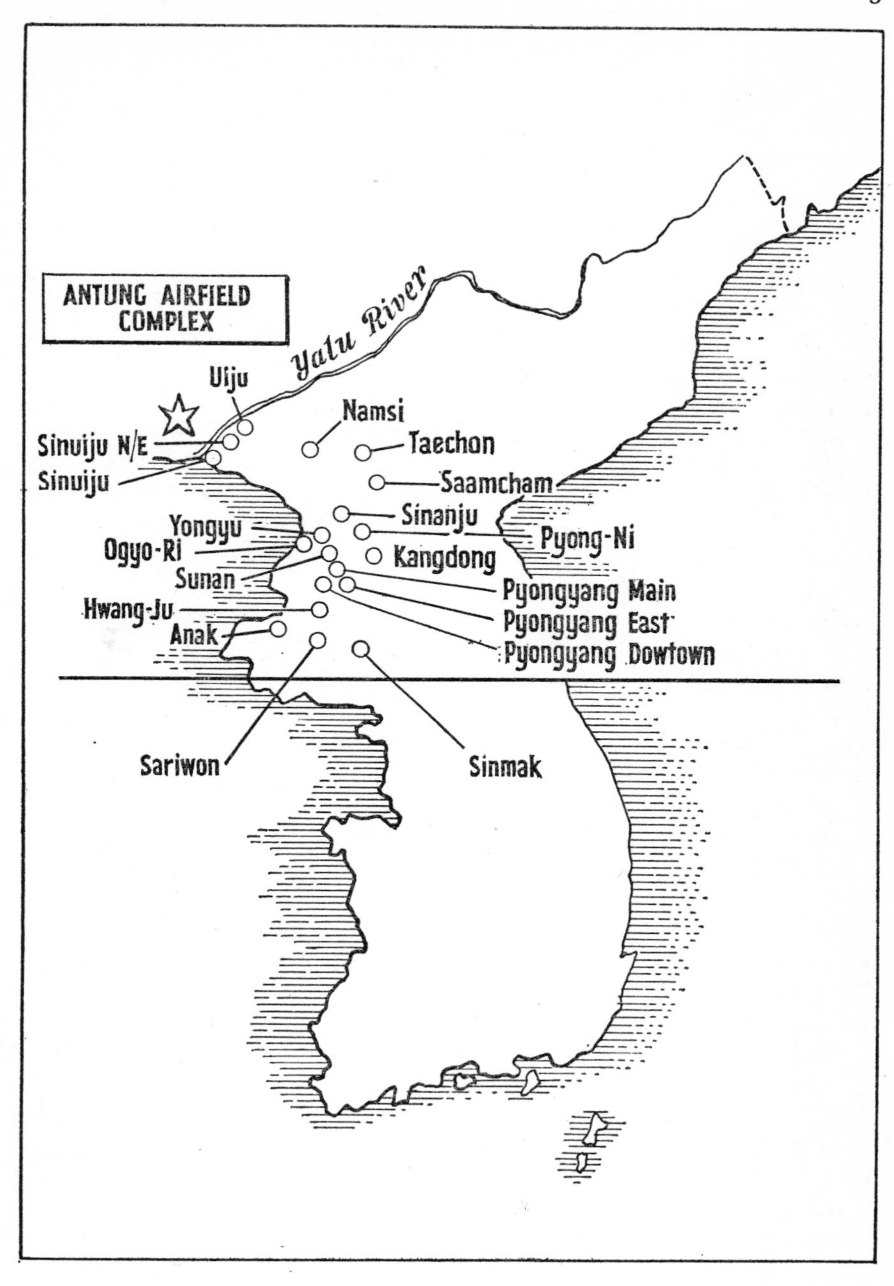


Principal Communist airfields.

by a fighter umbrella from one of the others, and it was clear that the Communists planned to use them as a base in an attempt to establish air superiority as far south as Pyongyang.

The airfield complex was immediately targeted for a B-29 strike, but before this could take place it was essential that the Allies established a firm—if only temporary—measure of control of the sky over north-west Korea to prevent interference with the bombers. Beginning on October 1st, the 4th Fighter-Interceptor Wing accordingly stepped up its counterair operations with the object of bringing in the MiGs to battle and inflicting a severe defeat on them. The result was some of the bitterest fighting in the history of air warfare. During the first two weeks of the month the 4th Wing claimed the destruction of 19 MiGs, nine of them on the 16th alone, while F-80 pilots of the 8th Fighter-Bomber Wing claimed two more probably destroyed.

Meanwhile, plans for the B-29 attack on the three new enemy airfields at Saamcham, Namsi and Taechon were running into difficulties. For safety's sake it had been envisaged that small numbers of bombers would attack the targets by radar under cover of darkness and the B-29s had been specially equipped with Shoran transceivers to do the job, but the first two Shoran raids—in which 307th Wing B-29s bombed the airfield at Saamcham on the nights of October 13th and 14th—produced disappointing results. Since the rapid destruction of the enemy airfields was a matter of supreme importance there was no alternative but to carry out large-scale daylight attacks, banking on a strong fighter escort to keep the MiGs at bay.

The first such daylight attacks, carried out on October 18th by B-29s of the 19th Group and 98th Wing, met with only limited success; the 98th Wing aircraft, scheduled to hit Taechon, missed their escorts and had to divert to secondary targets, and only the 19th Group's bombers were able to attack Saamcham as planned. The 98th Wing once again failed to rendezvous with its fighter escort in another attempt to raid Taechon on the 21st and it was left to the 19th Group to carry out this mission the following day. Shortly after the Group's nine Superfortresses had bombed the target their escort of 24 Thunderjets was scattered by a strong formation of MiGs, and under cover of the diversion three more MiGs dropped down out of the overcast to attack the bombers. The fighters finished off one bomber, already badly hit by flak, although its crew were rescued when they baled out over the coast.

There was evidence that on this occasion the MiGs had come upon the bombers purely by chance, but it was a different story on October 23rd. This time the Communists knew the bombers were coming, and they were waiting for them.

At 09.00hrs, eight B-29s of the 307th Bombardment Wing rendezvoused with 55 Thunderjets of the 49th and 136th Wings and set course for the airfield at Namsi. Ahead and far above, 34 Sabres of the 4th Wing provided a fighter screen, quartering the sky south of the Yalu.

Suddenly, at 09.15hrs, over a hundred MiGs swept across the river. Within minutes the Sabres, effectively boxed in, were fighting for their lives. While this dogfight—during which two MiGs were shot down—was in progress, 50 more MiGs approached the B-29 and Thunderjet formation and circled it at some distance, apparently intent on drawing off the Thunderjets. The latter, however, refused to rise to the bait, and a few moments later the MiGs came hurtling in to the attack from all directions. For the bomber crews, the next 20 minutes was a nightmare as the speedy MiGs ripped through the helpless F-84 escort again and again to rake the B-29s with cannon fire as the bombers grimly made their run-in to the target. Two B-29s went down a matter of seconds after they had released their bombs; a third, burning like a torch, staggered towards the coast where its crew baled out—all except the pilot, Captain Thomas L. Shields, who had sacrificed his own life in keeping the crippled bomber flying until the other crew members were clear.

One Thunderjet also failed to return from this mission. Four MiGs were claimed as destroyed, three by B-29 gunners and one by an F-84 pilot. The surviving bombers, all with severe battle damage, staggered back to emergency landings in Korea and Japan, bearing their pitiful cargoes of dead and wounded. It was Bomber Command's blackest day since the war began.

The next morning, eight B-29s of the 98th Wing set off to attack a rail bridge at Sunchon, escorted by ten F-84s and by 16 Meteors of No 77 Squadron. The formation ran slap into a whirling dogfight between Sabres and about 60 MiGs, some of which turned to attack the bombers, and a running fight developed. One Meteor, flown by Flying Officer Hamilton-Foster, was badly hit almost immediately and went into a spiral dive as its starboard engine flamed out. He managed to recover and made a safe landing at Kimpo with both engines dead. Behind him, the fight still raged as the MiGs chased the B-29s almost as far as Wonsan. The Meteors and Thunderjets fought hard, but they could not prevent the MiGs from breaking through to inflict severe damage on one of the bombers. It ditched in Wonsan harbour and all the crew were picked up. The B-29 gunners claimed one MiG destroyed.

On the morning of Saturday, October 27th, 16 Meteors of No 77 Squadron and 32 Thunderjets of the 49th and 136th Wings were detailed to escort eight 19th Group B-29s in an attack on a rail bridge near Sinanju. Because of reports that MiG pilots were reluctant to fight over water, the bombers were routed to the target in such a way that they stayed over the Yellow Sea as long as possible. The trouble started when the formation turned inland towards Sinanju; 95 MiGs came tumbling down like an avalanche and the fighter escort was quickly overwhelmed. Fortunately, the MiG pilots seemed disinclined to press home their attacks, and in a fight lasting ten minutes three kills were claimed by the B-29 gunners. Flying Officer Reading of 77 Squadron severely damaged a MiG, and other hits were claimed by Meteor and Thunderjet pilots. Four B-29s were damaged, one of them seriously.

October 1951 drew to a close with the destruction, during the month, of 32 MiGs—24 claimed by Sabres, seven by B-29 gunners and one by a Thunderjet. It was the highest jet fighter loss suffered by the enemy so far—but there was no escaping the fact that the Allies had suffered too, having lost seven Sabres, five B-29s, two F-84s and an F-80 in air combat. In comparison with what they had achieved during the preceding months, October's operations had been a success for the Communists—so much so that they were encouraged, towards the end of the month, to take the bold step of dispersing combat aircraft south of the Yalu; Allied reconnaissance revealed 26 MiGs in revetments at Uiju and about 60 piston-engined aircraft—mostly La-9s, Il-10s and Tupolev Tu-2 twin-engined bombers—at Sinuiju.

This was the gloomy picture that faced the Air Force Chief of Staff, General Vandenberg, when he flew to the Far East late in October to make a brief on-the-spot survey of the situation. After reviewing all available intelligence and talking with FEAF commanders, he came away convinced that General Weyland was right; the Communist air threat was more serious than ever before. "Almost overnight," he commented in a press statement later, "Communist China has become one of the major air powers of the world."

Immediately on his return to the USA, General Vandenberg ordered the despatch of 75 F-86s, with air and ground crews and full supporting equipment, from Air Defence Command to the Korean theatre. General Weyland planned to use these aircraft to equip the 51st Fighter-Interceptor Wing, returning an equal number of F-80 crews to the USA in exchange. Transfer of the new batch of Sabres was carried out by sea between November 1st and 9th. Meanwhile, the whole of the 4th Fighter-Interceptor Wing—including the 335th Squadron from Japan—was moved to Kimpo, which it shared with No 77 Squadron RAAF and the 67th Tactical Reconnaissance Wing, newly transferred from Taegu.

The arrival of the Sabre reinforcements was eagerly awaited, for in addition to their overwhelming numerical superiority the Communist jet fighter squadrons now had another advantage. Allied pilots reported encounters with what appeared to be a vastly improved model of the MiG-15 with a far better all-round performance. The machine was in fact the MiG-15Bis with an uprated VK-1 turbojet, the latest type to equip Soviet fighter squadrons, and in the hands of a capable pilot it was more than a match for the F-86A.

The Communists had also, by this time, developed a whole new range of air fighting tactics that presented the hard-pressed United Nations pilots with severe headaches. Up to 80 MiGs would cross the Yalu in two separate 'trains' and head southwards at over 35,000 feet to rendezvous over Pyongyang before returning towards Manchuria, detaching flights to attack Allied aircraft as the opportunity arose—the favourite targets being Sabres or fighter-bombers on their way home, short of fuel. As the 'MiG train' approached the Yalu once more, the Red aircraft now themselves low on fuel, more MiGs would cross the river to cover their withdrawal.

These tactics meant that no United Nations fighter-bombers or reconnaissance aircraft could operate in the zone between Pyongyang and the border without risk of interference from the enemy jets, and all reconnaissance flights into the area had to be escorted by Sabres, F-80s, F-84s or Meteors. On October 1st RB-29 operations over north-western Korea were suspended, the majority of photo-recce missions from that date being carried out by FR-80s of the 15th Tactical Reconnaissance Squadron, escorted by formations of eight or 16 fighters. The RF-80s were bounced by MiGs 18 times during October and November, and although only one photojet was lost several sorties often had to be made before a target was photographed. Additional fast photo-coverage of targets in the north-west during this difficult period was provided by two North American RB-45s of Reconnaissance Detachment A, 84th Bombardment Squadron, which had been attached to the 91st Strategic Reconnaissance Squadron for trials since January 1951. These aircraft successfully ran the gauntlet of Communist interceptors for several months, but following a series of narrow escapes in November FEAF restricted them to night operations over north-western Korea.

On November 6th the Reds used their Tu-2 light bombers for the first time—in an attack on the island of Taehwa-do in the Yellow Sea, where ROK forces were fighting North Korean marines. Three days later there was a fierce air battle between eight F-80s of the 80th Fighter-Bomber Squadron and more than 20 MiGs near Kunu-ri; the Shooting Stars came out on top, shooting down two MiGs for no loss to themselves. On the 18th, a flight of 4th Wing Sabres strafed 12 MiGs which were dispersed on Uiju airfield, destroying four of them, and on the 27th four more Communist jets were shot down in an air battle over the Yalu. One of them was destroyed by Major Richard D. Creighton, making him the fourth jet ace of the Korean War.

Then came November 30th—and the biggest air combat success so far for the United Nations. That afternoon, 31 Sabres of the 4th Fighter-Interceptor Group. led by Colonel Benjamin S. Preston, sighted a formation of 12 Tu-2s escorted by 16 piston-engined La-9s and 16 MiG-15s heading for Taehwa-do. Two of the 4th Group's pilots, Major George A. Davis and Major Winton W. ('Bones') Marshall, became aces that day. Marshall later described the action:

"We entered the area right on schedule and sighted two large formations of MiG-15 jets coming across the Yalu River high above us. They were apparently out on their own fighter sweep, but they didn't come down on us. We held our formation and turned south in hopes of cutting into them.

"Just then, Colonel Thyng called out bogies coming across the river dead ahead of us and about 10,000 feet below. He said he was going down to look and instructed me to cover them as the air above was filled with MiGs and there were more coming every minute.

"The bogies turned out to be a large formation of Tu-2 bombers and their fighter escort. There were several boxes of bombers in groups of three. They were surrounded by an escort of propeller-drive La-9 fighters. Another formation of MiGs was flying top cover. The Colonel called for a head-on pass by two squadrons of the Sabres. I came over the bombers just as the Sabres struck. It was better than a seat on the 50-yard line in a football game. As our fighters poured it on, the whole sky became alive with smoke and flame. It was really a sight—our boys scoring hits all over the bombers, and their fighters could do nothing because of the Sabres' superior speed.

"Right after the Sabres made their first pass on the bombers Colonel Preston called me and said 'Bones, come on down and get 'em.' We were in a perfect spot for an overhead pass. The entire squadron went over on its back and came in on the bombers from six o'clock high, right on the Mach. As we dived, the remaining bombers turned their guns on us and their fighters nosed toward us in an attempt to turn us from the battle. The whole area was alive with bullets. The bombers that hadn't been hit still held a tight formation and straight course. They were like sitting ducks.

"I lined up the bomber on the right side of the last box. My first burst set him afire. As I continued to fire, he fell out of formation and the crew began baling out. Then two La-9s came into my sights and I gave the leader a short burst from my 0·50-calibres. He seemed to come apart at the seams and dropped like a stone to the ocean.

"Our first pass on the Tu-2s was over in a matter of seconds. I glanced to see if my squadron was still with me and then turned into them again for another pass. It gave me a thrill, for this was the first bomber formation I'd ever tangled with. By this time the area was so crowded with fighters I had to weave in and out between them to get in position for another pass. Finally, I squared away on the lead box of bombers and fired my remaining ammunition into one of them. He started smoking as my bursts cut into his wings and fuselage . . . I pulled away."

When the battle ended, the Sabres had destroyed eight Tu-2s, three La-9s and a MiG-15. Three of the bombers and the MiG had been shot down by Major George Davis. There was quite a party in the mess at Kimpo that night.

The Reds, however, seemed determined to avenge the mauling they had received, attacking United Nations aircraft with unparalleled ferocity during the early days of December. On the first of the month 12 Meteors of No 77 Squadron, led by Flt Lt Geoff Thornton, were carrying out a sweep at 19,000 feet when about 50 MiGs were spotted high above them. At that height the Meteor pilots knew that they had no hope of turning with the enemy fighters; the odds would be better if they could draw the MiGs down to their own level, although the Australians were at a great tactical disadvantage.

The MiGs saw them and broke off in pairs, making a fast diving attack on 'Charlie' Flight. The Flight broke on Thornton's command, but one pilot—Flying Officer Drummond—left it a little late and was hit in the fuel tanks. His Meteor went into a tight turn, streaming fuel, and Drummond yelled for help over the R/T. The frantic call was answered by Flying Officer Bruce Gogerly, of 'Able' Flight, who fastened himself on the tail of an MiG. The enemy fighter crept into Gogerly's sights as the Meteor turned inside it and the Australian got in a solid five-second burst with his 20mm cannon, seeing the shells bursting on the MiG's fuselage and wing root. The MiG suddenly pulled up in a steep climbing turn to the left, then went down with smoke and flames streaming from it.

There was no time for Gogerly to congratulate himself. The next instant, he was subjected to a series of head-on attacks by a pair of MiGs. Other Meteor pilots found themselves trapped in the same way. A MiG went down vertically, blazing fiercely; three or four Australian pilots claimed to have hit it and it was later credited to the whole squadron. Suddenly, the MiGs broke off the action, leaving the Meteors free to straggle back to Kimpo in twos and threes. Thornton called a radio check and all the pilots answered, but on arrival at base three aircraft—Charlie 3 and 4 and Baker 2—were found to be missing. A few minutes later Baker 2, flown by Sergeant Thomson, was heard calling for a QDM, but the aircraft never reached Kimpo. Flying Officer Drummond, who had been hit early in the engagement, was one of the two other missing pilots.

December 1st, 1951, also saw the first operation by the Sabres of the 51st Fighter-Interceptor Wing, which had formed at Suwon on November 6th under the command of Colonel Francis S. Gabreski, who had destroyed 28 German aircraft while flying Thunderbolts with the

Eighth Air Force during the Second World War and who already had two MiGs to his credit in Korea. Gabreski was to down another $4\frac{1}{2}$ MiGs while commanding the 51st—the half MiG shared with another WW2 ace, Major Bill Whisner.

With the long-awaited conversion of the 51st Wing the United Nations now had 127 Sabres in Korea, with a further 40 in reserve in Japan. The reinforcements came only just in time, for as December wore on the pace of the Red air offensive showed no sign of slackening. During the first week of the month the MiGs—coming down to lower levels to attack Allied fighter-bombers—destroyed two F-80s and an F-84, but ten enemy jets were shot down by the Sabres of the 4th and 51st Wings on the 2nd and 4th. The next day two more MiGs fell to the guns of Major George Davis of the 334th Squadron, who had wrought such havoc on the Tu-2 formation at the end of November, and on December 13th Davis claimed another four MiGs in the course of a series of air battles that flared up along the Yalu. The 4th Wing's Sabres met 145 MiG-15s in combat on that day and destroyed 13 of them. After that, serious encounters became more sporadic; only three more MiGs were destroyed before the end of December, one by the 4th Wing on the 14th and the others by the 51st Wing on the 15th and 28th.

Meanwhile, Bomber Command's B-29s were continuing to hit the enemy airfields in North Korea—but at night, when they were safe from the roving MiGs. By the end of November most of the Superfortresses had been fitted with Shoran radar bombing equipment, and although early Shoran raids met with only limited success the B-29 crews soon began to inflict heavy damage on the enemy fields as their experience accumulated. The Communists quickly set up heavy flak batteries along the arcs followed by the bombers on their radar bombing runs, but although several B-29s sustained damage none was lost. It might have been a different story if the Reds had possessed an efficient night-fighter force; as it was, the few night interceptions reported by the B-29 crews were carried out on a hit-or-miss basis by MiG-15s, relying on searchlights to illuminate their targets.

Although they had failed to wrest air superiority from the United Nations during November and December 1951, the Communists continued to send growing numbers of MiGs across the Yalu in the New Year. On some days in January 1952, up to 200 enemy fighters crossed the river at the same time at just under the speed of sound, their formations stepped up between 30,000 and 50,000 feet. The MiGs, however, persistently refused to come down and fight, and FEAF Intelligence formed the opinion that some of the enemy formations—especially those assigned to the higher patrol levels—were composed of 'green' trainee pilots. For the Sabre pilots—and particularly those of the 4th

Wing, whose F-86As simply could not get to grips with the high-flying MiGs—January 1952 was a frustrating month, with a series of mostly inconclusive combats that resulted in the destruction of only five enemy fighters. The 51st Wing, with their higher-performance F-86Es, fared a good deal better; entering the combat area at 45,000 feet, they shot down 25 MiGs during the month. Air combats during February accounted for a further 17 MiGs, 11 of them credited to the 51st Wing; the score would undoubtedly have been higher had not both Sabre Wings been plagued by a high unserviceability rate and an acute spares shortage during this period.

February 1952 was also a month of sadness for the 4th Wing, for it saw the loss of Major George Davis. On the 10th, Davis was leading 18 Sabres on an escort mission to Kunu-ri when he spotted a large number of contrails north-west of the Yalu, heading in his direction. Leaving the main body of the Sabres to defend the fighter-bombers he immediately sped towards the bogies, accompanied by his wingman, with the intention of breaking up the threat before it developed. The two Sabres encountered 12 MiGs and apparently took them completely by surprise; Davis shot down two of them and was pressing home an attack on a third when his aircraft was hit and crashed into a mountain-side. Davis was subsequently awarded a posthumous Congressional Medal of Honor. His score at the time of his death stood at 14 enemy aircraft destroyed, a record that was not bettered until the next year.

In March, the Red pilots suddenly turned aggressive again, with formations appearing below contrail level and dividing down to attack United Nations fighter-bombers. The new tactics were to cost them dearly: in the eight weeks up to the end of April they lost 83 MiGs and claimed only six Sabres, two Thunderjets and a Shooting Star. It was hardly surprising that several 4th and 51st Wing Sabre pilots suddenly found themselves in the 'ace' category during these two months, with five or more enemy aircraft to their credit. They included Captain Iven C. Kincheloe, who also destroyed four Yak-9s on the ground in two separate strafing attacks on Sinuiju airfield on April 22nd and May 4th, Captains Robert H. Moore and Robert J. Love, and Major Bill Wescott. They were joined in May by Captain Robert T. Latshaw, Major Donald E. Adams, Lieutenant James H. Kasler and Colonel Harrison R. Thyng, the 4th Wing's commander. James Kasler later increased his score to six; Colonel Harry Thyng, who—among other types—flew Spitfires with the 31st Fighter Group in North Africa, already had 11 enemy aircraft to his credit in World War II. He was perhaps the most diversified of all American aces, his victories including German, Italian, Japanese, French (a Dewoitine 520 of the Vichy Air Force) and Russian aircraft. He eventually retired from the USAF with the rank of Brigadier-General.

The Sabres' score for May was 27 MiGs and five Yak-9s destroyed for the loss of five of their own number. The Reds also shot down three F-84s and a Mustang, two of the Thunderjets in the course of one engagement between 12 MiGs and 24 F-84s of the 49th Wing over Sonchon on May 17th.

During these latter weeks it was clear that the Communists were making extensive use of radar in carrying out their interceptions. On several occasions, Allied fighter-bombers were 'bounced' by MiGs which dropped down through a cloud layer, obviously being vectored to their targets by radar controllers. The Reds were also developing radar countermeasures against the B-29 night strikes; these mainly took the form of radar-directed searchlights and anti-aircraft batteries, although by the end of May at least one specialist Red night-fighter squadron was operational, using MiG-15s equipped with airborne interception radar. These aircraft usually assumed the role of 'master night fighters'; having located the bomber stream they would fly immediately above it and guide other fighters to the scene. The B-29s would then be constantly tracked by searchlight batteries, with the aid of which the fighters would launch their attack. These tactics produced results: on June 10th, 1952, four B-29s of the 19th Bombardment Group were suddenly lit up by 24 searchlights after being shadowed for several minutes by an unidentified aircraft. A few moments later they were savagely attacked by a dozen MiG-15s, which shot down two of them and damaged a third so badly that it crashed on landing at Kimpo. The B-29s' protective veil of darkness had been stripped aside for good.

In the spring of 1952—with plans for the deployment of most of the Fifth Air Force to Korea well advanced—the threat of Communist air attack on airfields and other Allied installations in South Korea was very real. Air defence—and particularly airfield defence—suddenly became of paramount importance, and the organisation of a tightly-knit defensive system was one of the priority tasks set by Lieutenant-General Frank Everest, the Fifth Air Force's commander since June 1951. By the end of 1951 a fairly efficient warning network had been up, and the overall efficiency was increased still further when, in February 1952, a warning radar station was installed on Cho-do island off north-western Korea; this enabled Allied air defence operators to keep the enemy fighter complex at Antung under round-the-clock surveillance.

From the beginning of 1952, the Fifth Air Force kept between 30 and 40 fighters on dawn and dusk alert as a matter of routine. These included the Meteors of No 77 Squadron, which—following the disastrous combat of December 1st, which had left it with only 14 serviceable aircraft—had been detailed to carry out area and airfield defence. The Meteor, which had a better rate of climb at low altitude than the

Sabre, was considered to be particularly suited to this role. For the Australian pilots, it was a period of stagnation and frustration; they sat there day after day, waiting for an attack that never came. Finally, the Squadron's new CO—Wing Commander Ron Susans—managed to convince the authorities that the Meteors would be far better employed in the ground-attack role. The necessary approval was obtained and, on January 8th, 1952, Susans led a flight of four Metors in a cannon attack on a water-tower at Chongdan. From then on the Squadron was back in business, and ground attack was to be its main occupation for the duration of the war.

As it turned out, General Everest's fears of a massive Red air assault on his Korean bases was unfounded. Nevertheless, there remained one persistent thorn in the Fifth Air Force's side; the little Po-2 'Bed Check Charlies'. While these raiders continued their nuisance activities, the Allied night defences had to be kept on constant alert—but it was not often that they managed to score. In an effort to cope with the slow-flying biplanes, four T-6 Texans—specially fitted with machine-guns—were kept on readiness at Kimpo during the hours of darkness, but they never had any luck. Neither did the Fifth Air Force's latest acquisition—the F-94 Starfire all-weather fighter, which replaced the 68th Fighter-Interceptor Squadron's old F-82 Twin Mustangs in December 1951. One F-94 did manage to shoot down a Po-2 by throttling right back and lowering gear and flaps to reduce its speed, but the fighter stalled immediately afterwards and spun in, killing its crew. Another F-94 was lost when it collided with a Po-2.

Later in the war, the Po-2s were joined by other Red trainers, notably Yak-18s. Their heckling missions reached a climax on the night of June 16th/17th, 1953, when they destroyed five million gallons of fuel in a dump at Inchon. A few weeks later, Lieutenant Guy P. Bordelon—flying an F4U-5N Corsair from the USS *Princeton*—destroyed four Yak-18s and one Yak-11 in the Seoul area. His exploit was notable for two reasons: it was the greatest success achieved by any one pilot against the Red raiders, and it made Bordelon the Navy's only ace of the Korean War.

CHAPTER TWELVE

# The Railway Battle, September 1951—July 1952

On August 25th, 1951, 35 B-29s of the 19th, 98th and 307th Bombardment Wings, led by Colonel Harris E. Rogner—deputy commander of FEAF Bomber Command—droned high over north-eastern Korea. Near Songjin the bombers made rendezvous with 23 F9F Panthers and F2H-2 Banshees, launched from the USS *Essex* in the Sea of Japan. The carrier had joined Task Force 77 two days earlier, and this was the second combat mission flown by the Banshees of Squadron VF-172.

The B-29s' target on this brilliant August morning was Rashin, the vital port and communications complex close to the Siberian border. For a year, because of its proximity to Soviet territory, Rashin had been excluded from FEAF's target lists, but on August 1st General Ridgway had sought and obtained the approval of the Joint Chiefs and President Truman to attack the port in view of the importance of the extensive marshalling yards there. Approval had only been given on condition that the raid was carried out under visual bombing conditions—and that it was to be given none of the publicity that usually accompanied Bomber Command attacks on other North Korean targets.

As the bombers approached Rashin the Navy fighter pilots kept a watchful eye on the dangerous sky over the Russian frontier, but no hostile aircraft appeared and the run-in was made without incident. Two hundred and ninety-one tons of bombs obliterated Rashin's marshalling yards, only light flak was encountered and none of the B-29s or escorting fighters was hit.

The Rashin attack marked the beginning of a sustained air offensive against the enemy's rail communications; it was to last ten months. In August 1951, it became apparent to FEAF planners that Operation Strangle—the offensive designed to paralyse enemy movements by road—had achieved only a fraction of its objectives, and that the Reds were making extensive use of the North Korean railway network to move supplies up to the MLR. Apart from all other considerations, rail transport—which was kept moving with supplies of coal mined in North Korea itself—was costing the enemy far less than road transport, which depended on stocks of fuel shipped over the border from Manchuria or Russia.

From the Fifth Air Force's point of view, the prospect of attacking railways was an attractive one. Several experimental railway attacks had already been made during July by the 8th and 49th Fighter-Bomber Groups, using a variety of methods, and the results had been encouraging; not only were stretches of railway track easier to hit than roads, but it took the Reds far longer to repair them. Also, in setting up strong anti-aircraft defences on key roads, the Communists had neglected to defend their railways, and the fighter-bomber pilots had experienced only light opposition during their attacks.

On August 18th, 1951, therefore, the scope of Operation Strangle was extended to include the enemy's railway system. It was to be a collaborative effort, with Task Force 77 called in to interdict the main east coast and lateral railroads and Bomber Command to attack five important rail bridges at Pyongyang, Sonchon, Sunchon, Sinanju and Huichon. In the event Bomber Command declined to operate against the latter target, as it lay in an area where there was a strong risk of interception by enemy fighters.

The North Korean railway system was in the form of a big letter 'H', with north–south lines running along east and west coasts and joined by lateral routes running across country. The weight of the Fifth Air Force's attack fell on the north–south routes, with each fighter-bomber wing assigned the daily task of interdicting a selected stretch of track between 15 and 30 miles in length. Attacks were usually made by between 32 and 64 aircraft carrying pairs of 500lb bombs under a Sabre escort. Two methods of attack were generally favoured by the fighter-bomber pilots; dive-bombing or a long, shallow glide approach. The latter method was found to be more accurate, although the attacking aircraft was exposed to greater risk from ground fire. Communist anti-aircraft defences were thickest along the lateral rail route running from Samdong-ni to Kowon, which soon became known as 'Death Valley' by the Navy pilots. In fact, after suffering disproportionately heavy losses during early attacks on this objective, Navy fighter-bombers from TF 77's three attack carriers—the *Bon Homme Richard*, *Essex* and *Antietam*—turned their main attention to the east coast routes, and in particular to 27 rail and road bridges.

Although the continual air attacks in August and September slowed down the movement of enemy rolling stock and caused damage to lines to such an extent that the Reds were cannibalising hundreds of miles of track to keep other more important routes open, the Communists were still able to keep the bulk of their rail traffic flowing. Except where bridges had been destroyed, the Reds were able to by-pass rail cuts with comparative ease; supplies would simply be unloaded from a train on one side of a cut and loaded on another at the other side. The old tricks of camouflage were also employed to the full to defeat post-strike reconnaissance. For example, FEAF Intelligence believed that Bomber Command had destroyed the bridge at Sunchon—until a night reconnaissance mission by an RB-26 revealed that the Reds were bridging the gaps with movable spans during darkness and taking them away again at dawn. All in all, the results hardly seemed to justify the UN aircraft losses—and the latter were substantial. In August 1951 the Fifth Air Force alone lost 26 fighter-bombers and had 24 damaged; in September the figures were 32 lost and 233 damaged, in October 33 and 238, and in September 24 and 255.

It was only in December, when Intelligence on the results of the rail attacks was substantiated by prisoner-of-war reports, that FEAF began to appreciate the full effect on the enemy of this phase of Operation Strangle. According to some prisoners, including one regimental commander, the attacks had compelled the Communists to shelve plans for another winter offensive. Nevertheless, General Ridgway and his subordinate commanders were aware of the dangers of over-optimism. If there was any let-up in the air attacks, it would not take the Reds long to sort out their logistics system and build up stockpiles of supplies near the front line once more.

It was therefore decided, in December 1951, to continue hitting the enemy's railway system until such time as even more important targets presented themselves. There were some changes in the overall plan; seriously worried about the build-up of Communist flak along the railways which had been repeatedly hit during the preceding three months, Fifth Air Force now directed its fighter-bombers against other, more weakly defended sectors. The immediate result was a higher percentage of rail cuts and a drop in aircraft casualties, although many fighter-bombers were damaged by blast when their bombs bounced off the frozen ground and exploded in the air during low-level attacks.

Intelligence, meanwhile, had been searching for a profitable rail target for the B-29s of Bomber Command. They found it in January 1952 near the village of Wadong, on the railway line running laterally across Korea. At this point the railway crossed a main north–south highway in a narrow defile, and Intelligence worked out that if the crossing was thoroughly plastered with bombs the Reds would have a hard time getting their supplies through the surrounding mountainous terrain.

For 44 days, beginning on January 26th, 77 B-29s and 125 B-26s dropped a total of nearly 4,000 500lb bombs on the objective. They achieved only 33 hits and succeeded in blocking the railway and road for just one week. After that, the B-29s went back to their more usual bridge targets.

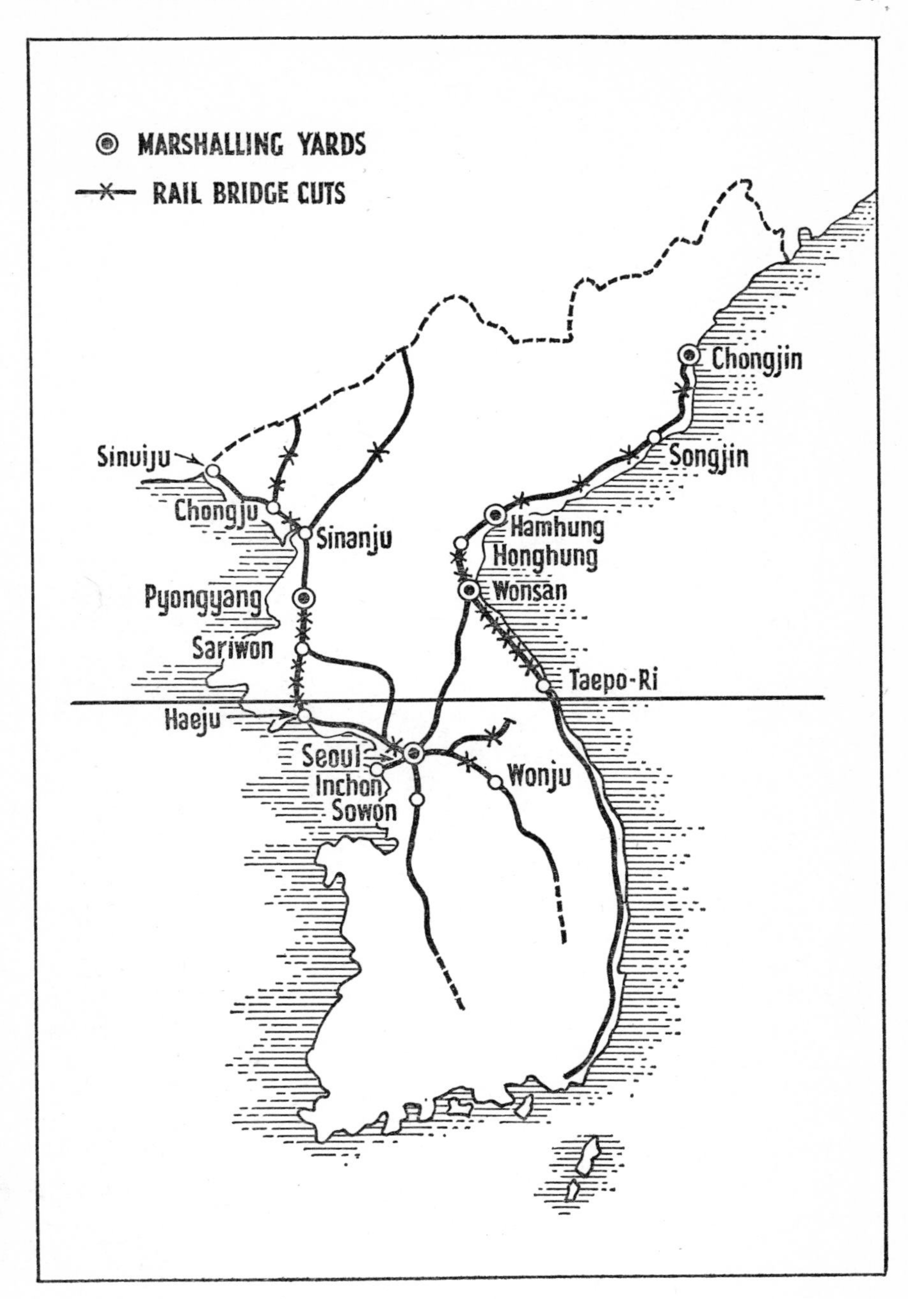


Rail points attacked by B-29s, Sept 1951.

Early in March, following recommendations made by Colonel Jean H. Daugherty, the Fifth Air Force Director of Intelligence, Operation Strangle gave way to Operation Saturate. Unlike Strangle, which had seen Fifth Air Force and Navy aircraft ranging over the length and breadth of North Korea's railways as far north as Chongchon, Saturate envisaged repeated maximum-effort strikes against short sections of track with the object of keeping them permanently out of action. Meanwhile, Bomber Command would mount large-scale B-29 attacks on selected bridge targets. To minimise losses, lightly-defended targets were to be chosen wherever possible.

Bad weather hampered the start of the operation, but on March 25th over 300 fighter-bombers dropped 530 1000lb and 84 500lb bombs on a stretch of track between Chongju and Sinanju. The same target was attacked that night by eight B-26s, which dropped 42 500lb bombs, and the next day 161 fighter bombers completed the assault with a further 322 1000lb bombs. Despite this weight of high explosive, the track was unserviceable for only five days; it was nevertheless considered to be a success and Operation Saturate was ordered to continue. Strikes against the Sinanju–Sinuiju line kept the latter out of action almost continuously during April and May, but the Fifth Air Force and TF 77 simply had too few fighter-bombers to permit maximum-effort interdiction against several rail targets at the same time—and the numbers of available fighter-bombers were dropping steadily through attrition. The Fifth Air Force's fighter-bomber units, for example, had already lost 243 aircraft, most of them during the railway attacks since the previous August, and a further 290 had sustained heavy damage—but only 130 replacement aircraft had been received. Among the worst hit were the 49th and 136th Fighter-Bomber Wings, whose authorised establishment of 75 Thunderjets each had been reduced to 41 and 39 respectively. Some of the losses had been caused by engine failure—a result of operating from Taegu's incredibly dusty and gritty airstrip. In an attempt to make good at least some of the attrition suffered by the F-84Es, USAF shipped a number of earlier model F-84Ds out to Korea—a move that was greeted adversely by both General Everest and the commanders of the two Thunderjet wings.

While the fighter-bombers continued to hit the North Korean railways by day, the Fifth Air Force's night intruder specialists—the 3rd and 452nd Bombardment Wings—were constantly seeking new and improved methods of striking at enemy rolling stock under cover of darkness. Despite the successes achieved the previous year with the use of Navy-type flares, satisfactory illumination remained a problem. Then, towards the end of 1951, several of the 3rd Wing's B-26s were fitted with searchlights of the kind used by the US Navy's 'blimps' for anti-submarine work. Once a target had been located and marked with incendiaries, the B-26s were able to make several strafing passes with the aid of the 80-million-candlepower searchlights. The only snag was that while the searchlight lit up the target, it also lit up the attacking aircraft and attracted heavy ground fire. After the loss of several B-26s while using these tactics, what had promised to be a good idea at the outset was finally abandoned.

Like most other Fifth Air Force units, both the 3rd and 452nd Wings were critically short of aircraft at the beginning of 1952. Many of the replacement aircraft sent out from the United States were useless for operations in the Korean winter because they had old-type flat topped cockpit canopies, which made it impossible for crews clad in winter clothing and parachutes to worm their way through the escape hatches in an emergency. There was also a shortage of crews; the operational training unit at Langley Air Force Base simply could not cope with the Fifth Air Force's requirements. Many of the crews that did reach the combat theatre lacked experience, and this showed up clearly in a series of poor bombing results early in 1952. By April of that year the attrition suffered by the B-26 Wings was out of all proportion to the results they were achieving, and it was rapidly becoming apparent that the old light bombers were approaching the end of their useful life in the Korean conflict.

By the end of May 1952, losses suffered by United Nations aircraft in the rail interdiction campaign had reached a new peak, the result of a denser concentration of enemy flak along all major routes. In fact, by the middle of the year the Reds had deployed a total of 850 anti-aircraft weapons of all types in defence of their railroads and rail bridges—about half their total arsenal of anti-aircraft weapons. Despite everything, however, UN airmen had claimed a total of 20,000 rail cuts throughout the North Korean system since Operation Saturate began, and although most of these had been repaired fairly quickly the sustained air pressure had at least disrupted and slowed down the enemy's rail supplies.

Nevertheless, Saturate had not stopped the enemy from getting ample supplies through to the front line by the summer of 1952; what it had done was prevented the Reds from mounting another offensive, and in that it had achieved its stated purpose. There were, of course, inevitable criticisms of the way in which the operation had been handled—many of them arising simply because the operation's aims had not been publicised clearly enough. When the operation failed to bring a sudden and dramatic halt to Communist rail traffic, it was immediately branded as a failure in many quarters—including some high-ranking ones. The fact was that the planners of the rail interdiction campaign had never claimed to be able to halt the flow of Communist traffic—merely to throw it into confusion.

Yet there was no denying that the execution of both Strangle and Saturate had suffered from a number of drawbacks that might easily have been avoided with more careful planning. Foremost among these was the lack of co-operation between the Fifth Air Force, Bomber Command and the Navy; although each had been assigned its own set of targets at the outset, attacks had been generally unco-ordinated. The whole interdiction programme might have worked a lot better had all operations been under one control.

To a great extent, it had been a victim of circumstances. Had it been carried out in conjunction with a major Allied offensive, it could probably have paralysed the enemy's ability to hold the battle line within a very short time. But the armistic talks still dragged on at Panmunjom, and it had already been decided that Allied politics and persuasion, and not Allied offensives, would be the principal factors in the bid to decide the outcome of the war. So air interdiction remained in essence a defensive weapon, designed to maintain the status quo in Korea—and time remained firmly on the side of the Communists.

CHAPTER THIRTEEN

# The Mounting Offensive

While the railway interdiction campaign went on during 1951 and the first half of 1952, FEAF planners had been giving a great deal of thought to the choice of a worthwhile target system in North Korea. What FEAF badly needed was a means of maintaining sustained air pressure on the enemy, and it was generally agreed that the best way to achieve this was through a series of maximum-effort attacks on selected strategic targets in the North—preferably those in which China and the Soviet Union had an interest. It was felt that the destruction of such targets would influence the North Koreans' Russian and Chinese masters into hastening the peace negotiations at Panmunjom.

The problem was that strategic targets—at least those that fitted the UN requirement—were scarce in North Korea. The exception was the country's hydro-electric power system, but up to the end of 1951 the Joint Chiefs had been reluctant to approve attacks on the hydro-electric plants. It was not until the spring of 1952, with the armistice talks apparently moving towards a total deadlock, that the attitude in Washington began to change and it was admitted that additional military force would be necessary to break the stalemate.

Although the hydro-electric plants were now regarded as profitable and justifiable military targets at the highest level, the proposal to attack them led to a sharp difference of opinion between General Weyland, who favoured the attacks, and General Ridgway, who did not. Ridgway took the view that so long as the Panmunjom talks continued, the use of additional force was fundamentally wrong. He insisted that before any attacks could be made on the hydro-electric plants, such a move would have to be recommended by him through the normal channels—a procedure which the Joint Chiefs were not willing to circumvent.

This particular problem, however, was resolved on April 28th, when Ridgway was replaced by General Mark Clark as the United Nations Commander in Korea. It was not long before General Weyland had obtained Clark's approval for the hydro-electric attacks to go ahead, and the FEAF operations staff were soon hard at work putting the finishing touches to the plan. Four principal plants—Sui-ho, Fusen,

Choshin and Kyosen—were scheduled for attack, and the planners realised that it would be necessary to carry out the entire operation in the space of about 48 hours to prevent the enemy defences from reacting fully. This would be a task of such magnitude that it could not possibly be accomplished by FEAF alone; the Navy was therefore called in to help, and by June 19th a joint Navy-Air Force operations team had worked out plans for a co-ordinated attack.

Everything depended on perfect timing. After negotiations between Vice-Admiral J. J. Clark, the new commander of the US Seventh Fleet, and General Glenn Barcus, who had recently succeeded General Everest as commander of the Fifth Air Force, it was agreed that the big plant at Suiho would be the target of a co-ordinated strike by Fifth Air Force fighter-bombers and carrier aircraft. Other fighter-bombers were to make a simultaneous strike on Nos 3 and 4 plants at Choshin and Fusen, while Naval aircraft would hit Kyosen and Fusen's Nos 1 and 2 plants. After dark it would be Bomber Command's turn, with a Shoran attack by B-29s on Nos 1 and 2 plants at Choshin. The Suiho attack was potentially the most dangerous, with 250 MiGs less than 40 miles away at Antung, but despite the risk many of the Navy pilots were looking forward to a chance of getting to grips with the enemy. It would be the first time since 1950 that aircraft of Task Force 77 had ventured into MiG Alley.

The attack was scheduled to begin at 09.30hrs on June 23rd, 1952, but heavy cloud over the target area delayed it for several hours. Finally, at 16.00hrs, the clouds broke and the aircraft-carriers *Boxer*, *Princeton* and *Philippine Sea* launched the first strike of the day: 35 Skyraiders, escorted by a similar number of Panthers. While 84 Sabres of the 4th and 51st Wings flew top cover, the Panthers went in and hammered the 80 flak emplacements around the target before the Skyraiders unloaded their bombs on the generator plant. In the space of the next hour the target was pounded by 79 F-84s and 45 F-80s, which—together with the Naval aircraft—dropped a total of 145 tons of bombs on it. Post-strike reconnaissance by RF-80s showed that the attack had been a complete success, with the generator plant virtually wiped out. The feared interception by enemy fighters never happened; early in the attack dust clouds at Antung showed that the MiGs were taking off, but instead of crossing the river they flew away into Manchuria. The most likely reason for this unexpected move was that the Reds believed that the Allied air armada was on its way to hit their bases.

Shortly after the Suiho attack began, Fifth Air Force Mustangs swept down on Nos 3 and 4 plants at Fusen, while Panthers of the 1st Marine Air Wing bombed Choshin's Nos 3 and 4. As these aircraft climbed away, the second Navy strike of the day—Skyraiders, Corsairs and Panthers from the *Boxer*, *Princeton* and *Bon Homme Richard*—hit Fusen's

Nos 1 and 2 and the complex at Kyosen. The onset of dusk prevented further attacks that day, but further heavy attacks were launched against the same targets by both Navy and Fifth Air Force on the 24th, and that night Bomber Command raided Choshin. Both Choshin and Fusen were bombed yet again by the Fifth Air Force on the 26th and 27th. When the attacks ended, nine-tenths of North Korea's prized hydro-electric system had been laid waste. The Allies lost only two aircraft, both to ground fire, and in each case the pilot was rescued. June 1952 would be remembered for a long time as the month when the lights went out all over North Korea.

In July 1952, FEAF set a re-organisation programme in motion in order to meet the requirements of a sustained air-pressure campaign following the highly successful hydro-electric strikes. Plans for the reshuffle were assisted by the fact that the equipment situation was a good deal easier now than it had been at the beginning of the year. Thanks to the purchase of 60 additional Sabres from the Canadair Aircraft Company by the USAF in February, FEAF was now able to bring both its F-86 Wings up to full strength while still retaining a 50 per cent reserve. The 51st Fighter-Interceptor Wing was brought up to three-squadron establishment by the transfer of the 39th Fighter-Interceptor Squadron from the 18th Wing early in June—the 39th being re-equipped with new F-86Fs.

Another significant stride was made during July when, for the first time, fighter aircraft crossed the Pacific using flight refuelling. The unit involved was the 31st Fighter-Escort Wing, led by Colonel David C. Schilling, whose F-84Es established themselves at Misawa on July 15th. The arrival of the 31st Wing, which was earmarked for the defence of Japan, meant that the Misawa-based 116th Fighter-Bomber Wing could now be released for service in Korea. The 116th was one of the two former Air National Guard Thunderjet units called up for combat duty; the other was the 136th Wing. Since ANG units could only remain in Federal service for a specified period, both Wings were relieved from combat duty in July 1952, their personnel and equipment being allocated to the newly-activated 474th and 58th Fighter-Bomber Wings. The 474th was the first of the new wings to go into action, staging its F-84s through Kunsan Airfield (K-8) from July 10th.

By September 1952, all the Fifth Air Force's Thunderjet units were once again up to full strength. The 'stop-gap' F-84Ds, which had been a continual source of trouble since their arrival in Korea, began to be phased out in August in favour of the latest model F-84G—production of which had finally caught up with the requirements of both the USAF and NATO air forces. Fifth AF's light bomber units also underwent some re-organisation during the summer, the 452nd Bombardment Wing being de-activated and replaced by the 17th Wing. By September both the 3rd and 17th Bombardment Wings were up to full strength, a sure sign to the crews that they were going to have to soldier on with the old B-26s for the forseeable future.

Meanwhile, Allied Intelligence in the summer of 1952 had once again revealed a number of alarming developments across the Manchurian border. By the middle of the year the strength of the Chinese People's Air Force stood at 22 Air Divisions, comprising 1,800 aircraft—1,000 of them jet types. In addition, there was a further potential menace in the fact that Soviet air strength in the Far East had climbed to over 5,300 aircraft. Not the least disturbing news to reach the Allies was that the Chinese Communists had been supplied with about a hundred Ilyushin Il-28 jet bombers, most of which were based in Manchuria.

The Reds were also hard at work on a new airfield complex across the Yalu during the summer of 1952, and some 25 early-warning radar stations gave coverage of Allied air space up to a considerable distance south of the 38th Parallel. There were also a dozen GCI stations, most of them situated in the west coast area, which were able to provide effective fighter control in all weathers over a 70-mile radius. South of the Yalu, important Communist installations were protected by a growing concentration of anti-aircraft artillery; by the autumn of 1952 the Reds had nearly 2,000 heavy AA guns and automatic weapons at their disposal, most of them Russian 85mm and 37mm pieces. A large proportion of these weapons were highly mobile, as were their associated searchlights—some 500 in all.

From the beginning of June 1952, the Reds showed a hitherto absent ability to co-ordinate all their air defence measures in a new challenge to Allied air superiority over north-western Korea. Their night-fighter force in particular reached a new level of efficiency in countering B-29 raids; on the night of June 10th/11th, for example, MiGs shot down two B-29s and badly damaged a third over Kwaksan. Red fighter pilots also began to show much greater proficiency in daytime air battles with Sabres, although this did not prevent Allied pilots from claiming 20 MiGs destroyed for the loss of three of their own number in June. One Sabre pilot, Lt James F. Low of the 4th Wing, joined the ranks of the jet aces during the month by destroying his fifth enemy aircraft.

The MiGs were up in strength on July 4th, when 50 of them crossed the Yalu to intercept Allied fighter-bombers attacking targets at Sakchu. All the fighter-bombers got away but the MiGs tangled with the Sabre escort and a frenzied dog-fight developed in which the United Nations pilots claimed 13 enemy aircraft destroyed for the loss of two Sabres. Six more MiGs were added to the Sabres' score during the remainder of the month, making a total of 19. In all, four Sabres failed to return from the July engagements.

The early part of August 1952 was characterised by several deep-penetration missions on the part of the enemy, the MiGs slipping through the Sabre screen and roving as far south as Haeju in search of Allied fighter-bombers. During one such mission, on August 9th, eight of them ran into the Sea Furies and Fireflies of HMS *Ocean*'s 802 and 825 Squadrons. Lieutenant P. Carmichael, of 802 Squadron, described what happened: "The encounter that my flight had with the MiGs took place at 06.00 hrs. My No 2, Sub-Lt Carl Haines, said 'MiGs five o'clock'. I did not see them at first and my No 4, Sub-Lt 'Smoo' Ellis, gave a break. We all turned towards the MiGs. Two went for my Nos 3 and 4, Lt Pete Davies and Sub-Lt Ellis. They were seen to get good hits on one, who broke away with smoke coming from him."

Carmichael also got in a good burst at a MiG, which went down and crashed. His report continues: "Though I have been credited with shooting down the first MiG, I feel that it was more of a flight effort than an individual one, because the one that crashed behind me was fired at by all of my flight. My Nos 3 and 4 then had another attack them and got hits on this one. He broke away and the rest of the MiGs broke off the engagement and escorted him away. The impression we got was that these MiG pilots were very inexperienced and did not use their aircraft to any advantage at all. I think it was the next day that we had another engagement with eight MiGs and we were very lucky to get away with it. I reckon they must have sent the instructors down! These pilots put their aircraft to the best use and we managed to ease our way to some cloud that was about 20 miles away. One MiG got on my tail and my No 3 fired at him and he broke away. The only MiG who made a mistake was one who made a head-on attack on my Nos 3 and 4 and was hit by them and seen to go away with a lot of smoke and flame coming from him."

During these two skirmishes the pilots of 802 Squadron claimed the destruction of two MiG-15s, with three more damaged. To Lieutenant Carmichael fell the honour of becoming the first piston-engined pilot to shoot down an enemy jet in the Korean War. It was a formidable testimony to the Sea Fury's ruggedness and its excellent dog-fighting characteristics.

All told, United Nations aircraft destroyed 35 MiGs in air combat during August 1952, six of them having been shot down in a scrap between 35 Sabres and 52 MiGs on the 6th. Only two Sabres were lost. Yet another ace was added to the United Nations list: Captain Clifford D. Jolley, who shot down a MiG-15 on the 8th to bring his score to five.

September turned out to be the most hectic month yet. The MiG pilots showed aggressive intentions right from the start, when—on the 1st—several of them penetrated as far as Haeju to attack Allied fighter-bombers. Once again, however, the Communist pilots threw away their advantage with poor gunnery and teamwork, and only succeeded in damaging one Mustang. On the 4th, the sky over the Yalu was criss-crossed with contrails throughout the entire day as Sabres and MiGs tangled in 17 separate dogfights that resulted in the destruction of 13 Red jets for four F-86s. One of the MiGs fell before the guns of Major Frederick C. Blesse of the 4th Wing; it was his fifth enemy aircraft, and before September was out he would have three more to his credit. On the 9th, no fewer than 175 MiGs crossed the river to intercept Thunderjets which were attacking the North Korean Military Academy at Sakchu, a frequent target since early in August. The Sabre escort was not strong enough to cope with all of them and some broke through to shoot down one fighter-bomber. Two more Thunderjets and six Sabres were destroyed in air combat during the remainder of the month, but the United Nations pilots claimed a record total of 63 MiGs. On September 21st Captain Robinson Risner destroyed his fifth MiG near Sinuiju to become the Korean War's twentieth jet ace.

Their heavy losses in September made the Red pilots more cautious during the following month. Most of the work was done by the 'honchos', the veterans; while the big MiG formations stayed safely upstairs at 40,000 feet or more, the experienced flight and squadron commanders would dive down to attack targets of opportunity. Alternatively, formations of 12 or 24 MiGs—all flown by experienced pilots—would seek out four-Sabre flights and attempt to box them in. To counter these new tactics, both Sabre Wings began to use flights of six or eight aircraft, with the higher-powered F-86Fs operating at 40,000 feet plus and the F-86Es working lower down. The new arrangement worked well and the Communists were only able to claim four Sabres and one Thunderjet destroyed for the loss of 27 MiGs. The MiGs, however, managed to score successes against Task Force 77's conventional aircraft in the Wonsan area, destroying two Skyraiders and a Corsair.

The fighter-bomber raids on the North Korean Military Academy at Sakchu, which the MiGs had tried hard to frustrate, formed part of a carefully-planned series of high-pressure air strikes against enemy targets whose destruction would, it was hoped, deal a severe blow to the enemy's morale. The biggest air attack of this campaign—and indeed of the Korean War—was launched on July 11th against 30 military targets within the North Korean capital, Pyongyang. Code-named Operation Pressure Pump, it involved almost every operational air unit in the Far East.

For several days beforehand United Nations aircraft dropped leaflets over the city, warning the population of the impending attacks. The latter began right on schedule at 10.00hrs, with a massive assault by Panthers and Corsairs of TF 77 and the 1st Marine Air Wing, Mustangs of the small ROK Air Force, Sea Furies and Fireflies of HMS *Ocean*'s 802 and 825 Squadrons, and Thunderjets of the Fifth Air Force. The attacks were repeated at 14.00hrs and 18.00hrs by the Fifth Air Force and Fleet Air Arm, and after dark eight targets in the city were hit by B-29s. In all, 1,254 sorties were flown during the day and night; three of the targets were totally destroyed and almost all the remainder badly damaged. Allied losses were a Panther, a Corsair and a Thunderjet. Radio Pyongyang, which was badly hit during the raids, was silent for 48 hours; when it finally did get back on the air it announced that 1,500 buildings had been destroyed in the city and 7,000 people killed or injured. Surprisingly, there was no reaction from the Communist delegation at Panmunjom.

The North Koreans had just begun to repair some of the devastation caused to their capital when, on August 29th, 1952, they were subjected to another raid that exceeded the previous one in size and fury. This time, in addition to military objectives, public offices were on the list of targets to be attacked. The three strikes—carried out at 09.30, 13.30 and 17.30hrs—were flown by Fifth Air Force Thunderjets and Mustangs, Marine Panthers and Corsairs, and Banshees, Panthers and Corsairs from the carriers *Boxer* and *Essex*. Flak suppression around the target was the task of the Thunderjets of the 474th and Mustangs of the the 8th Fighter-Bomber Wings, while 4th and 51st Wing Sabres and No 77 Squadron Meteors patrolled to the north along the Chongchon River.

The next day, photo-reconnaissance showed that the raids had been highly successful, with more or less severe damage inflicted on all the targets attacked.

These attacks on Pyongyang were supported by intensive raids on North Korean centres of manufacture and transportation. During July, an important cement plant at Sungho-ri, the hydro-electric plant at Choshin, a lead and zinc mill at Sindok and the Oriental light metals plant near Sinuiju all came in for the attention of the Fifth Air Force, TF 77 and Bomber Command, while in August fighter-bombers attacked the tungsten mines at Kiju and a chemical plant at In-hung-ni and B-29s pounded the Nakwon Munitions Plant. Attacking communications and troop concentrations was mainly the task of night-flying B-26s, which unloaded incendiary bombs in relays on targets marked by special 'pathfinder' crews.

The job of eliminating important industrial targets in north-eastern Korea fell to the pilots of Task Force 77, often working close up to the Soviet border. On September 1st, Banshees, Panthers and Corsairs from the *Essex*, *Princeton* and *Boxer* hammered the synthetic oil refinery at Aoji in the biggest naval air strike of the war, while a fortnight later more carrier aircraft from the *Bon Homme Richard* and *Princeton* struck at supply depots and barracks in the town of Hoeryong, right on the Soviet frontier.

By September 30th—on the night of which 45 B-29s wiped out the Namsan-ni chemical plant in a brilliant attack after confusing the enemy defences with electronic countermeasures and 'window'—the whole of North Korea's industry lay in ruins. Yet still the Communist negotiators at Panmunjom failed to show any sign of weakening, although intelligence reports indicated that both China and the Soviet Union were seeking a means of bringing the war to an end without a serious loss of face. At Panmunjom, the talks had reached a stalemate over the issue of repatriating prisoners of war; since several thousand Chinese and North Korean prisoners did not wish to return to their homelands when hostilities ended the United Nations were pressing for repatriation on a voluntary basis, but the Reds were insisting on the return of all prisoners. When they still proved intractable on this point early in October, the United Nations Command delegates recessed and indicated that they would be prepared to resume negotiations only when the Communists had something constructive to offer in the way of new proposals.

Meanwhile, the Allies had no intention of relaxing their air pressure operations, but selecting new target systems for a continuing air offensive presented problems. With most worthwhile fixed target systems in the north already shattered, the only way of hitting the enemy hard now was to lure his troops and equipment out into the open—and then turn the fighter-bombers loose.

To achieve this, General Clark and his commanders planned an ingenious hoax. They allowed the news to leak out that the Allies were planning a large-scale amphibious assault on the coastal village of Kojo, north of Wonsan, in conjunction with a ground offensive by the Eighth Army and an airdrop by the 187th RCT. For a week before the supposed assault was due to begin, FEAF aircraft hammered enemy supply and communications lines in the coastal areas, while an armada of C-46s and C-119s flew into Taegu. The air operations during this period provided the best example so far of inter-Service co-operation, with Banshees escorting B-29s and Sabres escorting Navy attack aircraft during missions against coastal targets.

Carrying out its part of the hoax to the letter, NavFE assembled the biggest naval armada since World War II—Joint Amphibious Task Force Seven—and sent it on its way up the Korean coast towards Kojo. On the night of October 14th the Eighth Army launched a two-battalion thrust into enemy territory—to all appearances the spearhead of a large-scale attack—and the following morning Task Force Seven sent a wave of landing-craft in towards the beaches. At the same time, 32 C-119s headed north to Chorwon, as though to make a paradrop. Both air and seaborne forces, however, turned away short of their objectives, the C-119s landing at Taegu and the naval craft returning to the Task Force.

Communist reaction to the hoax had not been as marked as General Clark and his staff had hoped, but nevertheless it had been enough to present the Allied air forces with a host of targets. Between October 9th and 19th the Fifth Air Force's fighter-bombers and light bombers flew 3,729 sorties, hitting 360 targets of all types, while Bomber Command attacked a further 43. During the same period carrier aircraft flew over 3,000 sorties, mainly against targets near the coast.

The biggest black spot of the operation had been the Eighth Army's limited offensive, which had been designed to capture two objectives north of Kumhwa: Triangle Hill and Sniper Ridge. Both objectives were taken, but only at the cost of heavy casualties, and the United Nations troops holding them were subjected to continual and heavy infantry attacks. In support of the UN forces the Fifth Air Force and the Marine Air Wing flew over 3,500 sorties, but despite this Triangle Hill was recaptured by the Communists early in November. The force on Sniper Ridge managed to hold out with air support, which was often delivered through intense automatic weapons fire. During one attack, on November 22nd, Major Charles J. Loring of the 8th Wing's 80th Fighter-Bomber Squadron deliberately crashed his F-80 into an enemy gun position after he was hit by flak. He was later awarded a posthumous Medal of Honor.

Although November 1952 was a fairly quiet month as far as air combat was concerned—the Communist fighter units encountered during previous weeks apparently having been withdrawn for a rest and replaced by new ones whose time was mostly taken up with operational training—the UN Sabre pilots nevertheless managed to increase their total score by 28 MiGs for the loss of only four 'friendlies'. The month saw three new aces: Colonel Royal N. Baker and Captain Leonard W. Lilley, both of the 4th Wing, and Captain Cecil G. Foster of the 51st Wing. Navy fighter pilots also tangled with the MiGs during the course of the month; on November 18th, the pilots of three Panthers from the USS *Oriskany*, covering an air strike on the frontier town of Hoeryong, spotted a formation of MiGs circling in the distance over Russian territory. Suddenly, several of the MiGs broke away and headed towards the carrier aircraft; they were immediately intercepted by the Panthers, which shot one of them down. There was no doubt about the MiGs' nationality: the fighters bore the plain red star of the Soviet Air Force. For fear of international implications, the incident was hushed up until years after the war.

The Red fighters enjoyed an increased success rate during December, but it had little to do with the fighting ability of individual pilots.

About the middle of the month the Communists suddenly launched a variation of their air tactics; a formation of MiGs would by-pass the Sabre screen and head southwards to the Chongchon River, where they would lie in wait for Sabres going home short of fuel. A number of Sabre pilots found themselves trapped in this way, and at least four had to bail out when their fuel ran out. Apart from that, only two Sabres were lost in actual air-to-air combat during the month, while United Nations pilots claimed 28 MiGs.

The MiGs again made extensive use of these new tactics during January 1953, but homegoing Sabres were generally able to keep out of trouble by flying a curve over the Yellow Sea. Early in the month, UN pilots reported that although most of the MiGs—presumably still engaged in one of their habitual training cycles—still remained at over 40,000 feet, some of the MiG units they were meeting showed a skill that matched their own. These squadrons—whose aircraft were camouflaged pale blue underneath, with copper upper surfaces and bearing plain red stars—almost always stayed to fight it out and used every trick in the book. Once or twice, Sabre pilots caught a glimpse of their opponents' features; they were distinctly Caucasian, not Asian. The United Nations claimed 37 kills for the loss of one Sabre during January, but most of the victories were scored by high-flying F-86Fs which were fortunate enough to tangle with the enemy novices. Two 51st Wing pilots, Captain Dolphin D. Overton III and Captain Harold E. Fischer, both became aces during the month—Overton destroying five MiGs in just four missions. On the last day of the month, Lt Raymond J. Kinsey of the 4th Wing trapped a Tu-2 bomber south of the river and shot it down in flames.

February 1953 saw the beginning of a different kind of air battle; a friendly tussle for the position of top jet ace before the Korean hostilities ended. Major James Jabara, with six MiGs to his credit during his earlier tour with the 4th Wing, was back in Korea—and his score was already beginning to climb. The magic figure was 14 enemy aircraft destroyed—the score of the late George Davis before his untimely death the year before—and Jabara was coming up fast. But so were a number of other pilots, and one in particular stood out from among them.

Captain Joseph McConnell had been turned down for pilot training during the Second World War, and had flown a couple of tours as a navigator on B-24s. It was only after the war that he was accepted as a pilot, finally emerging as one of the first batch of USAF Shooting Star pilots in February 1948. When the Korean War broke out McConnell was in Alaska; he immediately applied for combat duty, but instead of being transferred to Korea he was sent to George Air Force Base in California. It was not until the autumn of 1952 that he eventually got his wish and joined the 51st Fighter-Interceptor Wing at Kimpo.

He destroyed his first MiG on January 14th, 1953. Just over a month later, by which time he was a flight commander with the 51st Wing's 16th Squadron, his score had risen to five and he was racing almost neck-and-neck with Captain Manuel J. Fernandez of the 4th Wing. Fernandez downed four more MiGs in March, bringing his score to ten, while McConnell accounted for three more, making a total of eight. Three other pilots also became aces during the month; one was Major James P. Hagerstrom of the 18th Fighter-Bomber Wing, which had been flying F-86Fs since February, and the others were Colonel James Johnson and Lt-Col George L. Jones, both of the 4th Wing.

The MiG pilots proved particularly agressive during March, penetrating as far as Chinnampo equipped with wing tanks and coming down as low as 17,000 feet to join combat, but the Sabres once again came out on top and claimed 34 MiGs for the loss of two F-86s. March was also the month in which the Meteors of No 77 Squadron met MiGs in combat for the last time. It happened on the 27th, when Sergeants John Hale and David Irlam spotted three enemy jets while on patrol over Sinmak, south-east of Pyongyang, and immediately went in to the attack. One MiG broke away, but the others turned and made passes at the Meteors. Hale jettisoned his ventral fuel tank and fired two air-to-ground rockets the oncoming MiGs, which broke wildly; one of them tried to get on the Meteor's tail, but overshot and presented Hale with the chance he was waiting for. "For a second", the Australian pilot said, "he was flying parallel to me, about 50 yards ahead. I could see the pilot clearly and swung behind him and hammered at him with my cannon. Strips of metal began to peel off the MiG and it rolled on to its back and headed straight down from about 10,000 feet. Black smoke was pouring out, but I didn't see him crash. Now there were more MiGs, and two came at me with guns blazing. Again I managed to S-turn on to their tails. The Meteor was flying like a bomb. They tried to climb away, and as I blasted one I saw bright flashes near the wing root and white smoke poured out. Then my guns stopped firing. There was no more ammunition and I had to turn for home."

Although the United Nations pilots continued to get the better of the MiGs during the daylight engagements of early 1953, the enemy defences continued to give Bomber Command's night-flying B-29s a hard time. Between November 18th, 1952, and January 30th, 1953, Communist night-fighters claimed five B-29s and severely damaged three more, using a combination of radar-directed searchlights and flare-dropping 'master' night-fighters. Bomber Command's electronic countermeasures—based on data gathered by RB-29 'ferret' aircraft of the 91st Strategic Reconnaissance Squadron—continued to improve, but although ECM was able to reduce the loss rate substantially it was by no means the answer to the B-29s' problem.

The Fifth Air Force had been trying to help since the middle of 1952, but the only aircraft really suited to the task of seeking out and destroying enemy night-fighters—the F-94B Starfires of the Suwon-based 319th Fighter-Interceptor Squadron—were forbidden to fly over enemy territory because of the advanced electronic equipment they carried. Marine Squadron VMF(N)-513 made frequent night sorties into enemy territory in support of the bombers with its F7F Tigercats, but these piston-engined machines were no match for the Reds' jet night fighters.

The situation began to improve slightly from November 1952, when VMF(N)-513 re-equipped with 12 Douglas F3D-2 Skynights. Carrying older and less secret airborne interception equipment than the F-94s, the Skynights were used to sweep the night sky ahead of the attacking bombers, and on their second offensive patrol on November 3rd one of them shot down a Yak-15 over Sinuiju. Five nights later, another Skynight crew destroyed a MiG-15 near Sonchon. In the new year the Skynights revised their tactics, flying several thousand feet above the bomber stream on the lookout for night-fighters positioning themselves for an attack. Two enemy aircraft were destroyed in this way before the end of January 1953, and on the 30th of that month Captain Ben L. Fithian and Lt Sam R. Lyons in an F-94 shot down a piston-engined La-9—the Starfires having by this time been cleared for night operations over the north. Between them, the Skynights and Starfires accounted for 15 Communist night-fighters during the first half of 1953. It was a relatively small contribution in terms of aircraft destroyed, but it helped the war-weary B-29s to survive those last months of conflict in Korea.

February 1953 saw the resumption by Bomber Command and the Fifth Air Force of strikes against selected industrial targets. On February 15th, for example, 22 Thunderjets of the 474th Fighter-Bomber Wing, each carrying two 1000lb SAP bombs, hit the Sui-ho hydro-electric plant, which was thought to be partly operational again. Attacking at low level, while 82 Sabres beat off a force of 30 MiGs that made an unsuccessful attempt to intercept, the Thunderjets pulverised the generator building. None of the Allied aircraft was damaged. This was followed, on March 15th, by an attack with 16 Thunderjets on industrial areas in Chongjin, while on the night of March 13th/14th 12 B-29s raided an ore-processing plant at Choak-tong. Three nights later, 21 more B-29s attacked industries in the Sinuiju area.

For most of the following month the Fifth Air Force, Bomber Command and TF 77 threw the weight of their attacks against enemy bridges and supply lines in a bid to disrupt large-scale Communist troop movements following the spring thaw. During this offensive the Red fighter pilots showed a marked reluctance to come up and fight, and air combats during April were sporadic. The Sabre Wings claimed the destruction of 27 MiGs for the loss of four of their own number; one of the latter was Captain Harold E. Fischer, the 51st Wing ace, whose score then stood at ten MiGs. He was taken prisoner. Joseph McConnell's Sabre was also badly hit during a scrap on April 12th, but he ejected safely and was fished out of the Yellow Sea by an H-5 of the 3rd Air Rescue Squadron. He was back in action within 24 hours, flaming his ninth MiG, and he got his tenth on April 24th. He was now neck-and-neck with Captain Fernandez, but that state of affairs was not to last; on April 27th Fernandez shot down his eleventh enemy fighter.

The MiGs were very much in evidence early in May, but now there was a difference. For the past few months, many of the MiGs encountered had carried the plain red star of Soviet Russia—but now they bore the markings of either Red China or North Korea. It has been suggested that the Russians decided to pull out their fighter contingents following a United Nations offer of a 100,000 dollar reward to any Communist pilot who defected and brought a MiG along with him, but it is far more likely that an agreement had already been reached between the Soviet Union and China to bring the Korean hostilities to an end—given a reasonable face-saving period—and that the Russians, having learned all they wanted to learn from nearly three years of jet combat, saw little point in involving themselves further. The pattern was not new; exactly the same thing had happened during the Spanish Civil War.

Whatever the truth, the Red pilots who now faced the United Nations were no longer 'honchos'. They were keen and aggressive enough, but they were inexperienced and they paid for it with their lives. The Sabre pilots who opposed them had orders now to seek and destroy; with Allied air superiority now totally assured, General Weyland had 'turned the tigers loose', and in May 1953 they chopped 56 MiGs from the sky for the loss of a solitary F-86. Some of the MiGs spun into the gound as a result of mishandling during high-speed manoeuvres; other pilots simply ejected as soon as they found a Sabre on their tail.

Either way, the Fifth Air Force's fighter pilots had a field day. At the beginning of May Fernandez led the field with a score of 14½, but by the 18th McConnell had destroyed six more MiGs to achieve a score of 16—a jet combat record that still stands unbroken. Fernandez never had a chance to get his revenge, for on May 19th both pilots were relieved from combat. Tragically, McConnell was killed on August 25th, 1954, while testing a new F-86H Sabre.

May 1953 saw the return to combat of Major James Jabara, the original Korean jet ace with a score of seven aircraft destroyed. On the 26th, Jabara shot down his eighth and ninth MiGs; just over a month later he was to become a triple jet ace by destroying his fifteenth enemy aircraft, moving into second place behind McConnell. The air battles of May also saw Lt-Col George I. Ruddell, commander of the 51st Wing's 39th Squadron, shoot down his fifth Red fighter.

It was as though both sides knew, in June 1953, that the great battle for supremacy in the freezing vault of the sky eight miles above the Yalu was drawing to a close. Sabres and MiGs hurled theselves at one another in a series of frenzied dogfights that resulted in the destruction of 77 enemy fighters, with a further 11 probables and 41 damaged. No Allied aircraft were lost. To the Sabre pilots, it seemed that the Reds were really scraping the barrel; often, when a Sabre got on a MiG's tail, the enemy pilot took no evasive action at all, but merely crouched as low as possible in the cockpit and held a steady course while the F-86 chopped his aircraft to pieces, relying on the thick armour plate at the rear of the cockpit to keep the bullets from him before he ejected. Sixteen of the Sabres' total kills were claimed on the last day of the month—a new record. The June battles saw the emergence of five new aces; Lt-Col Vermont Garrison, Captain Lonnie R. Moore and Captain Ralph S. Parr of the 4th Wing, and Colonel Robert P. Baldwin and Lt Henry Buttelman of the 51st.

The eagerness of the up-and-coming aces to add to their scores during July was frustrated by bad weather during the early part of the month, but on the 16th the murk cleared and the F-86s were detailed to escort a series of fighter-bomber missions flown against targets in the north-west. The July air combats started badly for the United Nations: on the 20th, two Sabres were trapped by six MiGs near the mouth of the Yalu and shot down. Other UN fighter pilots who joined in the combat reported that the MiGs were being expertly flown and appeared to be using an armament installation consisting of six rapid-firing cannon or heavy-calibre machine-guns. The Sabres quickly had their revenge, however, claiming a total of 32 enemy fighters destroyed in the course of the month. On the 11th, Major John F. Bolt, a USMC pilot flying Sabres with the 51st Wing, shot down his fifth and sixth MiGs to become the only USMC ace of the Korean War; on the 15th James Jabara scored his fifteenth and final kill; and on the 19th and 20th two more 4th Wing pilots, Captain Clyde A. Curtin and Major Stephen L. Bettinger, also became jet aces. Bettinger was in fact the 39th and last jet ace of the war, but it was several months before his status could be confirmed. After destroying his fifth MiG he was himself shot down and captured, and for fear of reprisals the UN kept his kills secret until he was eventually repatriated in October.

At 17.00hrs on July 22nd, three Sabres of the 51st Wing led by Lt Sam P. Young entered MiG Alley at 35,000 feet on an offensive patrol. Young felt slightly depressed; in 34 missions he had not yet fired his guns in anger, and it was beginning to look as though he would never get his chance.

On this July afternoon, however, his bad luck broke. Ahead and below, four MiGs swept across his path at right-angles. Young dived down, lining up his Sabre carefully, and blew the number four MiG apart with a long burst of fire. It was the last time that Sabre and MiG met in combat over Korea.

CHAPTER FOURTEEN

# North Korea's Dams: the UN's Last Target System

On April 26th, 1953, hopes for a speedy end to the war in Korea were raised when, after a lengthy recess, armistic talks were resumed at Panmunjom—only to be dashed once more when the Communists again rejected the Allied terms outright. There was another ray of hope early in May, when—after some hard bargaining—the Reds agreed to a UN suggestion that neutral nations should have custody of all prisoners of war pending repatriation, but there was still no agreement on what was to happen to those who did not wish to be repatriated and another breakdown of the talks appeared inevitable.

As a possible means of avoiding yet another prolonged recess, General Clark recommended to the Joint Chiefs that the air pressure operations against North Korea be maintained, and that if necessary the Allies should be prepared to launch a limited land offensive, and possibly an amphibious assault, in the autumn of 1953. At the same time, US Secretary of State John Foster Dulles hinted that authority might be given for a UN air offensive against China's Manchurian bases.

In October 1952, during their search for valuable target systems, FEAF planners had recommended an attack on one of the most vulnerable targets in North Korea: the Country's irrigation dams. Twenty of the latter, situated near important supply routes, provided 75 per cent of the water necessary for North Korea's rice production. The rice harvest was concentrated in two main provinces—Hwanghae and South Pyongan—and most of the production went to feed the Communist armies. By knocking out the 20 dams, FEAF calculated that a year's supply of rice would be destroyed in the resulting floods.

There would also be additional benefits. As well as destroying the rice crops, the floods would also inundate roads, railways and supply dumps. The destruction of the crops would mean famine among both the civilian population and the Communist armies, forcing the North Koreans to import vast quantities of rice from China—and in 1953 the Red Chinese economy was already strained to breaking-point. From the psychological point of view it would be better if the dams were destroyed gradually, rather than in an all-out air offensive; in this way it was hoped that in the eyes of the civilian population, the weight of the blame would fall on the Communists for prolonging the war.

The first attack was to be in the nature of an experiment, to see if the idea would work and to develop techniques for similar raids in the future. The target was the Toksan dam, a 2,300 foot earth and stone structure on the Potong River 20 miles north of Pyongyang. The dam was hit in the afternoon of May 13th by 59 Thunderjets of the 58th Fighter-Bomber Wing, carrying 1,000 pounders—and at first the result of the attack appeared disappointing. Apart from a slight crumbling of the structure, the dam still stood.

The next morning, however, photographs brought back by an RF-80 showed a scene of total devastation. Sometime during the night the pressure of water in the reservoir had caused the dam to collapse and a mighty flood had swept down the Potong Valley. Five square miles of rice crops had been swept away, together with 700 buildings; Sunan airfield was under water, and five miles of railway line, together with a two-mile stretch of the adjacent north–south highway, had been destroyed or damaged. In just one raid, the UN fighter-bombers had inflicted more damage on the enemy's transport system than they had done in several weeks of interdiction work.

General Weyland was not slow in following up this success. Two more dams—at Chasan and Kuwonga—were immediately slated for attack, and on the afternoon of May 15th 36 Thunderjets of the 58th Wing bombed the Chasan dam. The bomb-aiming, however, was poor, and no direct hits were registered, and it was not until five 1,000 pounders hit the dam squarely during a raid by a second wave of F-84s the next day that the structure crumbled and the waters burst through to inundate a large area of rice and destroy half a mile of a nearby railway line.

The Kuwonga dam had been assigned to Bomber Command, and it was attacked by seven B-29s using Shoran on the night of May 21st/22nd. Four direct hits were scored on the crest, but the dam held; anticipating the raid the enemy had reduced the water level in the reservoir, relieving a substantial amount of pressure on the structure. During a second attack on May 29th/30th the B-29s again scored five direct hits with 2,000 pounders on the dam, but even then the structure failed to crumble. Nevertheless, the damage was sufficient to require extensive repairs, and before these could be carried out the reservoir had to be drained completely—which meant that the ricefields in the area were deprived of their vital water supply and the crop suffered as a consequence.

Meanwhile, on May 28th, Communist forces had launched a strong thrust against advance units of the US I Corps in western Korea. This attack was a feint, the main Red offensive opening on June 10th against the ROK II Corps near Kumsong. For three nights, following up the daylight air offensive by the Fifth Air Force, B-29s of Bomber Command made radar-directed attacks on enemy supplies and communications, and on June 12th—when the ROK forces showed signs of breaking—TF 77 also threw everything it had into the battle. For seven days, Naval airmen flew non-stop from the carriers *Lake Champlain*, *Philippine Sea*, *Princeton* and *Boxer* in the Navy's biggest close-support effort of the war. In one day alone—June 15th—the carrier pilots flew 532 combat sorties, while the Marines and the Fleet Air Arm carried out an additional 478. Maximum-effort close support operations continued until the 19th, when the Allied front stabilized.

While this bitter fighting was in progress, the ROK Government took action that threatened to sabotage the armistice talks for good. The South Koreans had indicated quite firmly that they would oppose any armistice that left Korea divided, and dropped strong hints that they would even be prepared to withdraw their forces from United Nations Command and launch a unilateral offensive against the Communists. Matters came to a head on June 18th, when President Syngman Rhee —who was opposed to talks with the enemy of any kind—ordered the release of 25,000 anti-Communist North Korean prisoners from camps all over the South. These were the men over whose fate both sides had been digging in their toes for several months at Panmunjom.

It was a time for rapid action. In an emergency middle-of-the-night meeting, Secretary of State Dulles and Dwight D. Eisenhower—America's new President—agreed that if the Communist launched an all-out offensive as a result of Rhee's move the United States would carry the war to mainland China. Lists of targets beyond the Yalu had already been drawn up, and there was a stockpile of atomic weapons in Okinawa ready for use by Strategic Air Command if the need arose.

In Korea, the Allied commanders worked hard to strengthen their defences in preparation for a possible major enemy offensive. By June 25th the 315th Air Division—despite the fact that all its Globemasters were grounded with technical troubles at the time—had airlifted the entire 187th Airborne RCT to Korea, with full supporting equipment. During the next few days, operating in very bad weather, the Division's fleet of C-46s, C-54s and C-119s also carried the 24th Division's 19th and 34th RCTs to the battlefront.

The bad weather was of definite assistance to the Communists in planning their coming offensive. Not only did it severely curtail Fifth Air Force, Navy and Bomber Command attacks on bridges, roads and railways at the beginning of July; it also grounded reconnaissance aircraft, which meant that the UN Command had no real idea of the enemy's movements. It was only on July 12th, when a break in the weather permitted the RF-80s to fly a number of sorties, that Allied Intelligence discovered that the biggest Red troop concentrations—supported by a large number of anti-aircraft weapons—were assembled opposite the sectors held by the US IX Corps and the ROK II Corps.

Meanwhile, the Allied air forces had been devoting much of their effort to keeping North Korea's airfields out of action. One clause of the armistice agreement, approved by both sides, placed a ban on the introduction of any additional troops or equipment into Korea while the armistice was in force, and it was clear from the Communists, frenzied airfield construction activities that they were trying to get as many air bases as possible serviceable so that they could pour jet aircraft into them before the armistice was signed. General Weyland had no intention of allowing this to happen, and early in May 35 North Korean airfields—all big enough to accommodate MiG-15s—were listed for attack.

By June 23rd, following intensive operations by Bomber Command, Fifth Air Force and TF 77, 34 of the airfields had been neutralised. The exception was Hoeryong, on the Soviet border. Then bad weather brought a temporary halt to air operations, and when it cleared photo-jet sorties revealed that the Reds had repaired some of the damage with incredible speed despite several night raids by B-29s. At Uiju—which had grass landing strips—over 40 MiG-15s had been flown in and dispersed around the airfield; the fact that the jets could use this type of field at all was a fine tribute to their sturdy construction and short-field performance, something that Allied jet fighters lacked. Twenty-one propeller-driven aircraft were sighted at Sinuiju, and the concrete runway at Namsi had been repaired.

On July 18th both Uiju and Sinuiju were attacked by F-86F fighter-bombers of the 8th and 18th Wings, and there were several follow-up attacks during the next five days. The attacks destroyed 21 MiGs at Uiju and six other aircraft at Sinuiju; the surviving machines at the latter base were flown back across the Manchurian border. By July 27th all North Korean airfields were once again listed as unserviceable by FEAF Intelligence; what Intelligence did not know was that the Reds taking advantage of the bad weather at the beginning of the month, had flown no fewer than 200 MiG-15s and piston-engined combat aircraft into Uiju and had dispersed them in the countryside adjoining the highway running between Uiju and Sinuiju. These aircraft would form the basis of a re-constituted North Korean Air Force immediately after the armistice.

The Chinese offensive began on the night of July 13th/14th, 1953, with a strong drive down the valley of the Pukhan directed against the ROK II Corps, which was forced to retreat. The United Nations Command, however, was quick to react, and for a week beginning on

July 13th the full weight of Allied air power was unleashed on the Communists. By July 20th the Allied line was stable once more and the enemy had suffered 72,000 casualties—the equivalent of nine divisions—to gain just three miles of ground along an eight-mile front. It had been a bloody—and totally unnecessary—end to the land war in Korea.

On July 19th, as their offensive petered out, the Communists indicated that they were prepared to sign an armistice. Rhee's government—following a mixture of threats and promises of mutual aid from the United States—also agreed to the terms thrashed out at Panmunjom. The armistice was finally signed at 10.00hrs on July 27th, 1953, and was to come into effect at 22.01hrs that same day.

The air war was not yet over. From 10.30hrs that day Thunderjets of the 49th and 58th Wings made three strikes on airfields in the north, while the 4th, 8th and 51st Wings re-deployed half their Sabre force to satellite airfields just in case the Communists retaliated with a last-minute air attack. About a dozen MiG-15s were sighted by 4th Wing Sabre pilots escorting fighter-bombers on an airfield strike near Chunggangjin, but the Red fighters sped away across the Yalu and were not seen again.

A few minutes later, however, Captain Ralph S. Parr of the 4th Wing spotted a twin-engined aircraft on an easterly heading and went after it with his wingman. The machine was a twin-engined Ilyushin Il-12 transport, a type not previously encountered in Korea. Whether the pilot had decided to take a short cut across the narrow salient of Korean territory jutting into Manchuria at this point, or whether he was flying supplies to one of the North Korean airfields, will never be known—but he paid with his life. Parr made two passes and the Il-12 plunged to earth, blazing furiously. It was the last Communist aircraft to be shot down in the Korean War, and Captain Parr's tenth victory.

At 21.36hrs, a B-26 of the 3rd Bombardment Wing's 8th Squadron unloaded its bombs on enemy forces near the front line in the war's last close-support mission. A little over three years earlier, this same squadron had flown the first UN air strike against a target in North Korea.

A few minutes later, an RB-26 of the 67th Tactical Reconnaissance Wing flew southwards through the dark after a final reconnaissance sortie over the north. It was a clear night, with scattered cloud reflecting the moonlight.

It was exactly 22.00hrs as the RB-26 droned across the 38th Parallel; and all along the front, the guns were silent.

CHAPTER FIFTEEN

# The Reckoning

The Armistice of June 27th, 1953, brought to an end one of the bloodiest, dirtiest conflicts in modern history. It had lasted for a little over three years, and during those years three million soldiers—not to mention one and a quarter million civilian casualties—of both sides had suffered, bled and died on its muddy battlegrounds.

It was a war that had been started by naked, armed aggression—and ended by politicians; a war of wholesale and often pointless slaughter, a conflict of alien mentalities that time and again overturned tactics and strategy which, over the years, had been carefully laid to combat potential enemies who could be expected to make moves according to the accepted military manuals.

The enemy in Korea was different. His strategy was often totally illogical from the military point of view—yet, with hindsight, terrifyingly logical in that it always formed the key to some psychological jigsaw puzzle. He was incredibly resilient; he could be fought to a standstill, yet not even overwhelming firepower could inflict a decisive defeat on him—a fact that the Americans found hard to accept, and were still finding hard to accept in Vietnam much more recently.

Insofar as the use of airpower is concerned, any real appraisal of its contribution to the Korean War tends to be confused by the overwhelming victory of the United Nations fighter pilots over the Red air forces. An overall assessment, however, reveals that Allied airpower never played a decisive part at any time in the conflict; in fact, the ingenuity of FEAF in devising new methods of knocking out enemy targets was outmatched by the Communists' ingenuity in patching them up again. And the results that were achieved must be weighed against the fact that, in three years of war, the American lost the equivalent of 20 combat groups—in other words, roughly a quarter of the USAF's total first-line strength as it stood in June 1950.

Whether airpower might have been decisive is a different matter; whether far more impressive results might have been achieved had the full weight of the Allied air forces been unleashed on targets in Manchuria is a matter for conjecture. The one thing that does seem certain is that, right from the outset, the Allied strategists underestimated Red

China's reaction to the threat of nuclear attack; in fact, it was not until the spring of 1953—when the Americans made it clear that they were prepared to extend the war into China, using nuclear weapons if necessary—that they fully realised the power of the atomic bomb as a political weapon in forcing the Reds to conclude an armistice. "The threat of atomic bombs was posed," Admiral Turner Joy wrote later; "Defeat for Red China became a possibility. In understandable prudence they took the only step open to them to remove the growing threat of a holocaust. . . . It was as simple as that. It had always been as simple as that."

If the United States had been prepared to shoulder the awesome political and moral consequences of using atomic weapons at an early stage in the Korean hostilities, a decisive victory could almost certainly have been won without the necessity of carrying the war into China at all. As a US Army study indicated after the war, the time to employ atomic weapons against enemy ground forces with really devastating effect would have been in November and December 1950, when United Nations forces were in full retreat from the north before a massive Chinese onslaught. For example, on the night of November 24th/25th, 1950, there was a dense assembly of 22,000 enemy troops at Taechon; one 40 kiloton bomb, fused for an air-burst, would have killed or injured some 15,000 of them. A few weeks later, six 40 kiloton bombs bursting over 95,000 Communist troops in the Pyongyang–Chorwon–Kumhwa area would probably have wiped out half of them, while on the last night of December up to 40,000 of the 100,000-strong enemy force poised for an assault along the Imjin River would have been destroyed by six 30 kiloton air-bursts.

In theory, then, three atomic strikes at the end of 1950 could have destroyed the enemy's capability to wage war by eliminating 100,000 troops—a significantly smaller casualty list than the three million lost by both sides before the fighting ended. And from the moral standpoint, it might be argued that incineration by an atomic weapon is no less humane than incineration by napalm.

Any searching analysis of the causes of the Korean War leads to the inescapable conclusion that the Communists would not have risked aggression had it not been for the dangerous weakness of the Allied forces in the Far East—and, for that matter, throughout the world. Before June 1950, few US politicians realised just how ill-equipped the United States armed forces had become in the space of five short years to fight a war of any kind, let alone a global war; Korea at least helped to bring America and the Western World to its senses. It gave rise to a whole new range of military and strategic policies, not the least of which was the birth of the deterrent—the threat of massive nuclear retaliation which has remained the West's biggest single insurance for peace for the past two decades—and the lessons learned in combat formed the basis of a new military technology out of which were born the awesome weapons systems of the 1960s.

The Korean War had a dramatic effect on the USAF's organisation and equipment. Strategic Air Command was among the first to feel the wind of change; the martyrdom of FEAF's B-29s over North Korea tragically underlined the inadequacy of the conventional bomber, and re-equipment programmes were accelerated. By the middle of 1955 all SAC's B-29s had been phased out in favour of the Boeing B-47 Stratojet, and that the same year the Command's heavy bomber wings began to exchange their Convair B-36s for B-52 Stratofortresses. To facilitate rapid re-deployment SAC's tanker fleet was also greatly expanded, with orders placed for KC-135s to replace the existing piston-engined KB-50s and KC-97s. By the beginning of 1957 Strategic Air Command's strength had grown to 51 wings—a far cry from the 19 wings with which it might have been launched into a Third World War in 1950.

Great changes also swept through the USAF Tactical Air Command as a result of the war. Before the end of 1953 FEAF's remaining F-51 and F-80 units had re-equipped with F-86F fighter-bombers; the long-suffering B-26s had to soldier on for another few months, but by the middle of 1954 these units too had begun to re-equip with Martin B-57 jet bombers. Also in 1954 Tactical Air Command began to receive F-84F Thunderstreaks to replace its F-84G Thunderjets, while F-86 wings re-equipped with the first of the 'Century' series of fighters—the F-100 Super Sabre.

On both sides of the Iron Curtain, three years of jet combat experience over the Yalu was woven into the designs of new air superiority fighters. In the United States, the agile brain of Lockheed's Clarence Johnson and his design team gave birth to the revolutionary F-104 Starfighter, while Russia's answer was the MiG-21. Also from Lockheeds came the U-2—the solution to the glaring problems of strategic reconnaissance that had manifested themselves in Korea.

The United States Navy, too, had learned its lessons. The Korean War had proved beyond all doubt that the fast attack carrier was still the most vital naval unit in modern warfare; at the same time, the deficiencies of the Navy's standard jet types—the F9F Panther and F2H Banshee—in combat over Korea had aroused serious misgivings, and propellor-driven attack types could no longer hope to survive in a hostile fighter environment. These shortcomings gave rise to a US Navy requirement for an aircraft that could take over the task of the Skyraider, carry nuclear weapons at a speed twice that of the conventional aircraft, and stand in as an interceptor when the need arose. The result was the remarkable Douglas Skyhawk, which was rolled out of Douglas's El Segundo factory only 19 months after its inception and flew for the first time in June 1954. At the same time, work went ahead on what was to become the world's first multi-role supersonic combat aircraft—the McDonnell Phantom. Together, these types were to form the backbone of the US Navy's attack capability in the 1960s.

The pattern of development that followed the Korean War was not new. Less than 20 years earlier, a new generation of combat aircraft and techniques had evolved from another bitter conflict between opposing ideologies, half a world away in Spain. The tragedy was that it had taken another war to shake the free world out of its lethargy.

If the years before 1939 had not already taught the world that military weakness born of complacency is no standpoint from which to face a ruthless and determined enemy, Korea should have hammered the lesson home hard.

But did it? Twenty years ago, the United Nations fought one battle in a war that is still being waged. Today, a second battle is being fought in South-East Asia; the enemy has not changed.

Where will tomorrow's battleground be?

# Appendices

## 1 THE KOREAN ACES

| *Name and Rank* | *Unit* | *A/c Flown* | *Score* | *Remarks* |
|---|---|---|---|---|
| McConnell, Capt Joseph | 51st FIW | F-86 | 16 | KIFA 25.8.54 |
| Jabara, Lt-Col James | 4th FIW | F-86 | 15 | +3½ Ger in WWII |
| Fernandez, Capt Manuel J. | 4th FIW | F-86 | 14½ | |
| Davis, Lt-Col George A. | 4th FIW | F-86 | 14 | KIA 10.2.52. Post CMoH 7 Jap in WWII |
| Baker, Col Royal N. | 4th FIW | F-86 | 13 | +3½ Ger in WWII |
| Blesse, Maj Frederick C. | 4th FIW | F-86 | 10 | |
| Fischer, Capt Harold E. | 51st FIW | F-86 | 10 | Captured 7.4.53 |
| Johnson, Col James K. | 4th FIW | F-86 | 10 | +1 Ger in WWII |
| Garrison, Lt-Col Vermont | 4th FIW | F-86 | 10 | +7 Ger in WWII |
| Moore, Maj Lonnie R. | 4th FIW | F-86 | 10 | KIFA 10.1.56 |
| Parr, Capt Ralph S. | 4th FIW | F-86 | 10 | |
| Low, Lt James F. | 4th FIW | F-86 | 9 | |
| Foster, Lt Cecil G. | 51st FIW | F-86 | 9 | |
| Hagerstrom, Lt-Col James P. | 18th FBW | F-86 | 8½ | +6 Jap in WWII |
| Risner, Maj Robinson | 4th FIW | F-86 | 8 | |
| Ruddell, Col George I. | 51st FIW | F-86 | 8 | |
| Jolley, Capt Clifford D. | 4th FIW | F-86 | 7 | |
| Lilley, Capt Leonard W. | 4th FIW | F-86 | 7 | |
| Buttelmann, Lt Henry | 51st FIW | F-86 | 7 | |
| Marshall, Lt-Col Winton W. | 4th FIW | F-86 | 6½ | 4½ MiGs, 1 Tu-2, 1 La-9 |
| Gabreski, Col Francis S. | 4th & 51st FIW | F-86 | 6½ | +28 Ger in WWII |
| Adams, Maj Donald E. | 51st FIW | F-86 | 6½ | KIFA 1952 |
| Jones, Col George L. | 4th & 51st FIW | F-86 | 6½ | |
| Love, Capt Robert J. | 4th FIW | F-86 | 6 | |
| Bolt, Lt-Col John F. (USMC) | 51st FIW (Att) | F-86 | 6 | +6 Jap with VMF-214 in WWII |
| Kasler, Lt James H. | 4th FIW | F-86 | 6 | |
| Whisner, Maj William T. | 51st FIW | F-86 | 5½ | +51½ Ger in WWII |
| Becker, Capt Richard S. | 4th FIW | F-86 | 5 | |
| Gibson, Capt Ralph D. | 4th FIW | F-86 | 5 | |
| Creighton, Lt-Col Richard D. | 4th FIW | F-86 | 5 | +2 Ger in WWII |
| Moore, Capt Robert H. | 51st FIW | F-86 | 5 | |
| Kincheloe, Capt Iven C. | 51st FIW | F-86 | 5 | Later test pilot of Bell X-2 rocket aircraft |
| Westcott, Maj William H. | 51st FIW | F-86 | 5 | |
| Latshaw, Capt Robert T. | 4th FIW | F-86 | 5 | KIFA 20.4.56 |
| Thyng, Col Harrison R. | 4th FIW | F-86 | 5 | +6 Ger and Jap |
| Overton, Capt Dolphin D. | 51st FIW | F-86 | 5 | |
| Baldwin, Col Robert P. | 51st FIW | F-86 | 5 | |
| Curtin, Capt Clyde A. | 4th FIW | F-86 | 5 | |
| Bettinger, Maj Stephen L. | 4th FIW | F-86 | 5 | +1 Ger in WWII |
| Bordelon, Lt Guy P. (USN) | 5AF (Att) | F4U-5N | 5 | Night kills |

(KIFA: *Killed in Flying Accident*)

## Other Notable Pilots Claiming E/A Kills in Korea

| *Name and Rank* | *Unit* | *A/c Flown* | *Score* | *Remarks* |
|---|---|---|---|---|
| Amen, Lt-Cdr W. T. (USN) | VF-111 | F9F | 1 | First Navy pilot to shoot down a jet aircraft |
| Colman, Lt Philip E. | 4th FIW | F-86 | 4 | +5 Jap in China-Burma-India Theatre in WWII |
| Mitchell, Lt-Col John W. | 51st FIW | F-86 | 4 | +11 Jap in WWII |
| Mattson, Capt Conrad E. | 4th FIW | F-86 | 4 | +1 Jap in WWII |
| Preston, Col B. S. | 4th FIW | F-86 | 4 | |
| Price, Lt-Col Harold L. | 51st FIW | F-86 | 4 | |
| Samways, Lt-Col William T. | 8th FBG | F-80 | 4 | |
| Heller, Maj Edwin L. | 51st FIW | F-86 | 3½ | +5½ Ger in WWII |
| Mahurin, Col Walker M. | 51st FIW | F-86 | 3½ | +21 Ger in WWII |
| Arnell, Maj Zane S. | 4th FIW | F-86 | 3 | |
| Chandler, Maj Van E. | 51st FIW | F-86 | 3 | +5 Ger in WWII |
| Glover, Fg-Off Earnest A. (RCAF) | 4th FIW (Att) | F-86 | 3 | |
| Harris, Maj Elmer W. | 51st FIW | F-86 | 3 | +3 Yak-9s on the ground |
| Raebel, Lt-Col James B. | 4th FIW | F-86 | 3 | |
| Kelly, Lt-Col Albert S. | 51st FIW | F-86 | 2½ | |
| Brueland, Maj Lowell K. | 51st FIW | F-86 | 2 | +12½ Ger in WWII |
| Eagleston, Lt-Col Glenn T. | 4th FIW | F-86 | 2 | +18½ Ger in WWII |
| Fox, Lt Orrin R. | 80th FBS | F-51 | 2 | Both Yak-9s |
| Hulse, Sqn Ldr Graham S. (RAF) | 4th FIW (Att) | F-86 | 2 | |
| Kratt, Lt Jacob | 27th FEW | F-84 | 2 | |
| McElroy, Lt-Col Carrol B. | 4th FIW | F-86 | 2 | |
| Meyer, Col John C. | 4th FIW | F-86 | 2 | +24 Ger in WWII |
| Wayne, Lt Robert E. | 35th FBS | F-80 | 2 | Both Il-10s |
| Andre, Lt John W. (USMC) | VMF(N)-513 | F4U-5N | 1 | Night kill |
| Best, Lt-Col Jack R. | 51st FIW | F-86 | 1 | |
| Bertram, Lt-Col William E. | 523rd FES | F-84 | 1 | |
| Brown, Lt Russell J. | 51st FIW | F-80 | 1 | First MiG shot down in Korea |
| Burns, Lt Richard J. | 35th FBS | F-80 | 1 | Yak-9 |
| Carmichael, Lt P. | 802 Sqn FAA | Sea Fury | 1 | First piston-engined a/c to destroy a MiG |
| Chandler, Capt Kenneth D. | 4th FIW | F-86 | 1 | +4 MiGs on the ground |
| Dickinson, Fg Off R. T. F. (RAF) | 4th FIW (Att) | F-86 | 1 | |
| Dewald, Lt Robert H. | 35th FBS | F-80 | 1 | Il-10 |
| Emmert, Maj Benjamin H. | 4th FIW | F-86 | 1 | +6 Ger in WWII |
| Fithian, Capt Ben L. and Lyons, Lt Sam R. (Observer) | 319th FIS | F-94 | 1 | La-9. First F-94 kill in Korea |
| Gogerly, Fg Off Bruce (RAAF) | 77 Sqn | Meteor 8 | 1 | |
| Granville-White, Flt Lt John H. (RAF) | 51st FIW (Att) | F-86 | 1 | |
| Harrison, Lt J. B. | 18th FBG | F-51 | 1 | Yak-9 |
| Heyman, Capt Richard | 8th BS | B-26 | 1 | Po-2 |
| Hinton, Lt-Col Bruce H. | 4th FIW | F-86 | 1 | First Sabre pilot to destroy MiG-15 |
| Hockerey, Capt John J. | 51st FIW | F-86 | 1 | +7 Ger in WWII |

| Name and Rank | Unit | A/c Flown | Score | Remarks |
|---|---|---|---|---|
| Hovde, Maj William J. | 4th FIW | F-86 | 1 | +10½ Ger in WWII |
| Hudson, Lt William G. | 68th FAWS | F-82 | 1 | |
| Keyes, Lt-Col Ralph E. | 51st FIW | F-86 | 1 | |
| Kinsey, Lt Raymond J. | 4th FIW | F-86 | 1 | Tu-2 |
| La France, Claude A. (RCAF) | 4th FIW (Att) | F-86 | 1 | |
| Lamb, Lt William E. (USN) | VF-111 | F9F | 1 | +5 Jap in WWII |
| Levesque, Flt Lt J. A. O. (RCAF) | 51st FIW (Att) | F-86 | 1 | |
| Lindsay, Sqn Ldr James D. (RCAF) | 51st FIW (Att) | F-86 | 1 | |
| Little, James W. | 339th FAWS | F-82 | 1 | +5 e/a in WWII |
| Long, Capt E. B. (USMC) | VMF-513 | F7F | 1 | Po-2 |
| Lovell, Flt Lt J. H. J. (RAF) | 4th FIW (Att) | F-86 | 1 | |
| Martin, Col Maurice L. | 18th FBW | F-86 | 1 | |
| Marsh, Lt Roy W. | 8th FBW | F-80 | 1 | Il-10 |
| McGuire, Capt Allen | 27th FEW | F-84 | 1 | |
| McHale, Lt-Col Robert V. and Hoster, Capt Samuel (Observer) | 319th FIS | F-94 | 1 | Night kill |
| McKay, Sqn Ldr John (RCAF) | 4th FIW (Att) | F-86 | 1 | |
| Mullins, Maj Arnold | 67th FBS | F-51 | 1 | Yak-9 |
| Norris, Lt William T. | 8th FBW | F-80 | 1 | La-7 |
| Plog, Lt L. H. (USN) | VF-51 | F9F | 1 | Yak-9. First Navy kill in Korea |
| Sandlin, Lt Harry T. | 80th FBS | F-51 | 1 | Yak-9 |
| Schillereff, Capt Raymond E. | 35th FBS | F-80 | 1 | Il-10 |
| Simmonds, Fg Off W. (RAAF) | 77 Sqn | Meteor 8 | 1 | |
| Skeen, Capt Kenneth L. | 49th FBG | F-84 | 1 | |
| Slaughter, William W. | 27th FEW | F-84 | 1 | |
| Thomas, Lt John B. | 36th FBS | F-80 | 1 | Yak-9 |
| Van Grundy, Maj E. A. (USMC) | VMF-513 | F7F-3N | 1 | Po-2 |
| Visscher, Lt Herman W. | 51st FIW | F-86 | 1 | +5 e/a in WWII |
| Wilcox, Lt Stanton G. and Goldberg, Lt I. L. (Observer) | 319th FIS | F-94 | 1 | Po-2. F-94 crashed after interception; both crew killed |
| Wurster, Lt Charles A. | 36th FBS | F-80 | 1 | Yak-9 |
| Young, Lt Sam P. | 51st FIW | F-86 | 1 | Last MiG destroyed in Korea |

## 2 FEAF ORDER OF BATTLE, JULY 1st, 1950

*FIFTH AIR FORCE (JAPAN)*

| *Base* | *Units* | *Equipment* |
|---|---|---|
| Ashiya | 8th FBS | F-80C |
| | 3rd Rescue Sqn 'D' Flt | SB-17, L-5, H-5 |
| Itazuke | 8th FBG: | |
| | 35th FBS | F-80C |
| | 36th FBS | F-80C |
| | 80th FBS | F-80C |
| | 9th FBS | F-80C |
| | 4th FAWS | F-82 |
| | 68th FAWS | F-82 |
| | 339th FAWS | F-82 |
| Iwakuni | 3rd BG: | |
| | 8th BS | B-26 |
| | 13th BS | B-26 |
| | No 77 Sqn RAAF | F-51 (Attached 5th AF) |
| Johnson | 3rd Rescue Sqn 'A' Flt | SB-17 |
| Misawa | 49th FBG: | |
| | 7th FBS | F-80C |
| | 3rd Rescue Sqn 'C' Flt | SB-17, H-5 |
| Tachikawa | 374th TCG: | |
| | 6th TCS | C-54 |
| | 21st TCS | C-54 |
| | 22nd TCS | C-54 |
| Yokota | 35th FIG: | |
| | 39th FIS | F-80C |
| | 40th FIS | F-80C |
| | 41st FIS | F-80C |
| | 8th TacRS | RF-80A |
| | 512nd WRS | WB-29 |
| | 339th FAWS (1 Flt) | F-82 |
| | 3rd Rescue Sqn 'D' Flt | SB-17, L-5, H-5 |

*THIRTEENTH AIR FORCE*

| | | |
|---|---|---|
| Clark (Luzon, Philippines) | 18th FBG | F-80C |
| | 6204th PMF | RB-17 |

*TWENTIETH AIR FORCE*

| | | |
|---|---|---|
| Andersen (Guam) | 19th BG | B-29 |
| Kadena (Okinawa) | 31st StratRS | RB-29 (SAC unit) |
| Naha (Okinawa) | 51st FIG | F-80C |
| | 4th FAWS (2 Flts) | F-82 |

## 3 FIFTH AIR FORCE ORDER OF BATTLE, DECEMBER 31st, 1950

| *Base* | *Units* | *Equipment* |
|---|---|---|
| Chinhae (K-10) | 18th FBG: | |
| | 12th FBS | F-51 |
| | 67th FBS | F-51 |
| | No 2 Sqn SAAF | F-51 |
| Kimpo (K-14) | 51st FIG: | |
| | 16th FIS | F-80C |
| | 25th FIS | F-80C |
| | 336th FIS | F-86A |
| Pusan East (K-9) | 35th FIG: | |
| | 39th FIS | F-51 |
| | 40th FIS | F-51 |
| | No 77 Sqn RAAF | F-51 |
| | VMF-311 | F9F |
| Seoul (K-16) | 6147th TacCon Sqn | T-6 |
| Taegu (K-2) | 49th FBG: | |
| | 7th FBS | F-80C |
| | 8th FBS | F-80C |
| | 9th FBS | F-80C |
| | 543rd TacSptGp: | |
| | 8th TacRS | RF-80A |
| | 45th TacRS | RF-51 |
| | 162nd TacRS | RB-26 |
| | 6166th AWRecS | RB-26 |
| Itami | 1st Marine Air Wing: | |
| | VMF-312 | F4U |
| | VMF-214 | F4U |
| Itazuke | 27th FEG: | |
| | 522nd FES | F-84E |
| | 523rd FES | F-84E |
| | 524th FES | F-84E |
| | 68th FAWS | F-82 |
| | 4th FAWS (1 Flt) | F-82 |
| | 8th FBG: | |
| | 35th FBS | F-80C |
| | 36th FBS | F-80C |
| | 80th FBS | F-80C |
| | VMF(N)-513 | F4U-5N, F7F-3N |
| | VMF(N)-542 | F4U-5N |
| Iwakuni | 3rd BW(L): | |
| | 8th BS | B-26 |
| | 13th BS | B-26 |
| | 731st BS | B-26 |
| Johnson | 4th FIG: | |
| | 334th FIS | F-86A |
| | 335th FIS | F-86A |
| Miho | 452nd BW(L): | |
| | 728th BS | B-26 |
| | 729th BS | B-26 |
| | 730th BS | B-26 |

# 4 UN AIR FORCES' ORDER OF BATTLE, JULY 31st, 1953

| *Base* | *Units* | *Equipment* |
|---|---|---|
| K-1 (Pusan) | 17th BW(L) Det 1 | B-26 |
| | 6152nd Air Base Sqn | |
| | 366th EngAvn Battn | |
| K-2 (Taegu) | 58th FBW | F-84 |
| | 1818th AACS Gp | |
| | 6156th Air Base Sqn | |
| | 6157th Air Base Sqn | |
| K-3 (Pohang) | 1st Marine Air Wng | F4U, F2H, F9F, AD2 |
| K-6 (Pyongtaek) | Marine Air Gp 12 | F4U, AD2 |
| | 1st Shoran Bcn Sqn | |
| K-8 (Kusan) | 3rd BW(L) | B-26 |
| | 49th FBW | F-84 |
| K-9 (Pusan East) | 17th BW | B-26 |
| K-10 (Chinhae) | 7th Air Depot Wng | |
| K-13 (Suwon) | 8th FBW | F-86F |
| | 51st FIW | F-86F |
| | 319th FIS | F-94 |
| | VMF(N)-513 | F3D |
| K-14 (Kimpo) | 4th FIW | F-86F |
| | 67th TacRW | RF-80, RB-26, RF-86 |
| | No 77 Sqn RAAF | Meteor Mk 8 |
| | 6166th AWR Flt | RB-26 |
| K-16 (Seoul) | 6167th Ops Sqn | C-47 |
| | 6167th Air Base Gp | |
| | 6154th Air Base Gp | |
| | 30th AWS | |
| | 10th Liaison Sqn (Serving 5th AF HQ) | L-5, L-19, L-20 |
| K-18 (Kangnung) | ROK Air Force (Combat Wing) | F-51 |
| K-37 (Taegu West) | 930th EngAvnGp | |
| K-46 (Hoengsong) | 6155th Air Base Sqn | |
| K-47 (Chunchon) | 6147th TacCon Gp | T-6 |
| K-55 (Osan) | 18th FBW | F-86F |
| | No 2 Sqn SAAF | F-86F |
| | 934th EngAvnGp | |

# 5 STATISTICS

## (1) FAR EAST AIR FORCES

*Sorties Flown:*

| | |
|---|---|
| Interdiction | 192,581 |
| Close support | 57,665 |
| Counterair | 66,997 |
| Air Supply | 181,659 |
| Miscellaneous | 222,078 |
| Total: | 720,980 |
| Bombs Dropped (Tons) | 386,037 |
| Napalm Dropped (Tons) | 32,357 |
| Rocket Rounds Fired | 313,600 |
| Smoke Rockets | 55,797 |
| MG Ammunition | 166,853,100 rounds |

*Losses in Air Combat:*

| | |
|---|---|
| Sabres | 78 |
| Others | 61 |
| Total: | 139 |

*Casualties:*

| | *Killed* | *Wounded* | *PoW (Repatriated)* |
|---|---|---|---|
| Air Operations: | 1,144 | 306 | 214 |
| Ground Operations: | 36 | 62 | 6 |
| Totals: | 1,180 | 368 | 220 |

## (2) US NAVY AND MARINES

*Carriers Operationally Involved*

*Antietam*
*Badoeng Strait*
*Bataan*
*Bon Homme Richard*
*Boxer*
*Essex*
*Lake Champlain*
*Leyte*
*Oriskany*
*Philippine Sea*
*Princeton*
*Sicily*
*Valley Forge*

| | |
|---|---|
| Total Sorties Flown | 167,552 Navy, 107,303 Marines |
| Bombs Dropped (Tons) | 120,000 Navy, 82,000 Marines |
| Rocket Rounds Fired | 272,000 (Navy and Marines) |
| Aircraft Losses | 814 (Navy),<br>368 (Marines) |

### (3) *DAMAGE INFLICTED ON ENEMY AIR FORCES BY UN AIR POWER, 1950–53*

*FEAF Claims:*

| | *Destroyed* | *Probably Destroyed* | *Damaged* |
|---|---|---|---|
| In the Air | 900 | 168 | 973 |
| On the Ground | 53 | 25 | 36 |

*US Navy Claims:*
In the Air ..................................16 (Including 4 destroyed by Navy pilots in Sabres)
On the Ground ...........................36

*USMC Claims:*
In the Air ..................................35 (Including 15 destroyed by USMC pilots in Sabres)

*No 77 Sqn RAAF Claims:*
In the Air ..................................6 (3 while flying Mustangs)

*Fleet Air Arm Claims:*
In the Air ..................................2

Grand Total Destroyed: **1,050.**

### (4) *SABRE 'KILLS' BY AIRCRAFT TYPES*

| | |
|---|---|
| Tupolev Tu-2 | 9 |
| Lavochkin La-9 | 6 |
| MiG-15 | 792 |
| Ilyushin Il-12 | 1 |
| Others | 2 |
| Total: | **810** |

### (5) *COMMUNIST MATERIAL LOSSES THROUGH UN AIR ATTACK, 1950–53*

| | |
|---|---|
| Tanks | 1,327 |
| Vehicles | 82,920 |
| Locomotives | 963 |
| Railway Cars | 10,407 |
| Bridges | 1,153 |
| Buildings | 118,231 |
| Tunnels | 65 |
| Gun Positions | 8,663 |
| Bunkers | 8,839 |
| Oil Storage Tanks | 16 |
| Barges and Boats | 593 |
| Rail Cuts | 28,621 |

Estimated Number of Enemy Troops Killed by Air Attack: **184,808**

# 6 BRITISH COMMONWEALTH AIR UNITS SUPPORTING KOREAN OPERATIONS

| *Unit* | *Equipment* | *Remarks* |
|---|---|---|
| No 2 'Cheetah' Sqn, SAAF | F-51, F-86F | Attached to 18th FBW, 5th AF |
| No 30 Transport Unit, RAAF | Dakota | Part of No 91 Composite Wing, Iwakuni |
| No 36 Transport Sqn, RAAF | Dakota | No 91 Composite Wing, Iwakuni |
| No 77 Sqn RAAF | F-51, Meteor 7 and 8 | |
| No 88 Sqn, RAF | Sunderland | Detachment at Iwakuni |
| No 209 Sqn, RAF | Sunderland | Detachment at Iwakuni |
| No 391 Base Sqn, RAAF | | No 91 Composite Wing |
| No 426 Sqn, RCAF | North Star | Carried out airlift in support of Commonwealth Division for the duration of hostilities |
| No 800 Sqn, Fleet Air Arm | Seafire 47 | HMS *Triumph* |
| No 801 Sqn, FAA | Sea Fury | HMS *Glory* |
| No 802 Sqn, FAA | Sea Fury | HMS *Ocean* |
| No 804 Sqn, FAA | Sea Fury | HMS *Glory* |
| No 805 Sqn, FAA | Sea Fury | HMAS *Sydney* |
| No 807 Sqn, FAA | Sea Fury | HMS *Theseus* |
| No 808 Sqn, FAA | Sea Fury | HMAS *Sydney* |
| No 810 Sqn, FAA | Firefly 5 | HMS *Theseus* |
| No 812 Sqn, FAA | Firefly 5 | HMS *Glory* |
| No 817 Sqn FAA | Firefly 5 | HMAS *Sydney* |
| No 820 Sqn, FAA | Firefly 5 | HMS *Glory* |
| No 825 Sqn, FAA | Firefly 5 | HMS *Ocean* |
| No 827 Sqn, FAA | Firefly FR 1 | HMS *Triumph* |
| No 1903 AOP Flt | Auster AOP 6 | |
| No 1913 Light Liaison Flt | Auster AOP 6, L-19 | |

# Abbreviations

| | |
|---|---|
| AACS | Airways and Air Communications Service |
| AOP | Air Observation Post |
| AWRecS | All-Weather Reconnaissance Sqn |
| AWS | Air Weather Sqn |
| Bcn | Beacon |
| BG | Bombardment Group |
| BS | Bombardment Sqn |
| BW(L) | Bombardment Wing (Light) |
| EngAvnBattn | Engineer Aviation Battalion |
| FAA | Fleet Air Arm |
| FAWS | Fighter All-Weather Sqn |
| FBG | Fighter-Bomber Group |
| FBS | Fighter-Bomber Squadron |
| FEG | Fighter-Escort Group |
| FES | Fighter-Escort Squadron |
| FEW | Fighter-Escort Wing |
| FIG | Fighter-Interceptor Group |
| FIS | Fighter-Interceptor Squadron |
| FIW | Fighter-Interceptor Wing |
| PMF | Photo-Mapping Flight |
| RAAF | Royal Australian Air Force |
| SAAF | South African Air Force |
| StratRS | Strategic Reconnaissance Squadron |
| TacCon | Tactical Control |
| TacRS | Tactical Reconnaissance Squadron |
| TacRW | Tactical Reconnaissance Wing |
| TacSptGp | Tactical Support Group |
| TCG | Troop Carrier Group |
| TCS | Troop Carrier Squadron |
| WRS | Weather Reconnaissance Squadron |

# Bibliography


Appleman, R. E. 'South to the Naktong, North to the Yalu'. US Department of the Army, Washington, 1961.

Cagle, Malcolm W. and Frank A. Manson. 'The Sea War in Korea'. United States Naval Institute, Annapolis, 1957.

Dean, William F. 'General Dean's Story'. Viking Press, New York, 1954.

Futrell, Robert F. 'The United States Air Force in Korea, 1950–53'. Duell, Sloan and Pearce, New York, 1961.

Gurney, Gene and Friedlander, P. 'Five Down and Glory'. Putnam, New York, 1958.

Karig, Capt. Walter, Cagle, Comdr. Malcolm W. and Manson, Lt. Cdr. Frank A. 'Battle Report, Vol. VI: the War in Korea'. Rinehart, New York, 1952.

Long, Gavin. 'MacArthur'. Van Nostrand, London, 1969.

Miller, John Jr., Carroll, Owen J. and Tackley, Margaret E. 'Korea, 1951–1953'. Office of the Chief of Military History, Washington, 1956.

Montross, Lynn and Canzona, Nicholas A. 'US Marine Operations in Korea, 1950–53; Vols. I–III'. USMC Historical Branch, Washington, 1954–57.

Rees, D. 'Korea—the Limited War'. Macmillan, London, 1964.

Ridgway, General Matthew B. 'Soldier: the Memoirs of Matthew B. Ridgway'. Harper, New York, 1956.

Stewart, Col. James T. 'Airpower: the Decisive Force in Korea'. Van Nostrand, 1957.

Thompson, Capt. Annis G. 'The Greatest Air Lift; the Story of Combat Cargo'. Dai-Nippon Printing Co., Tokyo, 1954.

Westover, John G. 'Combat Support in Korea'. Combat Forces Press, Washington, 1955.